"The first hours belong to us. The last, to God and the straightest shot."

BERNARD PAUL COY

ALCA

'TRAZ '46

THE ANATOMY OF A CLASSIC PRISON TRAGEDY

Don DeNevi

Philip Bergen

Distributed by
ASTERON PRODUCTIONS
Pier 47
Fisherman's Wharf
San Francisco, California   94133

 LESWING PRESS
San Rafael, California

ALCATRAZ '46
Tenth Printing

The Anatomy of a Classic Prison Tragedy
Copyright © 1974 by Leswing Press. All rights reserved. No part of this book may be reproduced in any form without permission in writing from the publisher. Address inquires to Leswing Press, 750 Adrian Way, San Rafael, California 94903. Printed in the United States of America. ISBN 0-88339-296-8.

PRINTED by DELTA LITHOGRAPH CO. VALENCIA, CA.

This book is respectfully dedicated to
Patricia Rothschild,
Katherine Gray,
and Tony Firpo

THE CONTENTS

PREFACE

Isolated in the waters of San Francisco Bay, Alcatraz Island Prison was the source of innumerable myths embellished by second hand information and garnished by repetition. The fear-provoking, awe-inspiring reputation which had made it an international symbol of anachronistic penal philosophy, stubbornly lingers on today, even though "The Rock" has long given up its last inmate.

In its day, Alcatraz Prison served a useful purpose. The nation was experiencing an unprecedented wave of gangsterism and violence. Federal prisons were few in number and badly overcrowded. When it was converted from an old Army Disciplinary Barracks in the early 1930's, it was redesigned to be an escape proof civil prison.

The redesigned prison helped relieve the pressure of overcrowding in other federal penal and correctional institutions. It provided a much needed place for the safe and secure incarceration of problem prisoners — the "escape artists", the "big shots", the "intractably vicious and depraved outcasts of society" — and permitted the rest of the growing Federal Prison System to enter a period of penological progress unimpeded by confirmed criminals who were covertly, and sometimes openly, opposed to any official attempt to rehabilitate them.

With the inception of the prison came the myth. Perhaps the sensational tales and imaginative rumors of whips and chains, of gloomy, rat-infested dungeons, and medieval treatment of offenders circulated in popular magazines, movies, and newspapers helped to reduce the incidence of jailbreaks, bank robberies, kidnappings, and murders during the era that followed the repeal of the prohibition law. Certainly, they fostered the stories that Alcatraz Prison was a hell-hole of cruelty and repression.

The story presented here focuses on one segment from the island's long history. The focus is essentially an anatomy of the most ingenious and savagely daring escape attempt in U.S. penal history. It was "Six against the Rock" as the newspapers described it. It was six against every law-enforcement agency, civil and military, in the United States. The desperate attempt to escape and the massive reprisals which followed, relate an all too human tragedy.

Details of the story were compiled over a two year period from official documents, personal diaries, and interviews with retired Alcatraz personnel, and inmates still serving life sentences. Except for the fictitious name given one officer, Norman Anthony, the story is true. The characters and events have been carefully reconstructed from numerous pieces of information.

ALCATRAZ '46

Twenty-two thousand pages of trial testimony recorded by U.S. District Court reporter, Kenneth C. Gagan, hitherto designated "secret" in the Archives Branch of the San Francisco Federal Records Center, were disinterred and dissected. Under file 30316-S (FRC 305565), these 16 volumes, coupled with the official U.S. Department of Justice Federal Bureau of Investigation report, I.C. No. 70-12090, provided most of the sentence by sentence dialogue recalled by officer and inmate witnesses immediately following the tragedy. In many instances, the events were of such a nature as to remain indelibly in the minds of surviving officers. Every word, every obscenity, every slang expression and sentence encompassing terror, murder, and revenge can be documented.

To all who provided counsel and photographic resources toward the reconstruction of this story goes much sincere gratitude: Robyn Gottfried, Director of Archives, San Francisco Federal Records Center; Phil Dollison and John Brunner, collectors of material for an Alcatraz museum; Walter Bertrand, secretary to Warden James A. Johnston and co-author of *Alcatraz Island Prison*; Ivan Burtis, California Historical Society; Leo Dehnel, Chief of Graphics Officer, Federal Bureau of Prisons; Officers J. J. Hart and Gerald GeGraaf, U.S. Coast Guard, Western Engineering Division; Anthony Biggs, Oakland Tribune Public Relations Director; Gordon Peters and Anna Parker, San Francisco Chronicle photographers; George Eastham and Larry Lieurance, San Francisco Examiner; and John Hart, photographer. Unfortunately, Official Bureau of Prison photographs of the bomb-shattered, bullet-riddled cellhouses have disappeared.

Those who made available federal, state, and county documents, surveys, reports, and newspaper clippings: L. Patrick Gray, former Acting Director, Federal Bureau of Investigation; Norman Carlson, Director, Federal Bureau of Prisons; James V. Bennett, Director, Federal Bureau of Prisons (retired); James Gordon, California State Attorney General; Alice Buxton, Head Reference Librarian, California Room, Oakland Public Library; and John B. Tompkins, Director of Bancroft Library, University of California, Berkeley.

Former Alcatraz officers who aided in the research: Robert Baker, George Boatman, Isaac Faulk, Clifford Fish, Loring Mills, Glen Pehrson, Fred Roberts, Marshall Rose, Emil Rychner, Ed Stucker, Carl Sundstrom, George DeVencenzi, and Lou Nelson, now warden of San Quentin.

The wives of Alcatraz officers who contributed a great deal of useful information about family life on the island: Mrs. Philip Bergen, Mrs. Isaac Faulk, Mrs. John Hart, Mrs. Ernest Lageson, Mrs. Joyce Ritz, Mrs. Marshall Rose, and Mrs. Earl Waller.

Above all, deepest and warmest appreciation goes to Lieutenant Philip R. Bergen and inmate Clarence Carnes, two of the few surviving witnesses to the battle, who painstakingly clarified the tragedy's sequence of events.

PROLOG

"In our prisons, I want to see groups of highly
trained, enthusiastic men of law-enforcement,
properly supported by equipment, appro-
priation, and freedom from paralyzing
influence."

J. Edgar Hoover

"When they dumped us out here to guard
the nation's most vicious criminals, they
forgot about us. Conditions have always
been bad. We are understaffed, overworked,
underpaid. We eat as bad as the cons and
Americans don't care. We protect them
from wife murderers, perverts, the insane,
hired assassins and our annual salary is
$2,540."

Carl W. Sundstrom, Records Officer

ALCATRAZ '46

The Island

Appearing like an impregnable, white fortress surrounded by turbulent waters, the 12-acre island of solid rock was an easily identified landmark for early Spanish explorers who visited the bay. The rock had served as a protective habitat for countless generations of seabirds whose excrement had continually white-washed its surface, making it a distinctive visual feature. Ignored for exploration of the less rugged terrain of other and larger bay islands, the rock was drawn on 16th century maps, but left unnamed.

About the time the Declaration of Independence was being drafted, the Spanish explorer, Lieutenant Juan Manuel de Ayala. was assigned the duty of surveying the bay. Each island, point of land, and inlet was to be given a distinctive name. On a cool August morning, de Ayala and his men circumnavigated the rock. They observed slender-billed cormorants, long-winged gulls, and little petrels which darted erratically over the water and their ship. They noted the great number of pelicans that lived among and fished from the craggy cliffs. Finding the shoreline steep and barren, de Ayala anchored off shore on the rock's windward side. Although there is no evidence that either he or his men ever set foot ashore, the rock was described in his writings, and a name was penned onto his map. De Ayala called the unapproachable white rock "Isla de Alcatraces" — Island of Pelicans.

The island was unused for the next half century, then in 1846, Pio Pico, the last Mexican governor of California, granted it to Julian Workman, a San Francisco attorney. Ownership changed hands several times in the next few years, and the island became the central issue in legal suits involving a purchase price of $5000. In one transaction, General Charles Fremont acquired the island for the United States Government. This acquisition eventually allowed the

10

government to become the legal owner without paying the purchase price.

When the California gold rush began to fill the bay with sailing ships and the shores with treasure-seeking men, the U.S. Army Engineers started to develop fortifications for the harbor. An outer line of defense at the bay's entrance involved the construction of two, directly opposite batteries of artillery — at least 100 cannon each at Fort Point and Lime Point. The inner line of defense involved a fortress on the twelve acre rock and two opposing batteries of artillery at Black Point (now Fort Mason) and Angel Island. The defense plan was to hurl a continuous succession of shot and shell in a gauntlet of cross fire over the bay waters to a distance of about six miles.

Strategically, the island, which had by this time become known as Alcatraz, was in a fine location for the inner defense line, and its role in the defense plan required a construction program that spanned several years. In 1854, a lighthouse standing 160 feet above the bay, was erected. Next, wharves and buildings were constructed, then massive gun-emplacements were hewn out of the solid rock, and batteries of muzzle-loading, smoothbore cannon were installed. Finally in 1859, Company H of the Army's Third Artillery Regiment reported to Fort Alcatraz for duty. The San Francisco Bay seemed well protected.

The island did not remain a simple military fortress for long. Because it was separated from the mainland by more than a mile of shifting tides and treacherous currents, it was reasonable for the military to begin using the newly constructed fortifications to confine military prisoners. Forts and isolated islands had long been associated with secure imprisonment, and this association was strengthened by such vivid 19th century examples as Fort Drum — the coral island bastille in the Dry Tortugas; Lipari — Italy's small island institution off the northern coast of Sicily; Devil's Island — France's hot, humid, palm-covered isle in the Atlantic Ocean northeast of French Guiana; Solovetskiye — Russia's isolated prison in the White Sea north of Russia. In 1861, Asbury Harpending and 16 privateers, who conspired to aid the Confederacy by equipping the schooner "J. M. Chapman" to prey on U.S. shipping, became the first men to be imprisoned in the fortress on Alcatraz Island in San Francisco Bay.

In 1868, the U.S. War Department formally designated Alcatraz as a place for confinement of military prisoners with long sentences. During the Indian Wars, several troublesome Indian leaders, including the Chiricahua Apache, Kae-te-na, a close friend of Geronimo, were kept on the island for safekeeping. After the Spanish-American War, the prison became crowded with military deserters.

When some San Francisco jails crumbled in the 1906 earthquake, prisoners were temporarily housed in the undamaged island fortifications. The next year, the War Department approved Major R. B. Turner's plan for constructing a steel and concrete installation of barracks, shops, and powerplant. In 1909, the Army Disciplinary Barracks were erected on the massive foundations of the old fort. These barracks later held many World War I military offenders, but as the 1920's passed by, the number of prisoners gradually dwindled. By 1933, only a handful of prisoners remained, and many of the steel and concrete facilities had fallen into disrepair.

The Rock in 1862.

11

ALCATRAZ '46

The Prison

During the depression, outcries from citizens, frightened by a series of violent bank-robberies, kidnappings, and murders, resulted in the enactment by Congress of a number of statutes which gave the federal government jurisdiction over certain criminal offenses previously held under exclusive jurisdiction by the states. U.S. Attorney General Homer Cummings suggested, and Congress agreed, that a special penal institution of maximum security and minimum privilege should be established. Congress authorized the Justice Department to acquire control of Alcatraz Island and to redevelop its decaying facilities into an escape-proof site for the confinement of America's worst criminals. The first of four wardens, James A. Johnston (January 2, 1934 to April 30, 1948) and a staff of officers carefully selected from other institutions, began operations in early 1934.

As the island was redeveloped into a maximum security prison, seven of the twelve acres were enclosed in a prison compound. The remaining five acres were set aside for employee residences, apartments, and recreational space.

The dominant feature constructed within the prison compound was the main cellhouse which rested on a northwest by southeast axis. From San Francisco, where tourists could peer at the prison through "10¢-a-look" wharfside telescopes, the cream-colored main cellhouse appeared to be a single massive structure. Actually, the huge building consisted of four cellblocks plus facilities for feeding, bathing, clothing, and hospitalizing the inmates. The cellblocks were constructed in parallel and identified by the letters A, B, C, and D.

A-block retained the typical characteristics of the old Army Disciplinary Barracks and was located on the northeastern side of the cellhouse. It extended approximately 125 feet along the outer wall.

Not included in the modernizing of the prison in 1934, it was generally considered to be far less secure than the other cellblocks, thus was seldom used.

B and C blocks were interior cellblocks. Each was three tiers high and 150 feet long. The lengths were divided into two sections by a ten-foot wide space called the "cutoff". A utility corridor running between the rows of cells further subdivided each section. The broad aisle between B and C served as the main corridor through which most of the prison traffic flowed. The inmates had named the aisle "Broadway". The narrower outer aisles were known as "Michigan Boulevard" (A-B aisle) and "Seedy Street" (C-D aisle).

Each cellblock tier was 8½ feet high and contained 54 single-occupancy cells. 168 openface cells looked upon Broadway and 78 looked upon each of the outer aisles. Twelve of the original 336 cells in the main cellhouse were eliminated in 1933 to provide space for stairs. The remaining 324 cells housed all the inmates who did not need more restrictive confinement.

The cell fronts and the security facilities on all exterior windows were constructed of tool-resistant steel bars. The windows were of the detention-sash type with small glass panes set in tool-resistant steel frames. Cell doors were manually controlled, using mechanical locking devices, from control boxes located at the four corners of each cellblock tier.

Two patrol walkways, the west gun gallery and the east gun gallery, were constructed so that armed officers could look down the rows of cells at all tier levels. The presence of the armed gallery officer provided a measure of protection for the unarmed officers in the cellhouse.

D-block, on the southwest side of the cellhouse, was rebuilt and walled off from the other cellblocks in 1940. This three tier, modern steel cellblock was used exclusively for the segregation of intractable inmates and for the protective custody of a few emotionally disturbed men at their own request. All 42 security-type cells had tool-resistant steel bars, steel floors, walls, and ceilings. All the cells, particularly the six closed-front solitary confinement cells and the eight open-front isolation cells on the ground floor, were larger and more modern than the cells in the main cellhouse.

Adequately lighted and ventilated, all open-front cells in D-block were equipped with electric light fixtures, vitreous china toilets and wash-basins, and comfortable steel bunks. Thick battleship linoleum covered the floors of all but the solitary confinement cells. The eight open-front cells had regular barred cell fronts and doors. The six double-door solitary confinement cells were not quite as comfortable as the others. Two were stripped of all furnishings except a protected electric light fixture and a flush-rim toilet.

Although the sliding cell doors on the lower tier were, as a rule, electrically operated from a control box located in the west gun gallery, the two upper tiers had sliding doors which were key-controlled. The door key for these 28 cells was kept in the west gun gallery. Whenever it was in the hands of the block officer, the gallery officer posted himself in the D-block section of the gallery to cover him.

Meals for the inmates in the open-front cells were usually served by an inmate orderly selected from the D-block population. The menu was the same as that offered to the mainline prisoners,

Obsolete A-block, looking toward east gun gallery. Cell fronts and doors have no tool-resistant bars or modern locking devices.

13

ALCATRAZ '46

however, the food was carefully portioned by the block officer so that each inmate received his full share. Additional servings of unrationed items were usually available.

On the northwestern end of the main cellhouse was the dining room. On the southeasterly end, immediately adjacent to the light-house, were the administrative offices and the super-secure main gate entrance to the prison. This ingeniously designed and strongly protected sallyport-type entrance was manned 24 hours a day. In this area was the armory, the prison's control center and arsenal, constructed of reinforced concrete, hardened steel plate, and bullet-proof glass. The armory was positioned so that the armory officer was able to exercise supervision and control over all persons who passed through the main gate.

Outside the cellhouse were well-equipped industrial shops and recreational facilities. A double row of twenty-foot high cyclone wire fence topped with strands of barbed wire sealed off these areas from access to the bay. Watch towers of steel and shatter-proof glass were positioned to oversee and, if necessary, control the areas. Each tower was equipped with a high power rifle, a sub-machine gun, gas projectiles, grenades, searchlights, field glasses, and a telephone. Each tower officer carried a .45 calibre Colt semi-automatic pistol for self-protection.

Inmates marching to and from the work area were required to pass through metal detectors and to submit to random body-searches by specially trained officers. There were no inmates working unsupervised anywhere on the island.

To maintain security, one half of the 100-man correctional force was required to reside on the island within a restricted, fenced-off five acre area. Three apartment houses, six cottages, and a two-family duplex were constructed 47 feet above the bay. These buildings offered reasonably modern accomodations for some fifty families. The island post-office, the assembly hall where residents frequently gathered for religious services and social affairs, and a small general store were conveniently located within the residential area.

Strung out along the single lane road leading to and from the cellhouse atop the rock, were other housing units, a bachelor's quarters, residences for the warden and the chief medical officer, the Officer's Club building, and numerous service and storage buildings including the powerhouse. Apartments for employees of the Light-house Service were located in the base of the lighthouse which towered above the immediately adjacent cellhouse.

The powerhouse and pumping station were located at the north-west end of the island. They provided heat and electricity for the prison and the residential area. Salt water for the island's firefighting and sanitary systems was pumped from the bay via a screened intake pipe immediately adjacent to the powerhouse.

In the early days of the prison, the army steamer "General Frank M. Coxe" and two army waterboats, the "Aquario" and the "Aquador," were frequent visitors. They were later replaced by a water barge which transported freight and fresh water to the island several times each week. This was necessary since the island's deep wells had become brackish. A number of huge underground cisterns were used for the storage of water. One of these was located inside the solid rock below the prison basement that had been the officers' quarters in the old fort and whose massive walls were used as

The Road Tower, from which guards overlooked D-block, the recreation yard, and the work area.

foundations for the Army Disciplinary Barracks. The use of the old underground masonry and cistern contributed to a century old legend about ancient excavations or "Spanish Tunnels" which led down through the solid rock to the water's edge. In later years, a huge steel watertank was erected to increase the island's freshwater storage capacity.

Daily collections of miscellaneous trash from all over the island, were trucked to a huge incinerator in the industries work area. Garbage and raw sewage were flushed directly into the bay, accounting in part for the dense offshore crab and fish populations and for the prevalence of well-fed rats and seagulls on the island.

There were two types of telephone service on Alcatraz. One was a completely independent local system which served both the prison and the residential area. The other was the public telephone system, the only fixed connection with the mainland. It consisted of three trunk lines from San Francisco two of which terminated in a PBX switchboard in the prison armory while a third served a pay station located in the captain's office just outside the armory. Incoming calls for island residents could be relayed to them by the armory officer via the local telephone system, but to make an out-going call, a resident had to walk uphill to the pay station. The three lines ran through a telephone cable which was draped across the floor of the bay to San Francisco. This solitary link with the outside world was often severed by vessels that dragged their anchors along the ship channel between the island and the San Francisco wharves. Until the broken cable was repaired, the prison relied on a two-way short wave radio communication system. In the early years, prisoners were never permitted to use the outside telephone and it was only under very unusual circumstances that they were allowed to use the inside telephones.

Large sign warns vessels not to drop their anchors.

The shoreline of the island was well guarded. Unauthorized vessels were not permitted to dock, and the tower officers were instructed to fire "warning shots" if any unauthorized vessel attempted to do so. Occasionally a small vessel, lost in the fog, would run aground on the rocky shore. On one memorable occasion, a sailor on a foreign vessel anchored off Treasure Island, fell overboard and was carried by the swift ebb tide to the north side of the rock. By great good fortune, he reached the shore and was able to cling to the barnacle-encrusted pilings of the island dock. His presence in the icy water annoyed the seagulls nesting near the dock, and they set up a protesting clamor which effectively drowned out the sailor's feeble cries for help. Officers investigating the unusual behavior of the gulls, found the unauthorized visitor, coolly snatched him from what might have been his watery grave, and turned him over to the Coast Guard for return to his ship.

Bathing or swimming in the cold, treacherous waters around the island was discouraged, but occasionally a few daring youngsters would swim across the ship channel from San Francisco to the 200-yard marker buoys to wave at watching islanders before swimming back.

For the most part, non-prison life on Alcatraz was pleasant and interesting. Although confined to the five acre section, the residents were not unduly restricted. They could come or go on any of the twelve daily round trips of the "Warden Johnston," a diesel-powered prison launch built by inmates at the U.S. Penitentiary on McNeil Island, Washington. For emergency passenger transportation, the

15

The Rock in April, 1946, one month before the blastout.

institution had a second launch, the "McDowell." On the San Francisco side, employees could park their automobiles at the foot of Van Ness Avenue and board the launch near Aquatic Park. School children were transported to and from San Francisco on school days because there were no educational facilities on the rock. Island residents who were registered to vote in California were required to vote at a mainland polling place because the island was within the limits of the city and county of San Francisco.

Island employees and their guests enjoyed the Officer's Club which provided bowling alleys, billiard tables, dance floor, banquet room, card rooms, and a well-equipped kitchen. There was a handball court which doubled as a gymnasium, a children's playground complete with sand-box, swings, and slides, and facilities for picnicking, fishing, and crabbing from the island's shore. Friends and relatives could be entertained in the homes and throughout the residential area.

As a general rule, all women and children residing on the island were required to avoid contact or conversation with prison inmates. This rule was not at all difficult to enforce because only a few carefully selected, closely supervised inmates were permitted to enter the non-prison area of the island. Women and children were also routinely excluded from the prison area except the auditorium directly above the prison's main entrance, where moving pictures were shown once or twice a month. Male guests, vouched for by an employee, could be taken on an escorted tour of the prison by special permission of the warden.

Prisoners and guards in recreation yard. As a rule, the families of the guards residing on the island were required to avoid either contact or conversation with the prisoners.

Although employee life-styles appeared to be normal on the surface, there was always an undercurrent of apprehension, kept alive by the various riots, assaults, and escape attempts by inmates. Employees and relatives could never completely forget the kinetic potential within the collection of criminals housed in the cream-colored cellhouse high on the island. But recognizing the potential, they learned to live with it and were physically and psychologically prepared to deal with it. Morale was surprisingly high. Prior to 1946, only one officer had been slain (Royal Cline, 1938), although several had been assaulted and might have been killed if other officers had not promptly intervened. Confidence in colleagues and in the prison administration was demonstrated by the fact that there was always a long list of non-resident employees patiently waiting for a vacant housing unit on the island.

It appeared that the federal government had developed an escape-proof prison supervised by a hand-picked staff of correctional officers and administered by one of the best qualified penologists in the country.

ALCATRAZ '46

Interior view of an isolation cell.

The Myth

The most important factor which influenced the federal government to convert the out-moded Army Disciplinary Barracks into a super-secure penitentiary, was the need for effective segregation and safe incarceration of trouble-makers, escape-risks, and other malcontent federal prison inmates at Atlanta, Leavenworth, McNeil Island, and Lewisburg. Alcatraz was designed to meet this need, and the administrators of other federal prisons gladly sent their worst problem inmates — the confirmed criminals, the sex offenders and perpetrators of other heinous offenses, the most belligerent and physically aggressive, the wealthy and influential gangsters. "Scarface" Al Capone, members of the Toughy gang from Chicago, "Machine Gun" Kelly, and members of the Barker-Karpis gang arrived at the island chained to less known but equally troublesome individuals. The transferees to Alcatraz were shipped cross country in special railway coaches twice each year. No instances of violence, insubordination, mutiny, or escape attempt were ever reported in connection with these transfers.

At first, many of the tough, arrogant, determined law-breakers were not particularly intimidated by the change from one federal prison to another. "After all," they rationalized, "prisons are all alike and easy to beat." But they soon discovered that Alcatraz was not like the other prisons. Bribery, threat, and physical assault were frequently attempted to test the officer personnel and the system, but the hand-picked staff of correctional officers could not be bribed or intimidated, and the attempts were met with such a swift, sure hand, that they were seldom tried more than once by the same individual. The success of the Alcatraz system was due to the close and constant surveillance of inmates, the strict discipline and routine, and the swift and consistent punishment for misconduct.

Prisoners were never physically abused. Punishment usually involved segregation. When it was most severe, an individual was confined in an isolation cell (solitary confinement) on a restricted diet (1200 calories per day) for an indeterminate period followed by an indeterminate period of confinement in a segregation cell on a full diet.

For many criminals, the absence of physical abuse and the impartial use of segregation facilities, was a new experience. Every instance of insubordination, assault, or rebellion was met with inflexible, prompt disciplinary action. Force was used when force was required, but it was never coupled with brutality or deliberate mistreatment of inmates.

Throughout the decade following the prison's establishment, a deliberate veil of secrecy was dropped about the island. The lack of details about the prison's system was thought to be a deterrent to extreme offenders. The fact that troublesome prisoners were dealt with firmly and successfully was well-publicized within the federal prison system, and the word quickly spread through the criminal underworld that the federal government had ceased to tolerate vicious misconduct.

The secrecy, however, gave rise to fanciful speculations as to how and by what mysterious means the government was able to control the "uncontrollable" criminals. Some journalists alleged that the Alcatraz guards were sadistic brutes who routinely beat and tortured the inmates and confined them interminably in sub-terranean dungeons until they died or lost their will to resist. A sizeable number of self-serving inmate braggarts claimed they were starved, whipped, clubbed, chained, trussed up in straight jackets, or beaten with high pressure fire hoses. Some columnists wrote of "bread and water" punishments when in reality, the minimal diet given a prisoner in segregation was nutritional, even though it consisted of only 1200 calories per day. Prisoners not in segregation had more than an ample supply and selection of food. Other columnists wrote that "temperatures were kept at a steady 70° F so that if an escapee tried to swim to the mainland, he would become numb the instant he hit the water." In reality, the prison had no system for regulating temperatures. Because of its location in the bay, the prison was generally cool. Still other columnists wrote that officers "would keep the floors so well-polished you could see your face in them. If a prisoner tried to run, he'd go straight on his butt." Actually the floors were kept spotless, but highly waxed floors were considered as dangerous for the officers as for the inmates.

The public of the 30's eagerly sought and accepted sensational stories. They absorbed the bragging of inmate transferees who savored an imaginary distinction of having proved that they were tough enough to survive "The Rock". And from books, newspapers, and moving pictures, it became generally believed that Alcatraz was a dead-end dumping ground for federal prisoners.

Alcatraz was far from being a dead-end for prisoners. The population turnover pattern was fairly constant from the start. Each year, approximately 40 inmates were received and about the same number was transferred. The prison population never exceeded 300 at any time. Few inmates served more than three years on the island. From his date of arrival, each inmate was encouraged to work his way back to a less restrictive institution. Most were able to do this. A few

D-block, looking toward closed-front solitary confinement and open-front isolation cells.

ALCATRAZ '46

U.S. Coastguard lighthouse.

refused to change their unacceptable behavior patterns even though they knew they might serve out their entire sentence on "The Rock". Others had become so well-adjusted to the facilities, particularly the relative luxury of the one-man cells, that they petitioned the Bureau of Prisons to permit them to decline a transfer to a less restrictive but more densely populated institution.

The first inmate, a U.S. Army transferee, was registered as 1 Az (Az = Alcatraz). By mid-1934, the top register number was 250 Az. Throughout its operation, a daily count of less than 300 was maintained, and there was a relatively high turnover — about 40 persons per year.

By the mid-1940's, Alcatraz had become accepted throughout the civilized world as the symbol of the federal prison system of the United States, but the symbol was tainted by the myth that had become firmly established. Subsequent lifting of the island's veil of secrecy failed to materially alter the popular belief that Alcatraz was a hell-hole of sadism and inhuman repression.

A look at the cell and personal belongings of a prisoner.

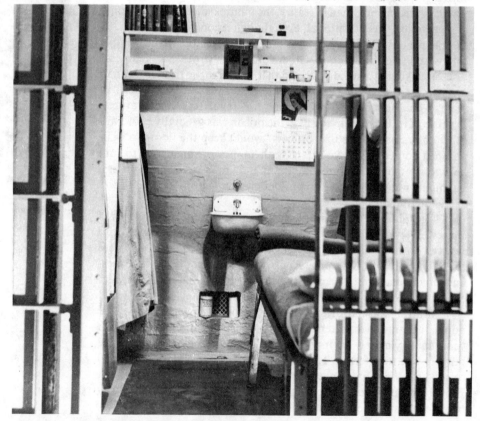

LOG

"There is no possibility of wiping out crime
by trying to reform criminals. The house has
been burned down. The tree has felt the blow
of the ax and has fallen in the forest. The
house cannot be re-erected, nor can the
tree again point its leaves to the sky."

J. Edgar Hoover

"Helen, death hovers over me day and night.
Here in isolation, there is no hope for me
to be different. I must come to you."

Marvin Hubbard
to his wife

Eighteen-year-old "Dutch Joe" Cretzer in 1929.

The Men

By Wednesday May 1, 1946, the San Francisco Bay Area had experienced nearly a month of unusually good weather. Temperatures had ranged from the low 60's to the high 70's, and fog had funneled through the Golden Gate on only three days.

Because of its location, Alcatraz was by far, the best ventilated prison in the federal prison system — *Air Conditioned By Nature: Hard To Heat But Easy To Ventilate*. On this particular day, however, the heat lingered on into the evening, and the air hung in a stagnant mass over the prison.

* * *

Joseph Cretzer lay perspiring on his cot in cell 152 and looked out onto the Flats of B-block. "That lousy food," he grumbled, the corner of his mouth shifting into a contemptuous sneer, "They're tryin' to starve us. The slop don't have no vitamins, no nothin'. It's just garbage, 'n we gotta eat it or starve." He turned his face into the pillow.

The combination of smells — sharp, salty air, after dinner kitchen aromas, and perspiring bodies — once again left him slightly nauseated. No matter how many years he had spent behind bars, it was always the same day after day — that sickening, repulsive, after dinner smell. This hot evening seemed to make the effect worse than usual.

Turning his head on the pillow, he folded his thick, hair-covered hands behind his head and studied the ceiling. "Tomorrow night at this time," his mind shifted, "with a little luck, I'll be with Kay in 'Frisco. We'll be havin' steak 'n pie a la mode."

Joseph Paul Cretzer when he was arrested in Chicago in 1939 after a bloody Los Angeles bank robbery. He was branded Public Enemy No. 5 by the F.B.I.

ALCATRAZ '46

Joseph Paul Cretzer (Dutch Joe) was 35. An Oakland, California burglar turned bank robber, he was serving a life sentence for the slaying of an elderly United States Marshal in Tacoma, Washington. Cretzer's penetrating, dark brown eyes were set beneath black, bushy eyebrows, and his shrewd, no-nonsense manner was communicated by the movements of his stocky build. Long strands of wavy black hair occasionally dropped across his forehead, and he had the habit of combing them back whether they had fallen there or not. He was distrustful of most people and events, and the wry smile that often crossed his face communicated sarcasm or doubt. Other inmates considered him to be wise about prison procedures and tended to look to him for advice. He knew a great deal about the loopholes in federal laws, the ins and outs of prison routines, and the personal characteristics of officers and prisoners. Although he was relatively young compared to most other Alcatraz inmates, he had quickly gained acceptance as a leader among the aggressive, escape-minded segments of the prison population.

Becoming restless, he arose from his steel cot and paced the five-by-nine cell. Pausing for a moment, he extended a small polished steel hand mirror through the cellfront bars and stared at the reflection down the aisle toward the West Gun Gallery. "That's where it all hangs," his eyes narrowed. "It's been one helluva long time since I first saw that damned bird cage."

Joe Cretzer, the youngest of three sons, was born in Montana to deaf mute parents. His family moved to the west side of Oakland, California before he was 10. The excitement in his young life centered around the criminal escapades of his two older brothers. Before he was 15, he had committed at least seven industrial burglaries in nearby Emeryville. In each instance he was caught, but because authorities felt sorry for his deaf mute parents, he was released to their custody.

In 1927 he was arrested in Livermore, California while traveling east and charged with the theft of the automobile he was driving. While awaiting trial, he escaped from detention but was recaptured near Lake Merritt, a few blocks from Oakland's downtown courthouse. He was sentenced to the Preston Reformatory Industrial School in Iones, California. On the way to Ione, he again escaped, this time from the parole officer's automobile, and remained at large until November 1929 when police found him at his parent's home in Oakland. While at large, his brothers had been imprisoned for long terms in the east for a variety of armed robberies.

Cretzer was again sent to the Industrial School at Ione to face his first prison term. Almost within hours of his arrival, he established a friendship with Arnold T. Kyle, a man somewhat shorter in stature and two years older. Originally from Oregon, Kyle had traveled to California and initiated a series of robberies. He had been caught in a

A-B aisle, looking toward west gun gallery.

24

grocery store holdup near Galt, California and convicted for an assault with the intent to kill. The friendship of the young inmates grew during their stay at Ione.

To their mutual surprise, both were paroled at the same time in 1931. Upon release, they stole an automobile, after mugging and robbing its occupants, and headed for Black Diamond Street in Pittsburg, California. Arriving in Pittsburg, the young pair abandoned the car and moved in with Kyle's younger sister, Edna, who was known in the vicinity by the alias of Kay Wallace.

Kay was the operator of a well-known and popular whorehouse in the Bruno Hotel near Pittsburg's busy wharf. She was somewhat attractive, sharp featured, red-haired, and outgoing. Strong self-assured men appealed to her, and she took a liking to Cretzer. They were soon married in nearby Antioch, and for the next few years, they and Kay's brother, Arnold, ran such an efficient and profitable whorehouse that the authorities left them virtually unmolested until Kay was arrested for forcing a 17-year-old Spanish-American girl into prostitution. When Kay was released on bail, the three decided to leave the Bay Area and look for easy-to-rob banks in California and Oregon.

With Kay as lookout and driver of the getaway car, Cretzer and Kyle committed scores of bank robberies up and down the West Coast. They were credited with at least 40 robberies in the San Francisco Bay Area alone. During this time, they were joined by two nationally sought bank robbers, John Hetzer and James D. Courey.

On January 23, 1938 the gang held up a branch of the American Trust Company at 40th and Piedmont in Oakland, stole $6,000, and severely wounded one bank official in the getaway. The Federal Bureau of Investigation placed Cretzer on its Most Wanted list, and he was considered to be one of the nation's most dangerous bank robbers. Agents of the Bureau began a nation-wide search for him and his gang. At age 27 he was receiving a press coverage comparable to that given John Dillinger, "Pretty Boy" Floyd, or "Baby Face" Nelson. Cretzer was proud to be billed as Public Enemy No. 5.

In 1939, when Kay was in Oakland working as a movie usherette at the Grand Lake Theater, Cretzer and Kyle were arrested in Chicago and returned to California to stand trial for a bank robbery in Pasadena. Cretzer proudly announced to newsmen that no prison could hold him and that he would soon become Public Enemy No. 1. While awaiting trial, an alert officer caught him trying to unlock his handcuffs with a lock pick made from the tongue of his belt buckle. The prosecuting attorney, as he prepared his case, observed that Cretzer and his gang were unlike any in California's crime history.

Before the trial could be held, the Federal Government indicted Cretzer and Kyle for the robbery of three Seattle, Washington banks and claimed jurisdiction for criminal prosecution.

Convicted and sentenced to the federal penitentiary on

Edna Kyle

ALCATRAZ '46

McNeil Island, in Puget Sound, the two immediately plotted another escape. Within three months of their arrival, they had familiarized themselves with prison routines and apparent gaps in security. On Wednesday morning, May 23, 1940, while on a labor detail cutting trees and brush, they jumped aboard a passing prison truck and threatened the inmate driver with their razor sharp axes. The driver sped them toward the island boat dock with bullets slamming into the back of the vehicle. Forced to abandon the bullet-riddled truck and seek refuge in the woods, both were recaptured within a few days. On August 22, 1940 they went on trial in the federal district court in Tacoma, Washington for the attempted escape.

As the district judge prepared to add another five years to each of their respective 25-year sentences, the two prisoners suddenly and viciously assaulted an elderly United States Marshal, A. J. Chitty. After striking him repeatedly with their manacled fists, they tried to remove his holstered pistol. The escape attempt failed, but Marshal Chitty suffered a fatal heart attack.

Now, instead of just additional escape attempt charges, Cretzer and his brother-in-law faced a murder charge. Their court-appointed attorneys pleaded that the killing of Marshal Chitty was not premeditated. They argued that the elderly Marshal died of a heart attack and not from the beating he suffered at the hands of their defendants. Evidently this argument saved them from the electric chair, for Federal Judge Neterer sentenced them to life imprisonment, and the Bureau of Prisons designated Alcatraz as the place of confinement. In the fall of 1940, they arrived in chains, leg-ironed and handcuffed together. Cretzer was registered as 547Az and Kyle as 548Az.

Cretzer turned the mirror he was holding and glanced toward the east end of the cellblock. "The Big House," he thought, brushing a strand of imaginary hair from his forehead, "No Cagneys or Bogarts in this dump. Only men like me, poundin' the walls, locked up tighter than animals in a zoo. Except that the animals eat better."

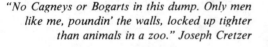

"No Cagneys or Bogarts in this dump. Only men like me, poundin' the walls, locked up tighter than animals in a zoo." Joseph Cretzer

During the routine receiving procedure when he arrived at Alcatraz, Cretzer warned Warden Johnston and other prison officials that he intended to escape at the first opportunity as he had done so many times before. More sophisticated inmates considered him to be stupid to announce his intentions, but neither officers nor inmates doubted that he would make the attempt.

His first try took place in May 1941. While working together in the industrial shops, he and Kyle planned an escape. They were joined by an ex-McNeil Island inmate named Lloyd Barkdoll and Sam Shockley, a 36-year-old transferee from Leavenworth who was serving a life sentence for robbery and kidnapping. The four men had been assigned to the prison mat shop at the west end of the island, only 20 feet above the bay. Nothing but a few steel bars and some rusty barbed wire separated them from the freedom they sought.

Cretzer's plan involved Kay. On several successive visits to the prison, Kay learned from him and Kyle the details of the plan and her role in it. She agreed to rent a fast motorboat. At 1:30 p.m. on May 21, she would be fishing in the channel between Angel Island and Alcatraz Island. She would watch the island through binoculars and head the boat toward the rocky shore as soon as she saw the escapees coming through the shop window. By the time they made their way through the barbed wire entanglements to the beach, she would be there to pick them up and speed them away to the mainland where guns and a fast automobile would be waiting.

As planned, the four men began their escape at precisely 1:30 p.m. Barkdoll approached the unsuspecting shop foreman and asked him to step into an adjoining room to inspect a faulty machine. The other three followed unobtrusively, then all four jumped the foreman and had him tied, gagged, and face down on the floor before he could utter a sound.

Several other inmates were in the shop, but they followed the standard inmate code of not intervening.

Industries shops and powerplant at northwest end of the island.

"She would watch the island through binoculars and head the boat toward the rocky shore as soon as she saw the escapees coming through the shop window."

ALCATRAZ '46

Lower level south side showing Road Tower, incinerator, and industries building in distance.

Grinning, they allowed themselves to be locked in the shop storeroom. For them it was an exciting change in the monotony of prison life, and whatever happened would not be held against them.

Cretzer expressed concern because he saw no sign of the speed boat in the channel. Kyle reassured him, "Don't worry, Joe, we can count on Kay. She'll be there."

They unbolted a grinding wheel from the work bench, plugged it into an outlet, and went to work on the window bars. Each inmate took turns grinding while the others guarded the foreman and kept a lookout for patrolling officers.

The next person to enter the shop was Cornelius Manning, the Superintendent of Industries. When asked to look at a faulty machine, he too, ended up bound and gagged on the floor.

An hour passed, and still the grinder kept grinding without making much impression on the bars. Barkdoll was openly disgusted, "Hell, the damn grinder isn't any good." Shockley added, "Where is that dame with the speed boat?"

When the work area officer reached the mat shop on his routine patrol of the area, the four took time off from their labors to add him to their increasing collection of captives. Returning their attention to the grinder, Cretzer and Kyle took turns. Working like maniacs, sweat dripping, their drawn faces tried not to express the growing hopelessness of their efforts. To get through the window, they would have to cut at least two of the bars, and they were still grinding away on the first one.

At 2:25 p.m. Captain Paul Madigan strolled into the shop and was immediately overwhelmed and bound, but not gagged. While Cretzer doggedly ground away at the bars and Kyle stared dejectedly at the empty ship channel, Madigan, speaking calmly and with conviction, pointed out that they would never cut through the bars with the grinder they were using. He carefully explained that the grindstone was not sufficiently abrasive to cut into hardened, tool-resistant steel and that this had been an important consideration when the grinders were purchased. He also reminded them that they had less than five minutes before the regular mid-afternoon count. If the count was not telephoned to the Armory by the shop foreman on time, the Armory officer would sound the alarm, and the riot squad would be sent to investigate. "Why not give up voluntarily," he suggested, "before anything serious happens?"

There was a long, tense moment of silence following the Captain's suggestion. A few years previously, three escaping inmates had wantonly slain their shop officer "just to let them know we meant business." Barkdoll looked at Kyle, and Kyle looked at Cretzer who stared bitterly at the empty channel, then at the undamaged window bars. Kyle spoke softly, "Joe, we're getting deader every minute. We'll come up again, wait and see."

With a final curse expressing his frustration, Cretzer hurled the useless grinder against the shop wall and numbly

Aerial view of Alcatraz.

ALCATRAZ '46

Interior of a solitary confinement cell.

stood by as Barkdoll cut the ropes which bound the captives. "Next time we'll have guns 'n a boat," thought Cretzer. "You can't depend on women, not even your own wife." It was much later that Cretzer learned that Kay's failure to appear with a rented speed boat was because she had been arrested on Market Street by the Vice Squad that same morning, and when they were grinding the mat shop bars, she was resting quietly in the women's section of the City-County jail.

The four men were placed in segregation for their attempt. Kyle settled down and made an effort to diminish his time through good behavior, but Cretzer, although less aggressive, remained bitter.

He spent nearly five years in D-block. During his long stay, the desire for certain foods bothered him most. He had always enjoyed eating even though he had little taste for subtle and delicate flavors. In D-block he was fed a monotonous prison diet which, although nutritionally adequate, was quite distant from the steaks and chops and pie a la mode of his freer days.

Much of his time in D-block was spent in idleness, but on a few occasions he tried his talent at poetry:

Solitary confinement, isolation, and segregation.

OLD ALCATRAZ POEM

Cretzer — 1945

"Habeas Corpus" — "Bill of Rights"
"Multiple Jeopardy" — "Too Much Time";
Good old Forma Paup'ris cites:
"This Indoor Sport don't cost a dime!"

RICH CONS, POOR CONS, CELL-HOUSE THIEVES
ALL ARE GUILTLESS — SO THEY PLEAD:
GATHERED IN, LIKE HARVEST SHEAVES,
THEY HOPE SOME JUDGE WILL SET 'EM FREE.

"Oh Noble, Honorable, District Judge,
Comes now on humble knee
Your ever-pleading appellant
Moves you for Liberty!"

BUY 'EM PENCILS — LET 'EM WRITE,
FINE WORDS LIKE "CORAM NOBIS."
SUCH SWEET PETITIONS, HONOR BRIGHT,
PRESENTED IN PROPER PERSONIS.

"Oh Circuit Court — Oh Noble Three Sirs,
Judge now, our valid appeal
Framed like dogs — without due process,
Affiant-Appellant, we wanna new deal!"

IGNORANT OF LAW'S ENDLESS PROGRESSION,
WITHOUT A LAWYER, THEY HADN'T A CHANCE.
THERE WEREN'T NO TRUTH TO THEIR CONFESSION,
THE "D. A." MADE 'EM "SING" AND "DANCE."

"Oh Supreme Court Judges, errors, torts,
Our honorable cause we bring to thee;
By the District and the Circuit Courts,
DENIED, in black conspiracy!"

COUNTLESS CONS, WITH WRITS GALORE
A HORDE OF DEADLY DING-BATS:
GUILTY AS HELL, BUT STILL THEY YELL,
"WE WANNA CHANGE OUR HABITATS."

"Oh Noble, Kindly Pres-i-dent,
Of this great coun-ter-ry,
Please Pardon Us — we'd love to fight
For life and Lib-er-ty!"

THEY'RE ALL INVENTORS, ENGINEERS,
BRAVE, BOLD, AND DARING MEN,
THEY'D SHOW YOU LOTS — IN SUICIDE SQUADS,
IF YOU'D RELEASE 'EM, THEN.

"Oh Judges, Court, and Pres-i-dent,
Appeals all seem to fail;
But writing reams of rancid writs
Is good, clean fun, in jail!"

SO DON'T YOU WORRY — DON'T YOU FRET,
WE DON'T DISCOURAGE EASY.
WE'LL TRY AND TRY AGAIN, YOU BET,
ON GROUNDS HOWEVER CHEESY!

ALCATRAZ '46

The Bay Bridge at sunrise, as seen from Alcatraz.

It was only in the past four months that Cretzer had been released on a trial basis to B-block in the main cellhouse. Now that he was again allowed the regular privilege of mixing with other prisoners in the recreation yard, he had informed them that doing time in D-block was "like bein' sealed up in an ancient submarine." He was told when to wake up, eat, and sleep. His letters and reading materials were carefully screened, and he was seldom allowed out of his cell. While prisoners in B and C blocks were allowed one 1-hour visit each month, Cretzer's visiting privilege was restricted to one per year. During his long stay in segregation, Kay had taken a job at the Hunter's Point shipyard and found a place to live nearby "to be at least that close to Joe." But she soon grew tired of waiting, divorced him on the grounds of abandonment, married a local truck driver, and began a respectable family life in a new housing area.

Cretzer moved back to his cot and slid the mirror under his pillow. Stretching out upon the mattress, he prepared to get a good night's sleep. "Kay'll put me up for a few days," he thought as he pulled a light blanket across his body, "Then I'll move on, 'n she can go 'bout her own business."

The first rays of the 7:10 a.m. sunrise foretold the coming of another beautiful Spring day. A slight westerly breeze, less than three miles per hour, had carried away the stagnant, warm air that had accumulated over the bay the night before. The placid waters around the island were disturbed only by the frothy wake of the "Warden Johnston" as it slowly circled the island on its regular morning inspection tour. Cutting inside the 200-yard marker buoys and carefully avoiding the semi-submerged tip of Little Alcatraz, a small outcropping of rock at the western shore, the prison launch skirted the shoreline for a few hundred yards, then swung away toward San Francisco where several day shift officers were waiting.

* * *

Through his cell window in D-block, Sam Shockley watched the launch diminish in size as it moved toward the city. The atmosphere was clear, and the sky was cloudless. "That's a helluva note," he grumbled. "No fog, no clouds, no nothin'. Why today, of all days?"

He removed a crumpled scrap of paper from his pocket, smoothed it out, and reread the scrawled message, "ok, 5/2." He replaced the paper, moved to the cell door, and glanced down the aisle at the cellhouse clock.

In the main cell house, an excess of cells facilitated the selective housing of inmates. Based upon the carefully considered recommendations of the prison's classification committee, emotionally disturbed inmates and others requiring close supervision, were housed in cells adjacent to the cellhouse officer's duty station where closer surveillance could be given. When there was need for maximum supervision, the cells in D-block were used.

Samuel Richard Shockley (Crazy Sam) was a typical inmate in D-block, although not all inmates were confined for the same reason. Inmate orderly Louis Fleish, the former leader of the Purple Gang which controlled the underworld rackets of Detroit, served meals to the D-block inmates. He was segregated because he seemed to be unable to avoid involvement in whatever undercover gambling

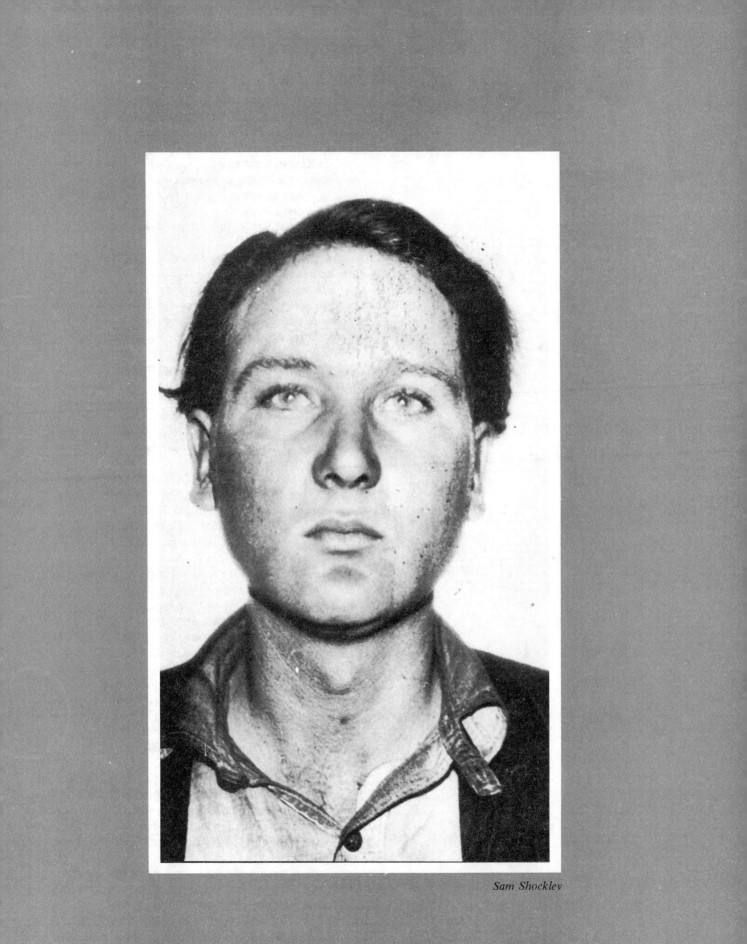

Sam Shockley

ALCATRAZ '46

went on in the prison. Robert Franklin Stroud, the "Birdman of Alcatraz," was in D because of his homicidal and suicidal episodes. Some men were housed in the segregation unit at their own request for protection. A number of aggressive homosexuals were also kept in D-block.

Shockley had claimed he heard voices which ordered him to create disturbances. When housed in the main cellhouse or assigned to work detail, his voices invariably led him into trouble with other inmates and with officers. A series of unpredictable outbursts brought about his placement in D-block.

Shockley was in his mid-thirties. High light colored eyes, set in an oval, youthful face, seldom expressed emotion. His mouth, however, smiled frequently, and his general manner seemed to be one that continually sought acceptance and approval from others. He had been imprisoned at Leavenworth for bank robbery and kidnapping.

While at Leavenworth, he was given a battery of tests. A Stanford-Binet Intelligence Test indicated his IQ to be 68. Other tests gave similar results. In situations of confusion or tension, he tended to break down and was unable to think clearly. Because his conduct in prison was erratic and unpredictable, he was considered to be dangerous to those around him, thus in late September 1938, he was transferred to Alcatraz.

During one of several reexaminations at Alcatraz, he indicated that he heard voices and felt sensations. He said that his insides were being bombarded with rays from lights. He could feel the rays in his head and spinal column. He believed that the rays were being sent out by some machine as directed by an organization called "The Public of Health" in order to treat people for different illnesses. He thought he was being helped by the rays.

Shockley was not the only inmate in D who claimed hallucinations. Several feigned insanity in the hope of being transferred to the federal prison hospital at Springfield, Missouri where the possibility of escaping was somewhat better. Officials, however, thought Shockley was incapable of faking the hallucinations he described because of the level of his intelligence. "He is probably mentally ill," stated one psychiatrist, "but he is not insane." Under consideration for removal to the Springfield hospital, it was likely he would soon be recommended for transfer.

Shockley's placement in D put him in a cell next to Cretzer. Having been involved in his earlier escape attempt with Shockley, Cretzer brought his old friend into a new escape plan. He was sure Shockley would keep the plan a secret and could be depended upon to follow simple orders. "Count me in, Joe," Sam agreed with an eager smile. "I'll do anythin' you say."

Cretzer would have preferred a more stable partner such as his friend Kyle, but Kyle was not in D-block at the time and Shockley was. The escape plan depended upon having a man in D. Actually Shockley was an ideal person to involve in the plan. Because prison officers considered him to be a nuisance among many nuisances, he would not be suspected of being up to something if he screamed, hollered, and threw stuff out of his cell. He was notorious for that sort of unacceptable behavior.

After Cretzer had worked his way back into the main cellhouse, Shockley's part in the plan was rehearsed twice. To set up the rehearsals, kites, secretly passed messages, were sent to Shockley. At a time predetermined by Cretzer, Shockley created a disturbance in his cell. While covered by the armed guard in the west gun gallery, the unarmed floor officer opened the cell and quieted him down.

Sometime later, Shockley received a second kite indicating another predetermined time. For this disturbance, he was given seven days in solitary confinement on a light diet. When he returned to his segregation cell on April 28, he sent a kite to Cretzer indicating he was ready and eager to continue with the plan.

"You'll get a kite when we're ready," promised Cretzer. "Remember, Coy'll bang on the steel door with his broom handle. You watch the clock, 'n give him five minutes to get down to the west end where Marve can see him. Then raise hell. Make it good. Maybe start a fire, 'n throw your stuff outta the cell. Get the D-block screw worried enough to call the screw in the gun cage to back him up while he calms you down. It's important to get that guy with the guns outta the main cellhouse 'n keep him out until we're ready to take him. Keep listenin' for a second bang on the door. Calm down when you hear it. The screw in the gun cage will think everythin' is O.K. in D 'n come back to the main cellhouse. We'll take care of him there, 'n we'll all be outta this joint before you know it."

Shockley thought back on the two trial disturbances. "It sure worked ok them times," he smiled. "The gun screw came runnin' every time."

*   *   *

View of B cellblock flats and Cretzer's No. 152 cell.

Southwest side of main prison building. D unit is in upper right hand corner and beyond it is a screened cage enclosing a catwalk outside the dining room windows.

ALCATRAZ '46

After disembarking the employees' school children and several women who planned to shop in San Francisco, the "Johnston" took on board the Day Watch officers who lived in the city and who were scheduled to go on duty at 8:00 a.m. Backing slowly from the dock, the prison launch began its return trip to the island at 7:45 a.m.

In Building 64, an old Army Barracks converted into apartments for employees, Officer Harold Stites was enjoying his day off by sleeping in. While he slept, Mrs. Stites had gotten their children quietly off to school, but now the noise of the approaching launch and its subsequent docking beside Building 64, awakened him sooner than he wished.

Lieutenant Simpson and several other Day Watch officers had come on duty at 7:15 a.m. to get an early start. Under their supervision, the 223 mainline inmates had been awakened, counted, and were fed by the time the launch docked.

In the cellhouse, Officer Jim Murphy in the east gun gallery, gathered his equipment preparatory to leaving the post unmanned as was customary during the less hazardous Day Watch. At the other end of the cellhouse, in the west gun gallery, Officer Frank Prindle was turning over his firearms, keys, and equipment to Bert Burch, the Day Watch Gallery Officer. In D-block, Paul Owens made the final entry in the Post Log as he awaited the arrival of Cecil Corwin. Throughout the institution, at the main gate, in the armory, the hospital, and gun towers, the midnight to 8:00 a.m. Morning Watch, under the supervision of Lieutenant Fred Roberts, was relieved by the Day Watch.

From a vantage point high on the recreation yard wall, Captain Weinhold made certain that the wall and towers were manned. When a new watch of armed officers arrived at their posts, each made a quick visual survey of his tower and equipment before reporting by phone to the armory officer.

All the gun towers, except the Powerhouse Tower, were constructed of steel and shatter-proof glass. Most were connected by catwalks raised high above the ground on spidery steel trestles festooned with barbed wire. The glass walls of the towers afforded excellent visual control of the areas surrounding them. Manderville was in the Main Tower on the roof of the prison building, Levinson was in

Officer Bert Burch

Officer Frank Prindle

Lieutenant Fred Roberts

36

the Road Tower, Besk in the Hill Tower, Metcalf in the Model Tower, Waldo in the Powerhouse Tower, and Comerford in the Dock Tower. Each officer was armed with a rifle, a submachine gun, and a pistol. Yard Wall Officer John Barker carried a Thompson submachine gun cradled in his arms and a .45 calibre Colt semi-automatic pistol holstered on his hip.

Clifford Fish, the armory officer, received the phone calls from the Tower Officers. The armory was the hub of communications on the island, and it also served as the custodial control center. The independent island telephone system, the 2-way short-wave radio, and the commercial telephone lines to the mainland were all centered in the armory. The prison's reserve supplies of guns, ammunition, and keys were also stored there.

When all tower officers had reported their respective towers manned and ready for duty, Fish relayed the information to Captain Weinhold. The captain's next task was to evaluate the weather. Since nearly all escape attempts occurred on foggy days or nights, the art of weather predicting had become a very important part of the captain's responsibilities.

If the fog, which frequently blanketed the bay, was slight, certain precautions were taken. Officers were assigned to patrol the path between the security fences, and inmates were locked in their respective work shops as soon as they reached them. If the fog was dense, the inmates were not marched to the work area but were allowed to return to their cells or to remain in the recreation yard. Inmates considered very foggy days to be holidays.

Captain Weinhold predicted a clear day.

Upon returning to their cells after breakfast, the inmates were once again counted. Lieutenant Simpson supervised this official count from his post at the west end of the cellhouse. Lageson, the officer in charge of the cellhouse, sat at a desk in the west end near the dining room gate preparing the count tally while in the gun gallery overhead, Burch kept a watchful eye on all that took place below.

An officer was detailed to count each tier of the two main cellblocks. As soon as the six officers were in position, the count bell was sounded, and throughout the cellhouse more than 200 inmates rose to their feet and stood quietly behind their locked doors while officers counted. Officers in the hospital, the Culinary Department, and D-block counted the inmates in their respective areas and reported by phone to the Armory officer. When the count totals from the cellhouse and all other areas had been added and checked with the official total, the count bell was again sounded to indicate that the count was correct.

Counting of the Alcatraz population was almost continuous through each day. There were 12 official counts and several unofficial counts every 24 hours. Not even inmates in the hospital or in solitary confinement cells remained unobserved or uncounted for any length of time. No talking or moving about was tolerated during an official count. If an inmate chanced to be perched on his cell toilet when the count bell rang, he was allowed to remain in that position while being counted. Many officers maintained that certain inmates demonstrated their contemptuous attitude by habitually jerking their pants down and squatting every time the count bell rang.

* * *

Officer Clifford Fish

ALCATRAZ '46

Inmate Carnes stood quietly by the open-face door to his cell. He unseeingly stared at the aisle in front of him as the sounds of the count echoed down the aisles.

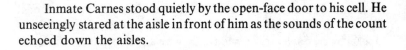

Clarence Victor Carnes (Joe/The Choctaw Kid) was born in 1927 in the hills of eastern Oklahoma. His Choctaw Indian parents were forced to move from place to place during his early years as his father sought work to feed his family. His mother would send him and his brothers and sisters to play with neighbor children, and when they returned she would ask if they had been fed. During the depression years, the neighbors always sent the children home when it came time to eat.

His father, Jimmie Carnes, had attended a government Indian school until he was old enough to work. He felt that the school had done much for him and that it would do his son good to attend the same school. Consequently, seven-year-old Carnes was enrolled in the Jones Academy, a boys school with grades from 1 through 12. While at the school, he associated with a gang of boys led by George Anderson, a large, husky boy of 12. He became George's best friend, and because George could whip any boy near his age, the two had no trouble from the older boys at school. Backed and coached by George, Carnes began to take on anyone he thought he could handle and discovered he had a natural ability for fighting. As he gained confidence, he acquired a reputation for being a fighter that was to be respected.

One evening the boys took in a Joe E. Brown movie. One outstanding feature about this prominent Hollywood actor was his extremely large mouth. In the movie, he put a whole apple into his mouth. Many of the boys tried to duplicate the feat with apples from the dinner table, but no one could do it. Carnes, however, selected a small apple which almost fit into his mouth. Giving it a thump with the heel of his hand, the apple went in. The boys laughed, then laughed harder when they realized he couldn't get the apple out. Embarrassed and angry, he was taken to the hospital to have it removed. From that day, Carnes was nicknamed Joe E. Brown. Eventually this was shortened to Joe E. and finally to Joe.

Carnes' first crime took place when he was eight. George decided to break into the school canteen for some candy. The door to the canteen was made of wooden slats nailed close together. Carnes' slender arms were able to reach through a small opening between the slats to the spring lock which held the door locked. Almost nightly the two boys would take a few candy bars, limiting the number in the hope that none would be missed.

On one occasion, George opened a small change box with a piece of wire. Carnes was impressed and thought he was associated with a master criminal, one who could open anything. The two took a quarter apiece and stole from the box from time to time. They were never caught.

Clarence Carnes in 1971 at a prison rodeo.

Clarence Carnes

ALCATRAZ '46

Carnes often remembered how scared he was the first time they stole. He remained scared all the next day, and the fear returned each time they went on their expeditions. There came a time when he began to enjoy the excitement and look forward to the next adventure. It became a pleasure to steal something, and the pleasure was transferred from one kind of stealing to another.

One night George and Carnes went hunting sparrows near a barn where potatoes were stored. They had constructed their own bows and arrows, and the flashlight they had, stolen earlier from one of the teacher's cars, was used to momentarily blind the bird so it could be shot with an arrow.

As they entered the barn, they met an old black man coming out with a sack of potatoes on his back. George fitted an arrow to his bow and commanded, "Stop or I'll shoot!" The old man was terrified and begged, "Please boys, dohn shoo me. Ah'm ony gettin sum food foh mah po famly." He carried on without let up. Carnes felt sorry for him and urged George not to shoot.

George lowered the bow and asked the man how many potatoes he had. After looking in the sack, George and Carnes each got sacks, loaded them up, and helped the man carry them to the wagon he had parked on a hill nearby. Telling the man to wait, the two boys broke into the dairy and took a can of milk, into the storage vault and took raisins, into the kitchen for a slab of bacon, and into the bakery for flour. When they returned to the wagon, the old fellow was overjoyed and couldn't thank the boys enough. After obtaining directions to the man's home, the boys continued to steal various food items for him. They were paid with candy and enough spending money to take them to the movies.

When Carnes returned to school in the fall of 1937, George did not show up. He had been caught in a jewelry store with his pockets filled with jewelry. He was sent to Pauls Valley Training School for boys, and Carnes never saw him again although he heard about him from time to time as he worked his way up the Golden Gloves ranks to become one of the better welterweights in the state.

Following in George's pattern, Carnes became the leader of a gang of boys and across a five-year period, he acquired a poor reputation at the school. When he was 15 and armed with a gun, he and a friend, Cecil Berry, tried to rob a service station in Atoka, Oklahoma. When the station attendant, W. M. Weyland, attacked Carnes with a coke bottle, the gun went off, and the attendant was killed. The young robbers were captured within the hour and placed in the county jail to await trial for first degree murder.

While in custody, they jumped their jailers, seriously injuring one, stole a revolver, and escaped. They were captured 12 hours later after an all-day chase by bloodhounds. Carnes pleaded guilty and was sentenced to life imprisonment on October 26, 1943.

He was sent to the Oklahoma State Reformatory at

Granite and put to work at a rock quarry where large rocks were broken into smaller ones to make gravel for roads. On a hot afternoon while the guards relaxed on duty, Carnes, Julian Blankenship, and Fred Newel escaped unnoticed from the quarry and made their way toward the town of Granite. On the way, they forced a farmer to give them the keys to his car, then taking him with them, they drove across the state line into Texas. Realizing they had violated a federal kidnapping law, they tied and left their prisoner near Shamrock, Texas, then doubled back with the intention of going to Tulsa, Oklahoma, but at 70 mph, Fred, the driver, couldn't make the sharp turn onto a bridge built temporarily alongside a washed out section of the regular bridge, and the car plunged 20 feet down the embankment into the river bed. The three were shaken, but unhurt. They walked back to town, stole another car, retraced their route, and were waved on across the temporary bridge by the sheriff and his men who were investigating the scene of the earlier accident.

The trio was spotted in Boise City, Oklahoma, and captured without a struggle. Carnes was convicted for kidnapping under the Lindberg Act and sentenced to 99 years in addition to his previous life sentence. His imprisonment began at Leavenworth, but he was transferred to Alcatraz because he became a serious disciplinary problem and an escape risk. On July 6, 1945, at the age of 18, the Choctaw Kid was registered as 714Az, the youngest inmate in the history of the prison.

The countbell sounded again, indicating that everything was in order in the cellhouse. Carnes turned from the open face cell door and began to straighten his bedding. Since he was not a part of any work detail, he planned to do some reading.

Carnes' thick, dark hair was parted on the right side. The dark skin of his face was highlighted by high cheekbones and thin, straight lips. His nose had been broadened by various fights both in and out of the ring. He seldom smiled, kept to himself, and was conversant only with close friends. One of his friends was Bernard Coy.

Coy distributed magazines to the inmates who ordered them and redistributed used magazines from one inmate to another. Every day he delivered the magazines after sorting and arranging them so that he could walk along a gallery and toss them into the cells as he passed. To inmates, this job was highly desired because it gave a greater freedom of movement than any other job in the cellhouse. Because Carnes did not have money to order magazines, Coy delivered discarded magazines to him on a regular basis. Often, he would stay and talk with Carnes. Talking was against the rule, but this rule was not strictly enforced against the magazine man.

During one prolonged talk, Coy, who had the reputation of being the best landscape painter in the prison, encouraged Carnes to try his hand at painting. Coy told him it was easy and that with all the time he had, he would

ALCATRAZ '46

Officer John Barker

quickly become good at it. For his first lesson, Carnes was told to put a shoe on a table and look at it. "Every principle of drawing is contained in that shoe," said Coy. "And if you can learn to draw that shoe, you can draw anything." For hours every day, Carnes practiced drawing the shoe. Sometime later he remarked to a friend, "To this day I can draw a helluva shoe but nothing else."

One morning Coy stopped by Carnes' cell and asked, "How much time are you doing, kid, life?"

"No, just 199 years," answered Carnes sarcastically.

"Well, I'll tell you, kid, that's too much time for anyone. You want to come with us? We're leaving soon through the Spanish tunnels. They'll take us right down to the dock."

Carnes had heard stories about ancient Spanish tunnels below the prison building. Many inmates half-believed the fantastic tales of hand-hewn passageways winding down through the rock to the water's edge. Rumors told that the entrance to them had been sealed when the Army Disciplinary Barracks were converted to a civil prison. Many inmates dreamed of a spectacular escape via the tunnels, but no one seemed to know the location of the sealed entrance.

"I thought the tunnels was all con talk," said Carnes.

"Naw, we know how to get through them to the prison boat. You want to go or not?"

Assuming that Coy had found the hidden entrance to the tunnels, Carnes answered, "Yeah, I'll go."

After giving his agreement, Carnes was slipped a small stiletto fashioned from one side of a compass and bound with tape at one end to form a handle. Later, Coy passed him some maps and a book with names and numbers in it. The book was labeled in large letters: LIFE ROUTE. If an officer saw the book, he would have thought it to be Coy's list of men who subscribed to Life Magazine. Actually, it contained the name of every man who had been involved in various aspects of the escape plan. Having been asked to keep the materials for Coy, Carnes hid them carefully in his cell.

Carnes checked the places where he hid the materials given to him for safekeeping, then he picked up one of the magazines Coy had delivered earlier that day and settled back on his cot to read it.

* * *

Following the official count, breakfast was served to the patients in the prison hospital and the inmates in D-block. Day Watch Officer Cecil Corwin brought a food cart and steaming kettle of hot coffee into D-block. Officer Owens checked the cart's contents, then locked the security door behind him when he left. Corwin unlocked the cell of Louis Fleish, the D-block orderly. Together they sampled the coffee before serving the breakfast meal to each hungry inmate in the three-tiered cellblock.

On the recreation yard wall, Officer John Barker patrolled the catwalk above the gate. Officer Al Shield waited below. Shield, like all Alcatraz officers who came in direct contact with inmates, was unarmed. He possessed no firearm, club, knife, or other defensive weapon. An unarmed officer's sole protection was something intangible, based largely upon his own aplomb and the indirect might of the federal government he represented.

In response to the clear day signal from the captain, Barker lowered two security keys to Shield who quickly unlocked the gate and entered the unoccupied recreation yard. Mentally noting that it needed a good cleaning, he crossed the yard, climbed two flights of concrete steps and passed through the metal detector booth to a platform outside the west wall of the cellhouse. Unlocking the barred outer gate, he peered cautiously through the vision panel in the solid steel inner door to make certain that everything was normal inside. The lock to the inner door was accessible only from the cellhouse side. Finding everything in order, he switched on the metal detector so that it might warm up for maximum operating efficiency by the time the prisoners arrived, then retraced his steps to his post outside the yard wall gate, locked the gate, and retained the key.

Outside the gate at the head of a long, narrow flight of steps which lead to the industries work area, was a second metal detector booth. This booth was situated on a small plateau close to the workshops from which most contraband weapons, tools, and other illicitly fabricated metal items came. To inmates, the detectors were "the worst stool pigeons in the prison." If Box No. 1 failed to detect a metal object, Box No. 2 would usually find it. Less hazardous but equally prohibited non-metallic contraband was more difficult to find, and a considerable number of nuisance items were carried into the cellhouse almost every day.

Officers who came in direct contact with the inmates were not armed.

ALCATRAZ '46

To supplement the detection devices and to discourage inmates from carrying materials into the cellhouse, officers would routinely frisk individuals selected at random from the marching line.

Inmates assigned to outside work details, changed into work clothing. Before leaving his cell, each inmate usually made a last minute check to be sure that everything was neat and clean enough to pass the inevitable daily inspection. An inmate could easily forfeit his work and/or yard privilege for having a slovenly cell or for being neglectful of his personal hygiene and appearance. Cleanliness and Order were in the forefront of the prison's inflexible requirements, and oddly enough, most inmates, once convinced that the officers really meant what they said about keeping things clean, fell into line and even developed a certain personal pride in following the rule.

Work detail officers and shop foremen responsible for the supervision and control of the outside details, assembled at the west end of the cellhouse. On a nod from Lieutenant Simpson, Burch lowered Key No. 107 to the cellhouse officer who unlocked the yard door, retained the key temporarily, and stepped outside to check the controls of the metal detector. Several officers and shop foremen walked past him down the stairs into the yard, parading teasingly through the metal detector booth to test the machine and Miller's temper.

When all officers were present at their assigned posts, Simpson gave the signal to unlock the cells and tier by tier, 125 inmates emerged from their cages to march downstairs through the metal detector booth to the yard floor. Miller counted the inmates as they filed past. When the last in line had passed unchallenged through the detector booth, he switched off the machine and reentered the cellhouse, locking the door behind him. Burch lowered the cord to retrieve Key No. 107 as required by the safety regulations. An unofficial count of inmates in the cellhouse and other inside areas was taken immediately.

* * *

On Alcatraz, a work assignment was considered to be a privilege because there was not enough work for all inmates when the population exceeded 250. There were 110 paid positions in the laundry, clothing factory, furniture factory, mat shop, and other units operated by the Federal Prison Industries, Inc., a non-profit government corporation. This organization, with branches of all federal civil prisons and correctional institutions, supplied manufactured goods and services to federal civil and military agencies. Inmates assigned to industries work shops, acquired training in a useful trade and could earn as much as $40 per month. Many inmates earned well over $400 per year and banked every penny of it.

Before an inmate was eligible for assignment to a paid position, he was required to accept and perform satisfactorily on an unpaid maintenance job in the hospital, culinary department, clothing exchange, bathroom, or cellhouse. Some inmates preferred to remain on a particularly satisfying maintenance detail, such as the kitchen or bake shop, rather than accept a paid position in one of the industries shops. Others scornfully refused to accept any work, preferring to remain idle in their cells.

On this typical day, the inmate population of 280 men was divided into: 125 outside workers, 77 inside workers, 8 hospitalized patients, 26 D-block isolates, and 44 individuals in idle status in the cellhouse. 18 of the 44 idle inmates had, for one reason or another, forfeited their yard privilege and therefore spent most of their time in their cells. Cretzer was in idle status on this day because officers could not decide upon an assignment in which he could be trusted.

On the concrete floor of the recreation yard the inmates were milling about, a few engaging in good-natured horseplay. Simpson blew a sharp blast on his police whistle, and all 125 men stopped talking and moved to their customary places on the painted lines which were established for the assembly of the various work details. Under the watchful eyes of the captain, the lieutenant, and the armed officers on the wall, the inmates were carefully identified and counted.

As is usual in most closely supervised prisons, every detail officer was required to know the name and register number of each and every inmate assigned to his detail. At Alcatraz, where most of the officers knew every inmate in the institution by name and number, instances of mistaken identity were virtually unknown. Detail officers knew their men almost as well as they knew the members of their own families.

When the count was complete, Shield, on a signal from the captain, unlocked the yard wall gate so Simpson could step outside to check the metal detector. Satisfied that the machine was operating properly and that all armed officers were alert, he indicated to the detail officers that it was time to take their men to work. With the lieutenant controlling the metal detector, Shield counted the inmates as they passed through the gate to the work area.

First through the gate were the 58 laundrymen under the supervision of George Manry. Manry paused briefly to check his tally with Shield before following the line to the laundry entrance where Officer Walter Hanson was waiting. The prison laundry occupied the entire top floor of the two-story industries shops building. It's modern, well-equipped plant provided laundry services for military establishments in the Bay Area as well as for Alcatraz inmates and employees. As the long line of inmates passed Mr. Hanson, who was carefully counting them, they broke formation and proceeded to their respective work stations. These inmates, thoroughly trained by prison industries technicians, were able to produce a huge volume of high quality, clean laundry.

Second through the gate were the 38 clothing factory workers followed by Officer Milton Amende. Shop Foreman Haynes Herbert, a jovial, elderly Texan, waited at the shop door to greet and joke with the tailor-trainees who were learning the trade under his tutelage.

The furniture factory detail of 11 inmates under the supervision of Officer Harold Henry filed into the carpenter shop. The five mat shop workers under Officer Marvin Orr were soon at work next door. Several other inmates worked under normal supervision in the dry cleaning plant, the blacksmith shop, and in the industries business office. While the inmates settled down to their assigned tasks, the officers counted them and reported count totals to the Armory officer.

After Shield totaled his count and checked it with Simpson's record of inmates released from cellhouse to yard, he closed the yard wall gate and returned the security keys to Barker. The lieutenant headed back across the yard toward the stairs leading to the cellhouse. Shield switched off the metal detector and jogged down the outside stairs to allow the incinerator operator and the gardeners through the electromagnetically controlled security gate to their work places below the Road Tower. The remainder of Shield's 3½ hour morning duty was devoted to routine patrolling through the industries shops and checking on the work area's security perimeter.

Officer L. O. Kelley marched the freight handlers and dock utility men along with his garbage detail to the island boat dock where Lieutenants Faulk and Rychner, who were responsible for the efficient operation of the innumerable dock area activities, accepted custody of the dock crew. Above them, on the platform of the Dock Tower, Officer James Comerford quietly counted and identified the inmates as they walked to their dressing room. Officers Kelley and Padget herded the garbage detail and the gardening detail into the trucks assigned to them. The 'outside' work details started routinely.

* * *

Inmate Miran Thompson made his way slowly across the tailor shop workspace toward Foreman Herbert. Thompson's face looked drawn as he said, "I don't feel so good."

"You do look a little under the weather," remarked the foreman.

"I oughta lay in, but Captain Simpson says I have to wait 'til Sick Call to see the doc."

Thompson was brought to Alcatraz on November 22, 1945.

Miran Edgar Thompson (Buddy) was in his early thirties. Like Foreman Herbert, he was from Texas. He had left home before finishing school and wandered about the southern states during his late teens.

He was stocky and square-shouldered. His dark hair, balding slightly at the temples, was always neatly combed. His mouth was narrow, his lips were thin and set high above a squared jaw. His eyes sloped at the lids, giving him a perpetually sad and forlorn look.

In the previous decade, he had accumulated a series of major and minor offenses throughout Alabama, Mississippi, and Texas. Caught and convicted of several crimes, he escaped from jails on eight different occasions. In the fall of 1945, he was found guilty of car theft and kidnapping and sentenced to 99 years in the Leavenworth Prison, but a more serious charge appeared and he was taken to Texas to be tried for the murder of a Texas policeman. Found guilty, Thompson was sentenced to life imprisonment, and the federal government claimed jurisdiction. He was brought to Alcatraz on November 22, 1945 and registered as 729Az.

Foreman Herbert responded to Thompson's complaint sympathetically although he suspected that the inmate just wanted a day off from his work. "O.K.," he said. "Take it easy this morning if you don't feel good."

Thompson slowly made his way to a far corner of the shop and sat down.

Miran Edgar Thompson, 35, serving two consecutive ninety-nine year sentences for kidnapping and murder.

ALCATRAZ '46

Bernard Coy had observed Thompson during the previous several months, carefully appraising his capacity for deceit, violence, and bravery. To Cretzer, Coy said, "We can use him. He'll stay the distance, and he'll be handy if we have to shoot it out with the screws on the dock or the boat."

It was the middle of April before Coy, with Cretzer's reluctant approval, approached Thompson in the recreation yard.

"We ain't talking about how or when we're going, but it's a sure thing," Coy explained.

"Hell, count me in," grinned Thompson.

"We'll take the gallery guns first. Too bad there's only a rifle and pistol there, but that'll be enough until we can knock off the tower screws. Once we get over the wall and into the towers, we'll have all the damn guns and ammunition we want. Shotguns, machine guns, everything. You can take your pick."

Thompson grinned more broadly, "Hell, I'll take one of each."

Thompson sat watching the other inmates at work. He tried to look ill everytime Herbert looked at him.

* * *

Lieutenant Simpson plodded up the steep concrete steps to the cellhouse entrance gate. The gun gallery officer, expecting Simpson's return, quickly lowered Key 107 to the cellhouse officer who admitted the lieutenant, relocked the gate, and returned the key to the gun gallery.

A tower guard stands watch.

William Miller, like other officers on cellhouse duty, carried a large ring of heavy keys snapped to a loop on his uniform belt. These keys allowed him access to cellblocks, utility corridors, cutoffs, dining room, and library. Security keys, such as 107, were never carried on the key ring.

As soon as the count had been checked and verified, the lieutenant signaled to unlock the inside workers. In a prison where no inmate was trusted, it was mandatory to keep all cell doors locked to curtail any incidence of theft, vandalism, homosexual activity, and other abuses or misuses of a cell, its furnishings, or its occupant. Each cell door was routinely closed and locked as soon as its occupant stepped out on the cellblock tier walkway.

Inside workers released from their cells proceeded quietly to their respective work places. Officer Lageson escorted the library workers to the fenced off library area where they immediately plugged in the coffee pot and prepared for a busy morning. Their regular daily chores included the selection and preparation of books and magazines for D-block and the hospital, as well as for the men in the main cellhouse. Some inmates took advantage of this security weakness to establish an avenue for the kiting of communications between main line inmates and those who were hospitalized or segregated.

Officer Ed Stucker assembled his seven-man detail of clothing handlers, showerbath attendants, and barbers at the screened entrance to the basement steps at the northwest corner of the cellhouse. Miller passed the inmates through the entrance saying, "Call when you're ready for the haircuts. I've got a flock of wooly ones waiting to be shorn."

Twelve inmate janitors gathered at the east end of A-block where Lageson issued the necessary equipment for their work in the cellhouse. The concrete floor of the aisles and the tier walkways were kept spotlessly clean and highly polished. Cellhouse walls were painted battleship grey and trimmed in black. Cell interiors were white with dark grey trim. Cell furnishings, such as the steel cot, folding table and bench, and wooden shelf, were painted grey. If not particularly colorful, all was at least clean and sanitary.

Inmate painters, directed by Officer Marshall Rose, carried their drop cloths, paint cans and brushes, and other equipment to three vacant cells which were scheduled to be painted that day. Each inmate painter was locked in a cell which had been carefully stripped of all its removable furnishings. As a general rule, each man painted and trimmed one cell per day, hurrying to complete the job in the morning so he could spend the afternoon in the recreation yard. When foggy or rainy weather prevented outdoor recreation, inmates who had the yard privilege were allowed to congregate in the basement area for indoor recreation.

The men of the culinary detail, 23 kitchen and dining room workers, were housed next door to each other at the west end of the cellhouse. Stewards Bob Bristow and Charles Scanland, together with Officer Larry O'Brien, supervised the a.m. activities in the Culinary Department. Because his workday ran from 6:00 a.m. to 6:00 p.m. seven days a week, a man on the culinary detail was permitted to return to his cell as soon as he had satisfactorily completed his assigned tasks. There he rested, read, wrote, studied, or worked on some handicraft until recalled to assist in preparing or serving the

Officer Ed Stucker

Officer Marshall Rose

49

ALCATRAZ '46

next meal. Although not compensated monetarily for their labors, many inmates considered the culinary detail a preferred job.

Every afternoon, weather permitting, inmates on the culinary detail, as well as other inside workers, were allowed to spend a few hours in the recreation yard, remain at their work place, or return to their cell. The principal requirement during this period was that the cellhouse officers knew exactly where each inmate was at any given time.

Three inmate yard cleaners, generally called the 'yard birds,' were the last of the inside workers to be released from their cells. Miller obtained the 107 key from the West Gun Gallery Officer and passed the three men out of the cellhouse. The recreation yard, approximately 100′ wide and 200′ long, was small but adequate for the inmate population. The yard birds enjoyed their assignment in the fresh air and sunshine of the yard. Under the watchful supervision of the Yard Wall Officer, they began cleaning the yard area. The handball courts, baseball diamond, domino/bridge and checker playing areas, and concrete bleachers were to be readied for the afternoon recreation period.

Throughout the prison, the inside work details were underway. Janitors, painters, plumbers, and electricians went about their duties. Supplies were delivered and trash was removed via the kitchen and clothing room sallyport gates. The one-man print shop was busy preparing the Daily Charge-out Sheet which maintained a daily-revised record of inmate assignment and privilege status. This sheet was the closest thing to a newspaper since daily papers were classed as contraband on Alcatraz.

With all counts verified and the routine operations of the cellhouse and adjoining areas proceeding smoothly, Simpson strolled back to the kitchen for a chat and a cup of coffee with the stewards.

* * *

On the roadways and lawns outside the prison building, the gardening detail and the garbage pickup crew went about their closely supervised duties of keeping the exterior of the island neat and clean. In the residential area, Lieutenant Philip Bergen strolled around the concrete plaza, formerly the parade ground of old Fort Alcatraz, checking the children's play area and the lawns and flower gardens which the island residents were required to maintain.

The lieutenant had been transferred to Alcatraz from the U.S. Penitentiary at Lewisburg, Pennsylvania and had resided on the island with his wife and two daughters for six years. The Bergens liked living on the island and had adjusted well to its routines and restrictions.

When friends asked how he happened to be assigned to "Uncle Sam's Devil's Island," Bergen would smile enigmatically and reply, "I was volunteered." The truth was that in 1939, the island prison was desperately short-handed, and volunteers for duty on the island were unobtainable, partially because of the unsavory, mythical reputation that the prison had acquired. Bergen and a dozen other seasoned correctional officers from Atlanta, Leavenworth, Lewisburg, and McNeil Island, had been informed that they were needed at Alcatraz much more than where they were presently working. Some were bitter about the prison bureau's arbitrary action of transferring

Lieutenant Phil Bergen

50

them without recourse, but others, like Bergen, "took it in stride" and slowly began climbing the promotional ladder.

This day was Bergen's day off. He and his wife planned to go to San Francisco on the 10:00 a.m. trip. As he passed the handball court, the departure whistle blew, telling residents that they had ten minutes to reach the island dock and board the steamer. While the signal still echoed from the cliff below the lighthouse, Mrs. Bergen joined her husband on the plaza. As they walked toward the dock, they were passed by the passenger bus coming down the single lane road from the warden's home.

"Looks like the old man is heading for town again, Evelyn," said the lieutenant.

"Does he still go to town every day?"

"Most days. He has an office in the Federal Building, you know. I'll bet he's the only two-office warden in the whole federal prison system."

"I never understood why he needs two offices."

"I suppose all the 'inside' business of the prison is handled in the office here, and all the 'outside' business is transacted over in the Federal Building on Mission Street."

"Some of the wives say he has a third office — in the Commonwealth Club."

"That may be. The old man is a real wheel. Belongs to all the best clubs in town. Lectures the other old boys every now and then, so I hear. But one thing you can't fault Warden Johnston for, he puts in his full forty-plus hours a week. Pretty darn good for a 70-year-old man."

The prison dining room.

The Alcatraz launch, "Warden Johnston."

When the Bergens reached the dock, the Army steamer "General Frank M. Coxe" was securing its mooring lines. The portable gangway was being wheeled into place. The lieutenant stepped into the dock office and spoke to Lieutenant Faulk while his wife walked ahead. "Keep everything peaceful and happy 'til we get back, Ike. Evelyn's got a session with the eye doctor ahead of her, but we ought to be back on the 3:45 with the school kids."

Bergen paused, looked around, then asked, "Isn't the old man going to town today?"

"No," replied Faulk. "I sent Winegar up with the bus, but he came back with the message that the warden is in bed with a cold or something."

Bergen followed his wife and several other island residents onto the steamer. The gangway was wheeled back, the mooring lines were released, and the steamer swung away from the dock and headed toward the mainland.

* * *

After downing his third cup of coffee, Lieutenant Simpson left the Culinary Department and made a quick inspection tour of the hospital, the basement area, D-block, and the main cellhouse. Waving a friendly greeting to the library workers as he passed the well-stocked shelves, the lieutenant casually inspected the visiting section at the east end of the cellhouse, then proceeded to his office in the administration area.

Miller and Lageson patrolled the aisles and the tier walkways, supervising and watching for loiterers or illicit activities. The cellhouse workers, knowing their work would have to pass critical inspection before they would be eligible to spend the afternoon in the yard, accomplished their simple tasks efficiently and well. Inmates who were on call to the prison hospital, barber shop, bathroom, clothing room, or for interview with the Warden, Associate Warden, or Captain, were routinely released and relocked as soon as they returned.

A tower guard stands watch with San Francisco in background.

As the two officers moved from tier to tier along the walkways, they conducted their daily inspection, carefully noting the cells which were not neat and clean. Individuals were given warnings if their cells were not satisfactory. A period in solitary confinement could be expected if personal appearance or cell-sanitation were not materially improved. Particular attention was given to recently arrived inmates.

In the afternoon, while most inmates were at work or in the yard, the officers would usually conduct a systematic, section-by-section search of the cells, the cell fronts, and the cellhouse windows. Officer Earl Waller, who possessed skill as a locksmith and who had complete familiarity with the Stewart cell-locking mechanisms, devoted several afternoons a week to the inspection, repair, and general maintenance of the locking devices and related equipment.

By 11:00 a.m., all the 'inside' detail inmates other than those in the Culinary Department had completed their tasks to the satisfaction of their supervisory officers. Officer Stucker brought his basement work crew and the last barber shop customer to the cellhouse gate at the top of the basement steps where the cellhouse officers were waiting. While these men were being locked in their cells, the three yard birds were called in from the recreation yard.

As soon as all the inmates had been locked in, Officer Lageson, who usually ate a late lunch in the officer's lounge in the administrative area, walked to the west end of the cellhouse to take Officer Miller's place at the dining room gate. "Everybody is locked in. No one is missing," he said.

Stucker, Miller, and other employees, including several clerks from the administrative offices, lunched in the officer's dining room which was located inside the Culinary Department adjacent to the main kitchen. As Lageson passed them through the dining room gate, they met Officer O'Brien who was supervising the delivery of the D-block food cart and the diet trays for the hospital patients. Lageson checked the cart and trays and waved them on to their destinations.

At 11:30, the powerhouse whistle signaled the end of the morning work period. Freight-handlers, garbage collectors, and gardeners were assembled, counted, and transported to the work area entrance below the Hill Tower. Fenced in, between the electromagnetically controlled gates of the sallyport, the inmates stood patiently in a single line while their detail officers searched them.

Safeguarding the sallyport gateway, through which truck and pedestrian traffic moved in and out of the prison work area, was considered so important that it was under constant visual control by two heavily armed officers whose Hill Tower and Model Tower posts were connected by a network of structural steel catwalks, power-lines, and telephone lines. Their high-power rifles could reach out and stop anything moving through the area.

After making certain that the armed officers in the several towers and on the yard wall were in position, Captain Weinhold ordered the Hill Tower officer to start the inmate work details on their return trip to the prison yard. Officer Shield's two men waited near the metal detector booth while he warmed up the device outside the yard wall gate.

Captain Weinhold moved across the yard toward the detector booth. He was pleased to note that the yard birds had done a good cleaning job and made a mental note to compliment them.

In response to the telephoned "go ahead" signal, the Hill Tower officer activated the electromagnetic lock of the inner sallyport gate, allowing the officers and inmates to enter the prison work area. Marching around the west end of the industries building, they quickly vanished from the view of the Hill Tower officer but came immediately under the direct supervision of the Model Tower officer. As the group marched on in an irregularly-spaced double line past the industries office, the civilian clerk stepped out and added his three inmate clerks to the parade. Next, the mat shop men were counted out of the shop and added to the marching line. In turn, as the tail of the line passed the other shops, each officer counted out his workers and added them to the lengthening file of men.

Plodding single-file through the inspection booth and up the steep steps, the inmates and officers passed into the recreation yard. On the platform, Officer Shield counted and checked his tally with each detail officer's shop list. Then, as soon as the last of the 58 laundrymen at the end of the line had entered the yard, the captain switched off the detector and followed them. Shield locked the gate, returned the key, and headed for home via the Road Tower gate.

In the yard, the inmates who had entered detail-by-detail, broke ranks and reassembled on a tier-by-tier basis before starting the long, single-file climb upstairs, through the second detector booth and into the cellhouse. Conversation ceased abruptly as they passed through the cellhouse security door and marched across the flats, up the steel cellblock stairs, and along the tier walkways where their cells had been unlocked to receive them.

Silence was a discernible vestige of old prison rules. Inmates were not allowed to talk when moving in formation through the cellhouse, nor when a count was in progress. They could converse at work, in the yard, in the dining room when seated, in their cells, and in 'outside' marching formations. In the prison auditorium, inmates could talk only if their conversation did not disturb or interfere with the religious service, the lecture, or the show. The religious services, Catholic one week and Protestant the next, were sparsely attended and usually models of decorum. The movies were attended by nearly all B and C-block inmates. They frequently outnumbered the officers by a ratio of 20 to 1, and it was sometimes difficult to maintain order.

Although the use of profane or vulgar language by officers or inmates was emphatically forbidden, it was almost impossible to control. Many inmates were unable to express themselves except through unacceptable language.

When all the inmates were inside the cellhouse, Officer Miller switched off the detector, followed the captain inside, locked the security door, and returned the key to the gallery officer.

* * *

As soon as the official noon count was checked and verified, some of the officers went to lunch in the officer's dining room. Others stayed in the main dining room to inspect tables and to later seat the inmates when they were marched in to eat. Weinhold and Simpson strolled around the dining room, checking the menu posted above the steam table and making certain that all the listed food items were on the table ready to be served.

Inmate waiters, in their clean white jackets, white cotton gloves, and starched chef's hats, were at the serving stations. The two rows of

"Plodding single-file through the inspection booth and up the steep steps, the inmates and officers passed into the recreation yard."

ALCATRAZ '46

polished oak dining room tables were neatly set with stainless steel cups, tableware, and steaming hot pitchers of tea. Compartmented stainless steel trays, on which the meal would be served, were stacked near the center of the steam table.

Noting that the armed yard wall officer was at his mealtime post on the catwalk outside the south side dining room windows and that the gun gallery officer was at his post in the gallery overlooking the entrance gate and the east end of the dining room, the captain ordered Officer Burdette to lock the grille gate between the dining area and the kitchen. Steward Bristow and Officer O'Brien remained in the kitchen with the cooks and bakers, ready to handle any food-serving emergency.

In the minutes before lunch, the B and C-block inmates changed into neatly tailored coverall uniforms. Many relaxed and passed the time smoking. Tobacco and matches were freely supplied. Inmates were permitted to smoke when they were in their cells, while at work except when engaged in the preparation or serving of food, in the hospital, or in the recreation areas. Smoking was forbidden in the auditorium, dining room, kitchen, bathing room, and in marching formations.

When noon arrived, Captain Weinhold led the main line inmates from the cellhouse to the dining room steam table where serving was conducted in a cafeteria style. The men approached the stainless steel table in a double line, picked up their trays, split right and left into two lines, and had their trays filled from a variety of well-prepared, appetizingly displayed food.

* * *

The cellblock cutoffs, looking south from A-B aisle.

MARCH 13 1956
2 GRILLED FRANKFURTERS
1 HOT CHILI
PARSLEY POTATOES
POT FRIED SAUERKRAUT
BUTTERED CARROTS
1 MUSTARD
1 BANANA PUDDING
2 FRANKFURTER ROLLS

BREAD & TEA

The dining area as it appeared in 1956.

ALCATRAZ '46

Hubbard, along with Kyle, was on the culinary detail. He worked on the serving line with several other inmates. As Cretzer filed past the serving table where Hubbard served out generous portions of mashed potatoes and gravy, almost imperceptible nods were exchanged.

Thirty-six year old Marvin Franklin Hubbard (Meek Marvin) was raised in the backwoods of Alabama. He was 5' 8" tall, but appeared shorter because of his stocky build and barrel chest. Although he was a strong and powerful man, his movements were not athletic or graceful. His hair, worn short, almost to a crewcut, seemed lighter than it was, due to its contrast with his ruddy complexion. His eyes, enlarged by frameless glasses, were a milky grey, and he had the piercing stare that is characteristic of nearsighted people who try to see at a distance. He was a quiet person who read a great deal, mostly fiction. When he spoke, he would talk in a low voice and privately to individuals rather than loud and openly to several people at a time. People who did not know him, received the impression that he didn't want others to listen in on his conversations. When he became upset or angry, his face would lose its reddish color, but even when angry, his voice retained its soft and low quality.

Hubbard was a man of precise principles. There were no grey areas in his life. Decisions were clearly black or white. He would not bully others or try to make his way by using threats of violence. He despised such actions and thought them to be hypocritical. He believed that bravery, courage, and dependability were the characteristics of a man, and without these characteristics one did not deserve respect and could not have self-respect. His beliefs guided how he lived and behaved.

At age 17, after a series of robberies and an escape from the Alabama State Prison, he became associated with a tough-talking, violent man. In a series of robberies, the man proved to be vicious toward the victims. He would beat and pistol whip them at the slightest provocation. This behavior suggested to the young, impressionable Hubbard that his associate was a person who was tough and who could be depended upon to fight to the death if the occasion demanded it.

An occasion arose in a small log cabin in the backwoods of Tennessee. The two committed a robbery and took a policeman hostage. They left him tied in a barn near the cabin. The policeman managed to free himself, and before they knew he was gone, he had returned with a posse which surrounded the cabin. The inhabitants were surprised when they heard, "Throw out your guns, and come out with your hands up!"

Hubbard's reaction was quick and decisive. He grabbed a rifle, threw it to his partner, and said, "You cover the front, I'll cover the back." Holding his rifle ready to fire, he looked out the back window for a target. He heard a door squeak and thought his partner was opening a crack to

Marvin Franklin Hubbard, 36, studious looking Tennessee kidnapper serving thirty years.

ALCATRAZ '46

shoot through, but in a moment realized that he was walking out the door with his hands up and yelling, "Don't shoot. I give up."

Hubbard was stunned. As the color left his face, he stared in disbelief. It was not the fact that his partner was giving up so much as what his action implied. His partner had behaved like a 'man' when he was on the controlling end of a gun and the other person had nothing, but he was not so brave when the balance of power was reversed. Hubbard had given him his respect, now he was proving to be all the things Hubbard despised.

Feeling rage, contempt, and disappointment in his own judgment, Hubbard took careful aim and shot the man in the buttocks. The man fell momentarily, then jumped to his feet yelling, and ran in fear of his life. The posse did not comprehend his actions, opened fire, and brought him down.

Hubbard, however, put up a battle. He fired from one window, then another, always moving, keeping the posse members guessing as to just where he was and making them reluctant to charge the cabin. In his thinking, he had decided to die "respectably as a man" by taking others with him in a fight. The battle went on for hours, and the cabin became riddled on all sides.

By evening reinforcements arrived. As the sky darkened, a ring of fire was built around the cabin so that not even a Tennessee rabbit could slip through unseen. The posse ceased firing, and its members discussed how to capture or kill their quarry. Hubbard also stopped firing. He watched, listened, and made his own plans. "It is better to die out there than in this cabin," he decided. "It is going to happen anyway if I stay here. Out there I would at least die running towards freedom."

As he peered through an open window, he could see shadows moving now and then beyond the fires. He checked his rifle, making sure it was fully loaded, checked his knife and the small box of fishhooks he always carried for survival in the wilderness, then put all the remaining ammunition into his pockets. Beginning with his back against the opposite wall, he ran toward the open window, dived through, hit the ground, rolled over and up onto his feet. Not a shot had been fired at him. With his first stride, he fired his rifle, not knowing or caring where the shot would go. He wanted to create sudden noise and cause surprise. He continued firing and ran straight toward the ring of fire.

It had not occurred to the posse members that a lone man would charge them. They expected him to either die in the cabin or give up quietly in the morning after thinking it over. With bullets whizzing wildly, every man on the posse dropped to the ground to let someone else become the hero by stopping him. Before any of them had time to reflect upon what was happening and thus take positive action, Hubbard had passed the fire and leaped into the darkness. The posse had lost its prey.

Thirty-two-year-old Hubbard after capture on a Tennessee backroad in 1942.

As a country boy, Hubbard had no problem surviving in the forest. Living off fish, small game he trapped, and keeping track of directions by the stars and sun, he took his time before returning to civilization.

Based upon this experience, Hubbard teamed with various individuals as he moved from one robbery to another, carefully choosing his partner each time.

On one occasion, Hubbard and a newly chosen associate, found themselves trapped by police. They had been driving on a daily basis from a country hideout to the city to case a job they were planning to pull. Someone had tipped the police of their plans, and one afternoon the two drove into a roadblock. The police had planned well. The roadblock was set at a point where it could not be seen until the car started up an incline out of a ravine. Surrounding this ravine, placed at strategic positions, were 20 police officers. The trapped men could not drive back, and they could not go forward. The police would riddle their car before it had gone ten yards.

Both realized the situation at a glance, and both reacted in the same way. They came out of the car with guns firing, determined to die fighting. Hubbard's partner was hit as he stepped from the car, but he kept firing, as bullets thudded into him, until he could no longer pull the trigger. Several feet from the car, Hubbard's leg was shattered by a bullet, but he continued to fire, dragging himself across the roadway. A hail of bullets stopped him. For a while it looked as though he might not live, but a strong determination of will, helped him regain his health.

The partnerships in these experiences shaped Hubbard's concept of manhood, and he developed the habit of mentally categorizing all men on the basis of these prototypes.

In prison, Hubbard did not expound upon his beliefs, nor did he try to impose them upon others. It was clear, however, that he disliked the many bragging, bullying inmates whom he thought were really cowards. When an inmate mentioned that "Machine Gun" Kelly had not once attempted to escape in all the years he spent at Alcatraz, Hubbard, reminded of his cabin shoot-out, said, "Guys like that never had it in the first place." His soft voice did not convey contempt. He simply made a statement of fact as he saw it.

The steward's office in the prison kitchen. This office was not functioning in 1946.

Hubbard continued to spoon out potatoes and gravy onto a seemingly endless line of stainless steel trays. His mind thought ahead to the possible events in the coming afternoon. "This time," he thought, "I'll be working with a team of dependable men."

Once trays were filled, the inmates proceeded to the closest vacant table on their side of the dining room. As soon as the supervising officer had seated them, ten to a table, they were allowed to begin eating and could talk to their tablemates if they wished.

There was no official separation of the races in the dining room as there was in the main cellhouse, but of their own volition, the black inmates usually congregated at one particular group of tables on the

ALCATRAZ '46

north side of the room. This self-segregation was deplored but not forbidden because racial tensions were a serious problem in the prison.

The noon meal of hamburger patties, mashed potatoes and gravy, green beans, bread, oleo, and hot tea with sugar was quickly consumed. Desserts were seldom served at the noon meal, but there was usually a dessert at the evening meals. Although certain food items, such as meat, milk, sugar, and oleo, were rigidly rationed, an inmate could help himself to as much bread, vegetables, and unsweetened tea as he desired. He was required, however, to eat every scrap of edible food he took from the serving table. Failure to do so without an acceptable excuse, meant he would be called out for an "educational discussion" with Associate Warden Miller. This disciplinary action often resulted in the forfeiture of the offender's next meal. Chronic offenders were usually sentenced to several days in solitary confinement on a restricted diet.

Almost before the main line had been served and seated, the inmates who had entered the dining room at the head of the line finished eating and were ready to return to their cells. At a signal from the captain, officers who had seated the inmates now proceeded to dismiss them, first checking to make certain that none of the tableware was missing. Potentially dangerous pieces, such as knives, forks, and spoons, had to be spread out in open view on the table before the inmates at that table were permitted to stand up and march out of the dining room.

East end of C-block. Officer is opening cells on middle tier, so inmates may march to dining room.

By 12:30 p.m., all the main line inmates had been fed and returned to their cells. Again there was an official count of the entire prison population, after which the kitchen grille gate was unlocked. The culinary workers cleared several dining room tables for their own use. Officers Baker, the mail censor, Sundstrom, the records officer, and Bertrand, the warden's secretary, finished their lunch and strolled through the cellhouse toward the administration building. Steward Bristow accompanied them to the office area for a food-cost conference with the prison's business manager Loring O. Mills.

Associate Warden E. J. Miller entered the cellhouse and walked down Broadway carrying a handful of interview request slips. Captain Weinhold and Lieutenant Simpson, along with a dozen or more inmates and several officers, awaited his arrival near the west end of the aisle.

Noon hour was a busy time in the main cellhouse. Pedestrian traffic on Broadway and Times Square, the open area at the west end of the building, marred the appearance of the highly polished floor. The marring continued as two lines of inmates, one for sick call and one for interviews, assembled in the area. Noticing the associate warden scowl at the unsightly scuff marks, Officer Lageson thought, "Coy will really earn his keep today."

* * *

Cells in the main cellhouse.

Broadway, looking east to visiting area and east gun gallery.

63

ALCATRAZ '46

Bernie Coy, the p.m. cellhouse orderly, had finished his magazine distributing duties well before noon and was quietly resting in his cell. As he had done on numerous occasions, Coy skipped the noon meal, explaining that he had an upset stomach. His emaciated, bony frame no longer filled his once neatly fitting coveralls. But Coy did not appear to be ill. "Just lost my appetite for prison food," he explained to the few officers who were interested enough to question him.

In recent months Coy had slowly dieted away several pounds without attracting undue attention. His coverall uniform had been twice altered to match his changing size. Although he had given no hint, over the years, of being an escape risk, some officers were instinctively distrustful of him. "He watches and studies everyone and everything," they said. "He's biding his time, waiting for some opportunity."

Bernard Paul Coy (Bernie) was in his middle forties. He was thin even before his recent loss of weight, and his being nearly six feet tall seemed to emphasize the thinness. Inmates jokingly described him as being "skinny enough to slip through a knothole." He was always polite, respectful, and efficient as he diligently swept the cellhouse aisles and distributed the library books and magazines. At meal times, inmates often saw him staring at some spot as though he were lost in thought or in a daydream.

Coy was intelligent and did a fair amount of reading in the fields of psychology and law. To pass leisure time, he painted. He was full of energy and overtly nervous. When he walked, he was always in a hurry. One could always tell when Coy was approaching because his shoes squeaked from his quick steps on the waxed floors of the cellhouse. His facial features were drawn and taut. His hair was straight, dark, and turning grey. When he didn't shave, his beard was white. His dark eyebrows hung over sunken blue eyes. Because his false teeth gave him trouble, he was often without them.

Coy liked to talk. When he did, he shifted from one foot to another or cracked his knuckles. When he was silent, he continually fidgeted. In conversations, he seemed to want to do all the talking. Although he called younger inmates "old men", he respected them and did not talk condescendingly or try to make them feel inferior because of an age and experience difference.

There was little pleasure in Coy's childhood. His parents, a common-law husband and wife, rejected him when he was born. He recalled vividly how they openly talked about abandoning him because he was an unwanted mouth to feed. He remembered that there was always little food and money, that his parents were always fighting, and that his home was a haphazardly furnished shack in the Kentucky hill country. When his sister was born, she became the favorite child. His father, a dominating, unaffectionate man, paid attention to him only to cuff or kick him when he came too close, and his mother, an uncaring, sub-

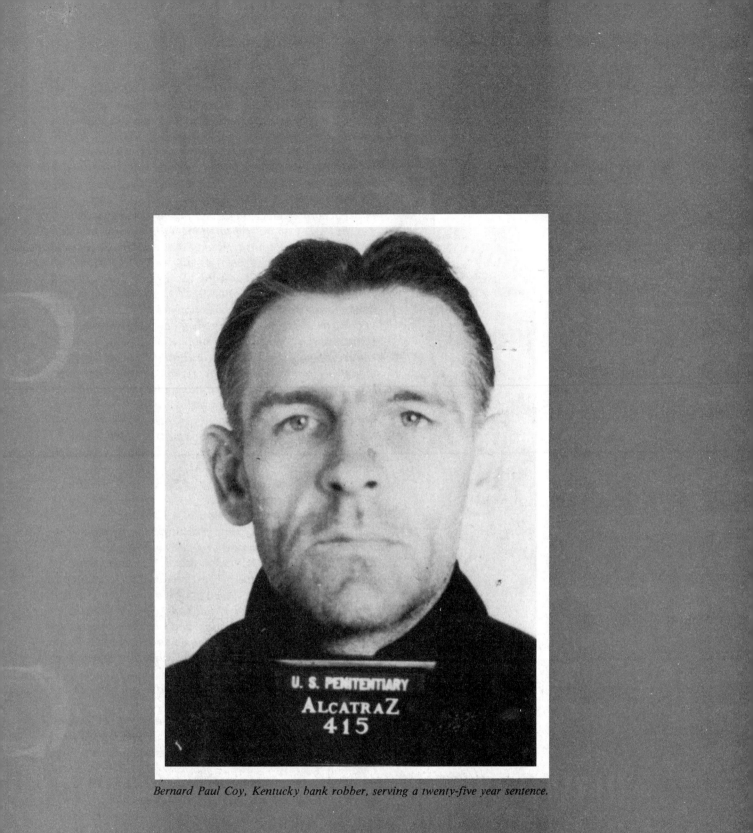

Bernard Paul Coy, Kentucky bank robber, serving a twenty-five year sentence.

ALCATRAZ '46

missive woman, cried easily and was often moody for long periods of time.

At age three, Coy frequently manifested temper tantrums for which he was severely punished. At five, he began stealing pennies from his mother's purse. At six, he was expelled from the first grade of a one-room schoolhouse for physically attacking the teacher. At nine, he was taken into custody for stealing automobile parts. He soon acquired a police record of petty thefts and juvenile misbehavior.

In 1931, Coy was captured in an unsuccessful attempt to rob a western Kentucky bank. Sentenced to four years in the state penitentiary, he was released in 1935. In March of 1939, he and Delber Stiles took $2,175 from the National Bank of New Haven, Kentucky. Coy was identified by the bank cashier as the man who calmly walked up to his cage and shoved a sawed-off shotgun against his head while his companion scooped up the cash. Coy and Stiles were captured but escaped and hid for three days in a small cave along the Rolling Fork River. Telltale smoke from their campfire gave them away to a posse of outraged citizens. Each man was sentenced to 25 years. The bank robbery and the interstate transportation of a stolen automobile were federal offenses. Coy was sent to the U.S. Penitentiary at Atlanta where, after a series of aggressive assaults on other inmates with a weapon contrived from razor blades and a toothbrush handle, he was labeled "incorrigible" and was transferred to Alcatraz.

Coy never accepted prison life. He never considered that he would do a lot of time because he always had something in the making, some plan that was going to come off next week, next month, or next year. This made his life in prison bearable. Through his reading of elementary psychology, he tried to understand himself. He reasoned that his overly aggressive childhood behavior must have stemmed from parental rejection, and while growing up, his feelings of insecurity and inadequacy probably turned to a resentment which found outlets in vandalism and brutal aggression. He told himself, "Now that I understand who I am and why I am always getting hurt, I'm not going to let anyone hurt me anymore."

In March 1942, Coy unsuccessfully sought release from Alcatraz on a writ of habeas corpus. He pleaded that his consecutive sentences were excessive and therefore illegal. When his writ was denied, Coy glumly confided to an inmate, "Now I got nothing to lose." Convinced that an escape was his only way out, he abandoned all consideration for further appeals to the courts and concentrated on the seemingly impossible task of finding a weakness in the system.

Prior to 1941, he had detected a structural weakness in the bars at the top of the west gun gallery face. Near the ceiling, the bars protecting the gallery like the bars of a cage, were not imbedded into the ceiling. They were slightly curved and secured to the west wall. At the time of his discovery, the west gun gallery, like the east gun gallery, was all in one large cellhouse building, and every portion of the building was constantly watched over by armed officers who were positioned so that they could immediately detect and prevent any inmate effort to reach the gallery. Coy kept his observations to himself.

In the early forties, D-block was reconstructed to serve as a segregation block. In the reconstruction it was isolated from the other blocks by a concrete wall. For the first few years following the walling-off of the reconstructed D-block, two correctional officers were stationed in the West Gun Gallery during the day Watch, one in the main cellhouse overlooking B and C blocks, the other in D-block. The vulnerable bars at the top of the gallery face still seemed inaccessible, but Coy was patient. He watched and waited.

By 1946, the economy-minded efficiency experts in the Washington Office of the Bureau of Prisons abolished the second officer's position in the West Gun Gallery. The bars were now left unguarded from time to time whenever the gallery officer was called into the D-block section of the gallery. For Coy, patience had paid off. He now firmly believed he had a way out.

Main cellhouse, B-block. This photo gives a good shot of the cellblock stairs. There were four such staircases in the main cellhouse.

Repairing D-block windows, after the 1946 blastout attempt.

67

ALCATRAZ '46

Restlessly, Coy turned on his cot. He cracked the knuckles of his fisted right hand in the open palm of his left. He was more nervous than usual. He thought momentarily about Hubbard, Thompson, Shockley, and Cretzer. He was sure they could be depended upon. They were chosen carefully over a long period of time. Each had proven in some way to be forceful and escape-minded. Each had nothing to lose.

Cretzer was Coy's first choice to help him with his plan. He had watched Cretzer from the time he arrived, and with well-concealed approval, Coy saw him gradually establish a leadership role among the other inmates. Cretzer made himself the focal point of almost everything. Cretzer, however, paid little attention to the quiet Coy. He considered him to be a 'good" inmate who was earning a parole. He cursed the skinny library runner whenever he failed to deliver choice magazines, books, and art pictures to him.

Coy ignored the insults until his plan was developed. He then employed a regular early delivery service of newly arrived magazines to Cretzer to develop a friendly relationship. Cretzer was suspicious, then realizing his preliminary judgment of Coy was in error, he scented the escape plan. He listened intently when Coy finally outlined his plan. Without hesitation, Cretzer agreed to participate.

The scheme required a change in the Alcatraz inmate work schedule, but prison routines being rooted in habit and tradition, were difficult, if not impossible, to change. Thus in 1944, Coy, using an ingratiating and servile manner, suggested to Associate Warden Miller that he be given an afternoon assignment as cellhouse floor orderly in addition to his morning work as library runner. "I seldom go to the yard, anyway," he explained. "Too cold and windy out there for this old man. I like to keep busy. Makes my time pass faster to have something to do besides sitting in my cell."

Coy needed to gain access to the main cellhouse floor in the early afternoon when, for a half hour each day, there was very little activity. Between 1:30 and 2:00 p.m., the big room was almost empty of inmates and officers. During the first 15 minutes of the period, two inmate floor orderlies were routinely held in from the recreation yard in order to repolish the cellhouse aisles which had become scuffed and littered during the noon hour traffic.

Coy knew that the orderlies hated being held in from the yard and knew that some had complained to the associate warden.

Miller was pleased to have someone volunteer to stay in and work while the other workers relaxed. The staff took pride in having all cellhouse aisles highly polished. Because of his problems with the grumbling orderlies and because Coy was a better than average floor polisher who could be relied upon to work quickly and efficiently with minimum supervision, Miller gave Coy the assignment. Coy now had access to the main cellhouse aisles.

"The loneliest walk in the world is the one we make to our cells each evening. Nothing but cliffs of steel and cement. We've been ground into dust. Nothing but silence. We're always alone." Marvin Hubbard

As he had done through many noon hours of self-imposed starvation, Coy rested and waited for the mid-day activities to cease and for the crowded, bustling cellhouse to become empty. Soon Lageson would release him and order him to clean the messed-up floors.

Most of the inmates used the half hour between 12:30 and 1:00 p.m. to rest and smoke an after-meal cigarette. A few had personal problems to discuss with the associate warden, and those who thought they were ill were unlocked for a quick consultation with the prison medical staff.

Among the first to line up for Sick Call was Miran Thompson who had been trying to get off work detail all morning. When he returned from the hospital, he displayed the sick slip given him by the prison doctor. The sick slip allowed him to remain in his cell rather than return to work. Captain Weinhold looked him over skeptically and said, "Well, you still don't look sick to me, but take it easy this afternoon. Maybe you'll feel more like working tomorrow."

Thompson turned his eyes from the captain's and replied, "I hope so, Cap'n, I sure do hope so."

The sick call and interview lines dwindled to nothing as the hands on the cellhouse clock slowly moved toward 1:00 p.m. Associate Warden Miller gathered his notes and headed for the administrative area where he paused briefly to ask Sundstrom to check a number of inmate complaints against the official record. To Bertrand, who was typing the warden's responses to the previous day's mail, he smiled knowingly, "Take it easy, Bert. The warden's not coming in today."

He slipped a battered hat on his balding head and strolled down-hill to his residence by the old Army parade grounds at the eastern point of the island.

Bertrand watched him until he was out of sight past the light-house before he quietly closed the door to the warden's office and settled down for a short siesta in one of the comfortable armchairs. Bertrand's siesta usually meant that Warden Johnston was off the island.

Chief medical officer's residence.

ALCATRAZ '46

Many unsuccessful attempts to escape from Alcatraz were made.

The Blastout

BLASTOUT: An antiquated prison term emanating from the 19th century when it was common for prison inmates to utilize firearms and hide behind hostages in escape attempts. Shielded by the bodies of their captives, the escapees would blast out of their confines.

From the opening of Alcatraz as a federal civil penitentiary until May of 1946, many escape schemes had been tried. It was a rare month when officers failed to uncover escape paraphernalia, contraband tools, or improvised weapons. Often, the escape plots were carefully planned. Sometimes, the escape attempt was an act of sudden, irrational desperation.

Joe Bowers, serving 25 years for assault and robbery, was the first to attempt an escape from Alcatraz. One day, on an apparent impulse, he climbed the perimeter fence which topped the brink of a cliff on the island's south side. A tower officer ordered him to stop and fired a warning shot, but Bowers swung over the top of the fence and scrambled down the outside. The officer's second shot was fatal. The escapee fell from the fence into the surf below. Correctional Officers aboard the prison launch, "McDowell," later recovered the body.

A more elaborate escape plan was conceived by Theodore Cole and Ralph Roe, both serving life terms for bank robbery and kidnapping. On December 16, 1937, a day when the entire Bay Area was shrouded in fog, the two escapees sawed through the detention sash of an outside window in the prison laundry. When their detail officer walked into the toilet room for a few minutes, Cole and Roe squeezed through the window and dropped into the icy water. No trace was ever found of the two, but the waters were numbingly cold and the ebb tide, sweeping out toward the open ocean, was particularly strong that day.

Alcatraz under siege.

ALCATRAZ '46

Rufus "Whitey" Franklin, the lock and key expert Cretzer was depending upon. Franklin remained in solitary confinement throughout the siege.

The third attempt was violent. On May 23, 1938, three paranoid inmates brutally beat their shop officer with a sledge hammer. They then climbed through a maze of barbed wire to the roof of the industries shop building. They intended to kill the gun tower officer, seize his weapons, and blast their way down to the island wharf and the prison launch. As they darted across the roof toward the tower, the tower officer opened fire on them. Two of the escapees were severely wounded, the third surrendered unhurt. One of the wounded, Tom Limerick, was serving a life sentence for armed bank robbery. He died later that night. Royal Cline, the shop officer, died of a fractured skull the following afternoon. Harold Stites, the tower officer, fortunately escaped the fate of Officer Cline. James Lucas, who emerged uninjured from the event, and Rufus Franklin, who was wounded in both shoulders, received life sentences for the attempted escape and the murder of Officer Cline.

About 2:30 a.m. on January 13, 1939, five inmates housed in the D-block segregation unit (before it was redesigned), managed to cut through the mild steel cellfront bars and the window bars in the south wall. Although a thick fog enveloped the island, within 30 minutes of their emergence from the cellhouse, the escapees were discovered. They were on a rocky beach at the foot of the cliffs on the windward side of the island constructing a raft from driftwood. When ordered to surrender, two of the escapees dove into the fog-shrouded water. The others attempted to flee along the base of the cliffs. Prison officers opened fire on the two in the water. One of them, Arthur Barker, serving a life sentence for kidnapping and bank robbery, was killed. Cowed by gunfire, Dale Stamphill, the other swimmer, surrendered. The three remaining escapees, Rufus McCain, Henry Young, and William Martin, were quickly recaptured.

On May 21, 1941, Joe Cretzer, Arnold Kyle, Sam Shockley, and Lloyd Barkdoll, all serving life sentences, failed in an escape attempt when they found that their grinding wheel would not cut through the tool-resistant window bars of their work shop.

John Bayless, serving 25 years for bank robbery, slipped away from an inmate work detail on the island dock on the morning of September 15, 1941. Minutes later the detail officer sounded the alarm when he realized that Bayless was missing. Officers rushing to the area found Bayless feebly struggling in the cold water near the dock. He was so cramped and cold from his few minutes in the water that it was necessary to hospitalize him.

On the morning of April 14, 1943, four inmates were mixing concrete and molding concrete blocks in the work area at the west end of the island. When their work detail officer strolled into the material storage building, the quartette followed and overpowered him. Later, when the captain appeared on a routine inspection tour of the work area, he too was seized, bound, and gagged. Cutting through one of the shop's outside window bars, the escapees dropped onto the barbed wire entanglements on the cliff side. Making their way through the rusted wire, they found an area where they were out of view of any tower officer and dove into the icy water. Meanwhile, the captain freed himself and the detail officer, then sounded the alarm. Tower officers spotted the escapees swimming from the island, ordered them to stop, and opened fire when they disregarded the order. Within minutes, Harold Brest, serving life for kidnapping, and Fred Hunter, serving 25 years for mail robbery, were recaptured by officers in the prison launch. James Boarman, serving 20 years for bank robbery, was shot and killed. Floyd Hamilton, an associate of the notorious bandits, Bonnie and Clyde, serving 30 years for bank robbery, swam underwater and hid in a half-submerged, debris-filled cavern. Two days later, cold and hungry, he emerged from the cave and surrendered.

Huron Walters, serving 30 years for bank robbery, slipped away from his work detail just before the 2:30 p.m. count on August 7, 1943. He was found trying to conceal himself among the rocks on a hillside above the beach. With several fruit juice cans tied around his waist for buoyancy, he was preparing to leap into the cold waters and swim to San Francisco.

John Giles, serving 25 years for mail robbery, was assigned to the labor detail on the island dock. Over a period of several months, he had managed to pilfer enough uniform clothing from the military laundry to disguise himself as a technical sergeant. On the morning of July 31, 1945, he slipped behind the garage and suited up. He then pulled his prison coveralls over the uniform and returned to his assigned tasks on the dock until the army steamship "General Frank M. Coxe" docked. Giles waited until his detail officer walked over to help handle the gang-plank, then slipped out of line, dropped under the dock, removed his coveralls, donned an overseas cap, and brazenly stepped aboard the steamer's lower deck. After the steamship had pulled in its lines and set course for Fort McDowell on nearby Angel Island, the detail officer checked his men and found Giles missing. The army authorities on Angel Island were notified, and the Alcatraz launch with Associate Warden Miller and Lieutenant Bergen aboard, followed in pursuit. The launch reached Angel Island before the slow-moving steamship, and the two Alcatraz officers were waiting at the gang plank when the escapee stepped ashore. Upon seeing Miller and Bergen, Giles said disgustedly, "Hell, I thought this damn tub was headed for 'Frisco."

* * *

At 1:00 p.m., another official count was taken and checked with the armory officer who then reported that all armed posts were manned and ready for the p.m. exodus from the cellhouse. With Weinhold and Simpson again supervising the procedure, outside workers were quickly unlocked and sent to work under the same security precautions taken that morning.

When the recreation yard door was relocked and the key returned to the gun gallery officer, 15 culinary workers were brought to the dining room gate. Miller searched the inmates and locked them in their kitchen row cells. "Mr. Miller," said one worker, "Hubbard got delayed in the dish-tank room. He'll be out to go to the yard as soon as he's through."

Upon the return of Weinhold and Simpson to the cellhouse, the usual unofficial count was taken before they proceeded through the main gate to the captain's office where a small mountain of paperwork awaited them.

Miller received key 107 from Burch and released the three yard birds so they could organize the recreational equipment for ballplayers, sun-bathers, and domino-bridge enthusiasts. After relocking the yard door, Miller retained the key since other inmates who

Rufus Franklin, right, is escorted to Federal Court in San Francisco for 1938 trial in connection with the murder of Alcatraz Officer R. S. Cline.

ALCATRAZ '46

had yard privilege were soon due to be released to the yard. Retaining this security key was against the prison rules, but rules were occasionally stretched for the convenience of the officers involved. "After all," they rationalized, "How much sense does it make to run that key up to the gun gallery and back down again every few minutes?"

Lageson sent the clothing-bathroom workers, two inmate barbers, and 13 barbershop customers to the basement area with Officer Stucker. Two library clerks, who weren't interested in yard privileges, remained at work in the library. As usual, the library gate had been left unlocked to facilitate the delivery of books and magazines to cellblocks B and C.

Lageson and Miller unlocked all the inside workers and men on idle status, who had yard privileges. When cell doors were relocked, 55 impatient inmates lined up in the aisle near the recreation yard door. Many clutched small denim bags, fondly called 'Rock Sacks'. These sacks contained specially designed dominoes, known as 'rocks,' which substituted for playing cards because cards were prohibited in the prison.

After passing the men through the metal detector booth, Miller relocked the recurity door and again retained the key since he was expecting Hubbard to emerge momentarily from the dining room to be released to the yard.

Lageson released Coy, the only Alcatraz inmate with two distinctly different work assignments, and directed him to polish the floor with his blanket-swathed, long-handled floor brush. Coy began on Broadway at the east end and worked his way toward the visiting area below the east gun gallery. This area, known by inmates as 'Pekin Place' because it was the only place where people outside the cellhouse could peek inside, was equipped with four tiny cubicles

"By 1:20 almost all the 280 inmates were out of the cellhouse."

where inmates, who were fortunate enough to have visitors once every 30 days, could gaze at their relatives through bullet-proof glass and could converse over a monitored telephonic device.

By 1:20 almost all the 280 inmates were out of the cellhouse. The outside workers had been marched off to work. The inside workers and inmates from the Culinary Department were in the recreation yard enjoying the fresh air and sunshine. Six inmate patients and an inmate nurse were in the prison hospital above the main dining room. In the basement area were five inmate workers and 13 inmates on call to the barbershop. Seven inmates, including Hubbard, were at work in the kitchen. Two librarians were sorting magazines in the unlocked library. Eighteen inmates, who had forfeited their yard privilege, settled down to another afternoon in their cells. Among them were Cretzer, Thompson, and Carnes. Coy was polishing the main cellhouse floor. In D-block, 25 men, including Shockley, were locked in their cells while Fleish, the D-block orderly, assisted Officer Corwin with the distribution of supplies.

Miller waited patiently near the dining room gate for Hubbard and possibly other stragglers from the culinary detail. Above him in the gallery, was Burch. Lageson, on his way to the administrative office area to have lunch, strolled past Coy, who was still polishing the scuffed floor below the East Gun Gallery.

"Floor's messed up pretty bad today," Coy said. "It'll take a while to shine it up. What time you got now, Mr. Lageson?"

Lageson glanced at his wrist watch. "Almost 1:30," he replied. "I'll be back around 2:00. Will you be finished by then?"

"I think so," said Coy. Lageson passed through the massive steel doors. Gate Officer Phillips slammed the doors shut behind him.

* * *

Middle and top Broadway tiers at meal time.

"Floor's messed up pretty bad today," Coy said. "It'll take a while to shine it up."

ALCATRAZ '46

At both ends of the cellhouse, steel-barred gun galleries rose from the concrete floor on slim steel pillars. These galleries were built on two levels connected by steel stairways. Each lower level was 10 feet above the cellhouse floor. Each upper level was 10 feet below the cellhouse ceiling. The bottom face of the levels was constructed of light sheet steel about waist high. The top face was an imposing array of steel bars spaced five inches apart and strengthened at appropriate intervals with horizontal crossbars of half-inch flat steel. Through a design error, there was no horizontal bar at the top of the gallery face where the vertical bars curved inward toward the cellhouse wall.

Authorized access to the East Gun Gallery was through the prison's main gate and a security door. Generally, this gallery was manned only during the Morning Watch, the Evening Watch, and in emergencies. Known by inmates as "the east end shootin' gallery," it was similar in most respects to the West Gun Gallery except that it did not extend into D-block. The authorized entrance to the West Gun Gallery was through a security door which opened from an exterior catwalk near the southwest corner of the cellhouse and was under the protecting armament of the Road Tower officer.

Coy glanced at the gallery above him, then at the one at the other end of the cellhouse. Carrying his floorbrush, he moved swiftly across 'Pekin Place,' down 'Seedy Street,' and through the library to the steel emergency door at the east end of D-block. He tapped the door twice with his broom handle. Shockley, in D-block, recognized the signal. In exactly five minutes he would begin a disturbance.

The Road Tower

The new visiting area under construction after 1946. The prisoners called the visiting area of the prison "Pekin Place."

76

Not taking time to explain his actions to the open-mouthed library clerks, Coy hurriedly retraced his steps, then headed down 'Broadway' toward the west end. He knew that the only officers on duty at this time were Miller on the floor and Burch in the gallery. As he approached the scuffed floor area at the west end, he saw Miller standing with his back to the dining room gate. Miller was talking with Burch who stood directly above him in the gallery. They could see each other in the convex mirror mounted on the end wall of B-block.

Hubbard had been carefully pacing his labors in the dish-tank room. The trays, cups, bowls, and tableware from the noon meal had been moved through the dishwashing machine, and the machine had been cleaned and rinsed out properly so that there would be no reason for Officer Burdette to find fault and detain him in the kitchen past 1:30. Eyeing the kitchen clock, Hubbard leaned across a food preparation table and slipped a long, sharp butcher knife up his sleeve. He then reported to Burdette that his work was completed and that he was ready to go to the yard. With permission granted, Hubbard went to the gate and peered through the vision panel. Miller, standing with his back to the dining room, was talking to Coy as he swept the floor near the end wall of B-block. Through the glass panel, Coy saw Hubbard waiting quietly.

Muted by the thick concrete walls and padded doors, the faint sounds of a disturbance was heard coming from D-block. As Burch anxiously glanced down the long walkway toward D, the shrill ring of the gallery phone echoed throughout the cellhouse.

Rifle in hand, Burch hurried to the telephone that hung on the wall midway between Broadway and Seedy Street.

"Better get over here and cover me, Bert," said Officer Corwin on the other end of the line. "Shockley's at it again. I think he might set fire to his cell."

Burch hung up the receiver and turned toward D-block. The disturbance was almost completely muffled by the massive wall and the sound-resistant door located at the point where the gallery penetrated the D-block wall. These barriers were equally effective in preventing main cellhouse sounds from being heard by the occupants of D. Coy had taken this fact into consideration when he plotted the escape.

Not bothering to tell Miller he was crossing over into D-block, Burch passed through the heavily padded, self-closing door.

Coy paused at his work and signaled Hubbard by leaning the handle of his floor brush against the B-block stairs. Hubbard shifted the butcher knife from his sleeve to his hip pocket, then tapped on the shatter-proof glass for admission to the cellhouse. Hearing the tapping, Miller turned and opened the dining room gate as he always did, even though it was against prison rules to do so in the absence of the armed gallery officer. He was somewhat surprised to find only one kitchen worker seeking release to the cellhouse.

Hubbard stepped out from under the gun gallery to the designated spot where culinary detail inmates were always searched before they were passed in or out of the dining room. Miller closed the gate, snapped the key ring on his belt, and extended his hands to search Hubbard, saying, "I suppose you want to get out to the yard as quickly as possible. I left your cell door open so you can get in and change your clothes."

Officer Burdette

ALCATRAZ '46

Little did Hubbard or Coy expect a siege of the magnitude shown above to erupt as they started to execute their plan.

As Miller's hands moved from Hubbard's arms to his waist, Coy leaped across the aisle, grabbed Miller from behind, and pinned his arms in a crushing bear hug. Immediately Hubbard slammed his fists into the helpless officer's face. Miller crumpled, unconscious. Coy cautiously relaxed his grip and lowered Miller to the floor. Hubbard reached for the knife, but Coy waved him off. "Forget it," he whispered. "He's out cold."

Listening carefully, they found no indication that anyone had seen or heard the assault. Coy unsnapped Miller's key ring while Hubbard shifted the knife to the waistband of his pants. The eye-contact between the inmates conveyed the mutual feeling that they were now fully committed to carrying through the escape plan.

Hubbard dragged the officer around the corner of the cellblock onto Seedy Street while Coy used the keys to open the control box. Hubbard stopped at the first vacant cell and called softly to Coy, "Open 403."

Coy dialed the cell number and expertly manipulated the levers which opened the cell door. He called back, "I'm dropping that cell door off the hook. You can pull it shut after you take care of him." Leaving the control box unlocked, Coy headed for the nearby utility corridor entrance.

Alone in the cell with Miller, Hubbard quickly removed the officer's jacked and slipped into it. "Sure is a lousy fit," he gumbled, "but it should fool the screws until they get close."

The officer remained limp and unconscious throughout the hurried trussing, making it easy for Hubbard to complete his task. Using the necktie, he tied Miller's hands behind his back. The leather belt from the trousers tightly cinched his legs together. Hubbard's bandanna served as an effective gag. In his haste to rejoin Coy, he neglected to search Miller's pockets, one of which contained security key 107.

* * *

During the siege, Sam Shockley had time to fashion this razor-sharp plastic knife.

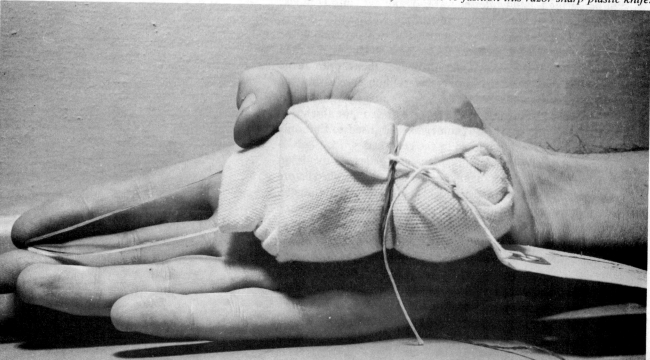

Arriving at the C-block utility corridor door, Coy knew exactly what to do. For years, whenever he moved about the cellhouse delivering library books and magazines, he observed officers locking and unlocking the security doors. He noted that although prison personnel were rotated from time to time, key identification numbers did not change. Coy had never handled any Alcatraz key, but he knew exactly which doors each of Miller's keys unlocked.

Selecting the proper key from Miller's ring, Coy unlocked the utility corridor door and moved swiftly into the dark, narrow alley. This passageway, which bisected C-block from top to bottom and end to end, contained the electrical conduits, the sewer and water pipes, and the ventilation ducts which served the cells. Its gloomy depths provided a variety of hiding places where contraband could be concealed. Coy's skinny arm reached high into a long ventilator duct that had not been used since 1933. The arm emerged with a grease-soaked 'Rock Sack.'

"This is the best key of all," smiled Coy.

Moving quickly, Coy emerged from the utility corridor, snatched Miller's keys from the door, and ran to the junction of Times Square and Michigan Boulevard at the northwest corner of B-block. He unlocked the control box and released Cretzer and Carnes from cells 152 and 146. In a few seconds, the three were together beneath the west gun gallery.

Convicts' Leader Once Nation's No. 1 Bank Robber

Joseph Paul Cretzer, leader of the bloody Alcatraz outbreak and labelled as the man who "cold bloodedly" shot four guards, was sought here in 1938 as the leader of the nation's No. 1 bank robbing gang.

The 35-year-old criminal is being held on three sentences—life, for the murder of a U. S. marshal at Tacoma, where he was on trial for escape from McNeil Island Penitentiary; five years for that escape, and 25 years for bank robbery.

Cretzer, now No. 548, was traced early in 1938 after the arrest f "Kay Wallace," who was arrested as the keeper of a Pittsburg house of prostitution in a notorious white slave case.

One of many newspaper articles that appeared in San Francisco newspapers during the siege.

Lieutenant Philip Bergen preparing the guard roster.

Dressed in Miller's uniform jacket, Hubbard left cell 403 and walked across the west end of the cellhouse. He was greeted by Cretzer's sardonic comments, "Marv, you're the screwiest lookin' screw I ever saw. That monkey suit fits you like a tent. Did someone die 'n leave it to you?"

"You don't savvy," replied Hubbard. "This is insurance. It's camouflage, a gimmick to fool the screws."

Coy handed Miller's keys to Hubbard. "Marv, hang on to these. Stand guard by the C-block stairwell, but keep an eye on Miller." He turned to Carnes. "Kid, go on down to the southeast corner of C-block, and keep your eye on the main entrance. Stay back out of sight so the gate guard can't see you. We don't want to be surprised by some fool screw wandering into the cellhouse. If anyone comes, let us know."

Carnes waved and trotted off. Hubbard checked cell 403 to make certain Miller had not come to and freed himself. Cretzer's unkind remarks about the jacket bothered him. As he moved to the lookout position by the C-block stairwell, he slowly unbuttoned the jacket and tossed it into a corner by the recreation yard door. "Maybe I'll get one that fits better. If not, maybe I'll put this one back on later when we go over the wall."

View of powerhouse workshop (note lack of bars or detention sash on windows).

Coy had selected the north end as the most logical place to force his way into the gun gallery. At the junction of Times Square and Michigan Boulevard, the barred and screened stairwell leading to the basement offered a means of reaching the lower level of the gallery.

Coy kicked off his unlaced prison-made oxfords and shrugged out of his soiled denims. With Cretzer's assistance, he smeared axle grease from the Rock Sack on his skinny, naked body, being particularly careful to thoroughly lubricate his head, shoulders, chest, and hips. Then, with the 'Rock Sack' gripped firmly in his teeth, Coy jumped atop the stairwell, reached high to grasp the gun gallery bars, and pulled himself up. Hand over hand, he climbed like a monkey to the top of the gallery face where the vertical bars curved inward toward the west wall of the cellhouse. Locking his thin legs around the bars with his emaciated thighs resting uncomfortably on a cross-brace, he reached into the sack and pulled out a crude but workable bar-spreader.

Surreptitiously fashioned in a prison work shop, the ingeniously designed bar-spreader had been smuggled into the cellhouse in the false bottom of a garbage can. Basically, it worked on the jack-screw principle. It was a five-inch long, coarse thread, case-hardened steel bolt, one-inch in diameter, and deeply notched across one end. Threaded on this bolt was a double-thick steel nut. A flat steel washer and a four-inch long cylindrical steel sleeve, also notched across one end, completed the assembly. The inside diameter of the sturdy steel sleeve was slightly larger than the diameter of the bolt so that it could slide smoothly over the bolt. When properly combined and thoroughly lubricated with axle grease, these four simple parts formed an efficient pressure-exerting device when inserted in the five-inch space between two parallel bars. With the notched end of the bolt firmly seated on one bar and the notched end of the sleeve firmly seated on the other bar, turning the nut toward the base of the steel sleeve would apply pressure to the bars, bending and forcing them apart. An end wrench to turn the nut and a liberal supply of grease to lubricate the spreader and Coy's body, were included in the sack's contents.

Prison Industries Building

81

Coy carefully placed the bar-spreader between two of the gracefully arched bars and twisted the nut with his fingers until the device was firmly seated. Then, using the end wrench, he turned the nut, exerting pressure to widen the space between the bars from five inches to approximately nine inches. When the spreader reached the limit of its effectiveness, Coy carefully unscrewed the device, stowed it and the end wrench in the 'Rock Sack,' and dropped the bundle into Cretzer's waiting hands.

"That's all the thing will do," he said to Cretzer. "The rest is up to me."

"Good luck, Bernie. I'll hide this thing like I promised."

Cretzer turned and strode across the west end to the open utility corridor and entered its dark depths.

* * *

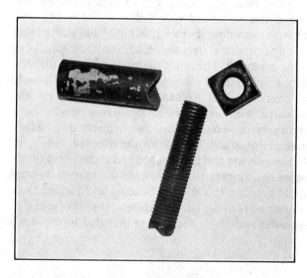

These two photos show bar-spreader Coy used.

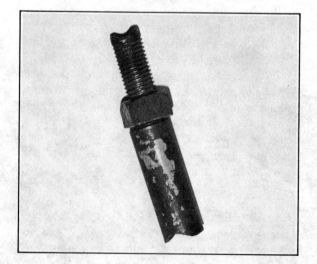

Hubbard periodically rechecked cell 403 to make certain his captive was still securely bound, returning each time to his lookout position in the C-block stairwell where he could watch the B-C aisle and the dining room gate.

Coy unwrapped his cramped legs from around the bars of the gallery face and inserted them through the space widened by the bar-spreader. It was, as he had expected, a tight squeeze for his hips, chest, and head, even though he had dieted just about all excess flesh from his bones. The lubricant helped, and finally he was where no other Alcatraz inmate had ever been — inside the 'west end shootin' gallery.' It was 1:42 p.m.

Cretzer emerged from the utility corridor in time to see Coy squeeze through the bars. He and Hubbard moved to the D-block entrance door. Looking down Seedy Street between C-block and the segregation cellhouse, they saw Carnes standing on watch at the southeast corner of the block, across from the library. Carnes waved assuringly, indicating that there was no suspicious activity in or around the main cellhouse entrance. Cretzer thoughtfully retrieved Miller's keys and left the utility corridor unlocked.

On bare feet, Coy raced down the steps, apprehensive that Burch might be waiting to greet him with a blast of gunfire. At the foot of the stairs, he crouched for a moment to scan the long, empty avenue to the D-block door. Burch hadn't returned, but he could come through that distant doorway at any moment. Coy ran to the doorway and peered cautiously through the vision panel. Thirty feet down the walkway on the other side was the armed Burch, leaning against the bars of the gallery face, talking to Officer Corwin and Fleish, the inmate orderly.

"Beats me why they keep Shockley here," Corwin muttered. "That little creep belongs in the loony bin."

"Springfield, Leavenworth, Atlanta, and the other joints are plumb full of nuts like Sam," drawled Burch in his Oklahoma accent. "This nut just happens to be an Alcatraz type."

Coy could not hear what they were saying. Moving away from the vision panel, he slipped a riot club from the wall rack, climbed the bars, and perched above the doorway.

"O.K., Joe," he called softly. "Hit that damn door, then you guys get back out of sight while I clobber old man Burch."

Cretzer banged Miller's ring of jail keys against the door. Shockley, who had been listening intently for the second signal, gave one last scream, then settled down to pacing and muttering.

Corwin, somewhat relieved, glanced up at Burch and said, "Looks like he ran out of steam or something. He's just talking to those voices he hears. I'm sure glad they didn't tell him to set fire to his cell. We won't have to put up with that smoke-stink all afternoon." He paused, then added an afterthought, "But I would have enjoyed wetting him down with the fire extinguisher."

"One of these times, he's gonna roast himself to death in one of those fires he's always starting," predicted Fleish.

"That'd be a small loss," shrugged Corwin. "I'll call the captain when he gets back from lunch and tell him our boy is off his rocker again."

Satisfied that the disturbance was over, Burch turned to leave. "I better get on back to Bill Miller. That rap on the door probably means he has some more kitchen inmates ready to go to the yard."

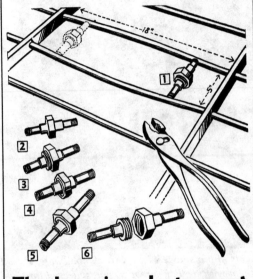

The Ingenious Instrument

Convict Bernard Coy had a home-made spreader made out of rods and screws from a toilet. He also had a pair of pliers. When he put the ends of the rod between the bars and twisted the nut it forced the ends — and the bars apart. (In diagram, number 2 would go where the phantom spreader is shown, and so on until the bars were spread.) He then squirmed through the opening.

Newspaper diagram showing how Coy used bar-spreader.

ALCATRAZ '46

This photo shows where Coy climbed bars, spread them with his bar-spreader, and squeezed through.

Corwin and the inmate orderly continued to discuss Shockley. Burch opened the self-closing door and entered the main cellhouse section of the gallery. As the door closed behind him, Coy slammed the riot club down on his head. Completely surprised, Burch was knocked off balance, but his uniform cap absorbed much of the impact. Dazed, he tried to raise the rifle to defend himself, but Coy grabbed the weapon and twisted it out of his hands. The two men struggled and the rifle and riot club clattered to the metal floor out of reach.

Desperately Burch tried to draw his pistol but was unable to free it from its buttoned-down holster. The naked, grease-smeared inmate was on top of him punching, pounding, and butting fiercely with his bony skull. The commotion in the metal cage made a racket that seemed to continue for a long time. Coy grabbed the officer's necktie and brutally twisted and tightened it around Burch's neck until he ceased to resist.

Thinking Burch dead, Coy leaned against the cold bars to catch his breath. Below, on the cellhouse floor, Cretzer and Hubbard grinned up at him.

"Man," smiled Hubbard, "What a battle. I'll bet it's been a long time since you slugged it out like that."

Cretzer handed Miller's keys to Hubbard and reached toward the gun gallery. His voice was insistent and urgent, "Give me the pistol, Bernie. Come on, give me the pistol."

In sole command of the dimly lit gun gallery, Coy quickly removed the officer's gun belt with its holstered pistol and leather clip pouch and lowered them to Cretzer. Selecting key 83 from the security keys hanging on the wall, he dropped it into Hubbard's waiting hands saying, "That'll open the D-block door. Get in there and grab Corwin, but don't shoot him unless you have to. We don't want anybody getting wise to us."

Keys — a way of life in a prison.

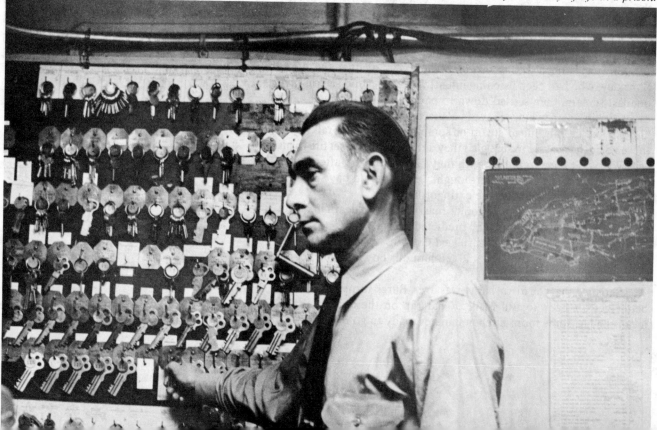

Cretzer buckled the gun belt around his chunky waist and drew the pistol to check it. "Six in the clip and one in the firin' chamber. O.K. Let's go, Marv."

"I'll cover you from up here," said Coy from the gallery.

Expertly, Coy loaded a cartridge into the rifle's firing chamber, slung the cartridge belt over his shoulder, and pushed through the doorway into the D-block section of the gallery as Cretzer and Hubbard burst in through the main floor entrance door.

The sudden invasion did not catch Corwin completely by surprise. He had heard some suspicious sounds from the general direction of the gun gallery during the fight and had turned toward the floor telephone, but Fleish was standing between him and the instrument. Fleish didn't say a word, but he looked at Corwin in a way that meant "Don't touch that phone." Corwin hesitated, then without saying a word, stood motionless by the door. Now, as he stared into the muzzles of Cretzer's pistol and Coy's rifle, he paled apprehensively.

Cretzer took Corwin's keys and his uniform jacket. Hubbard kept the cigarettes, wristwatch, and wallet. Prodded along by Cretzer's pistol, the unhappy officer was marched to cell 403 where Miller, still unconscious, lay bound and gagged. Coy, covering the movement, moved back into the main cellhouse section of the gallery. Looking up at him, Fleish said quietly, "Coy, you know you can't get off this rock. Go back to your cell before the other screws get wise and gun you down."

"Dummy up, Big Shot," snapped Coy. "I'm getting out. You want to come along, O.K., otherwise stay the hell out of our way."

Shoved untied into the cell with Miller, Corwin sagged to the floor beside the motionless body. He was relieved to feel the officer's pulse. "At least he's alive," he thought. "There might be a chance for us yet."

Coy barked, "Shut that cell door on those screws and come over here under the gallery. There's a lot of good stuff up here besides the guns and keys."

For several minutes a steady stream of clubs, tear gas grenades, gas masks, keys and miscellaneous defensive equipment poured through the gallery bars into the waiting hands of Cretzer and Hubbard. When finished, Coy, streaked with grease, sweat, and grime, surveyed the ravaged gun cage and decided, "Well, that's it except for the screw's monkey suit. He ain't going to need it, and it should fit one of us."

He stripped off Burch's uniform and dropped the garments through the bars leaving the officer, sprawled on the cold steel deck, clad only in his shorts.

Trailing the rifle, Coy trotted to the north end of the gun gallery. At the stairs, he waited until Hubbard had climbed atop the basement stairwell, then passed the rifle and the ammunition belt to him.

"Careful, Marv," he warned. "It's loaded and cocked."

Coy scurried to the top level of the gallery and squeezed his scratched, bruised, but still greasy body through the opening in the bars. In a few seconds, he lowered himself to the flats, climbed back into his discarded clothing, and accepted the rifle and ammunition from Hubbard.

As he crossed Broadway and made his way to D-block, a voice called to him, "Hey, y'all gonna let us out of here now?"

ALCATRAZ '46

Coy ignored the question because he knew the speaker was a Black. Another Black on the middle tier of B-block shouted, "You white trash. You let us out or we gonna raise hell."

Coy stopped in mid-stride and raised his rifle threateningly. "Nigger. This is a white man's caper all the way. You stay where you are at."

"You be sorry, mother fucker," shouted the man on the middle tier. "You be damn sorry if you don' let us out. You hear?"

"Hush up fool," cautioned another Black. "Can't you see he's got a gun? Let dem white fools go 'head and get theirselves killed."

Before moving on, Coy warned, "Make any more noise and I'll come up there and kill you, personally."

Cretzer had piled the miscellaneous equipment inside the C-block utility corridor and had pocketed the security keys and all the keys taken from Corwin.

"Bernie," he said. "It's time we got Whitey and Sam outta D. They'll think we forgot 'bout 'em."

"O.K. Get them out, but be careful of the electric locks over there. Get Fleish to show you how they work. I'll go get Buddy and maybe a couple of other guys. When I get back, we'll be ready to go." Coy turned and held out his hand toward Hubbard. "Marv, give me Miller's cellhouse keys."

Famous tough guy actor Edward G. Robinson poses with Warden James Johnston at Alcatraz.

86

Cretzer seated himself on Corwin's desk in D-block and spread his collection of keys on the desk top. "Fleish, come over here 'n tell me which key gets Whitey outta the hole."

Fleish pawed through the pile and sorted out two keys. "I've seen Corwin use these two," he said. "The 99 unlocks the outer doors of the dark cells. The 81 is for the control boxes and the cell doors on both upper tiers. I don't know about the box here on the flats. I never saw any officer open it. They always operate these cells down here by electricity from the gun cage. You got a helluva lotta keys here. Try 'em. One might open the box."

Cretzer thoughtfully studied the confiscated keys. "Perhaps it'd be smarter to wait for Coy," he thought. "Fleish isn't too sure 'bout anythin' but the 99 and 81 keys. Coy'd probably know which key'd set Whitey free."

He slid off the desk and hurried past the open front isolation cells on his way to the closed front cells at the east end of the block. Several inmates saw the keys and the Colt .45 and shouted, "Hey, Joe. Rack us open. We want out."

Joe grinned at them. "Later you guys. I'm gonna talk to Whitey first. Then we'll let everybody out."

Pictured here is Louis Fleish, one of the leaders of the notorious Detroit "Purple Gang," serving thirty years for possession of unregistered machine guns. Fleish was later cleared of any involvement in the escape attempt, although at first he was suspected of being one of the ringleaders.

87

ALCATRAZ '46

Using the 99 key as Fleish had advised, Cretzer unlocked the outer door to Franklin's cell and swung it wide. Franklin was standing at the inner grille door, his hands clenching the bars. "Get this door open, Joe. Hurry up. You know that damn siren is bound to start screamin' any minute."

"We'll get you out all right, but we're havin' a little trouble with the locks. What do you know 'bout 'em?"

"All I know is there ain't no key hole in these damn sliding doors. If there was, I'd been outta here a long time ago. The screws open these damn doors with electric motors from the gun cage. You know that, Joe. You've seen 'em do it often enough. That screw in the cage does it every time I go in or out."

"How 'bout that control box at the end of the block?"

"I don't know. It oughta open these doors. Ask Fleish. He should know. They didn't put that damn box there for nothin'."

"Don't worry pal, we're gonna get you out," said Cretzer as he hurried back to the west end of the block. He found Fleish talking to Hubbard who was standing in the open doorway watching cell 403.

"Marv," said Cretzer, "We're gonna hafta figure out a way to get Whitey's cell door open. I'm gonna go upstairs 'n let ol' Sam out."

Fleish cautioned, "Don't forget to open the control box first and take the dead-lock off. Use the 81 on all those locks up there. But remember, the key won't work the cell doors as long as the dead-lock is on."

Cretzer sneered, "Goddamn, I know that. You think you're the only con who knows his way 'round this lousy block?"

The 81 key unlocked the control box. Cretzer had no trouble moving the control lever off the dead-lock position. Leaving the box door open, he hastened along the tier to where Shockley was waiting. Again, inmate acquaintances locked in cells along the walkway clamored to be released, but Cretzer went straight to Shockley's cell and unlocked the door.

Shockley, brimming with self-satisfied pride, asked, "Joe, how did I do? Did you hear me raisin' hell in here?"

"We heard you, Sam. You did O.K. Those stupid screws really fell for it, 'n we took 'em without any trouble. Now we're goin' home."

"Joe, how 'bout all these other guys up here. They wanta go home, too. Ain't we gonna take 'em along, Joe?"

"Sam, you let 'em out. Here's the key. But tell them to keep out of our way. If they wanta follow us over the wall, it's O.K. with me. Just so they don't get in our way."

Cretzer returned to the flats at the west end of the block for another conference with Hubbard and Fleish. He was deeply concerned about the unexpected problem which was delaying the release of his friend, Whitey Franklin, and angry because Coy was not there to advise him.

Shockley, bursting with self-importance, gleefully loped along tiers 2 and 3, unlocking cells and shouting, "Everybody off the range. We're all goin' home!"

More than a dozen excited, grinning inmates rushed out on the tier walkways. Spotting the pistol in Cretzer's hand, one yelled, "Goddamn, the cons have taken over. Come on guys, let's go. The joint is ours."

Some of the segregated inmates, having little or no taste for high risks and possible violence, remained in their cells. Robert Stroud was one of these. He sauntered to the walkway railing and leaned over to observe the inmates milling around aimlessly on the flats. He could see Cretzer, Hubbard, and Fleish gathered around the spread out collection of keys. Shaking his balding head, he slipped back into his cell and drew the door almost closed. "Guys like them," he mused, "are always doing it the hard way. They'll be dead before the sun goes down, and a lot of other poor, ignorant bastards will perish with them."

* * *

In his cell on the middle tier of C-block, Thompson impatiently waited to be released. Although he used his hand mirror with the skill of long practice, he couldn't tell what was happening. So far, everything he had heard — whispering, scuffling, clattering, but no siren — seemed encouraging.

He knew that all of Coy's actions had to be precisely timed and accomplished with a minimum of time and effort. Any one of a hundred things could happen to upset the plan — failure of the untested bar-spreader, unexpected arrival of officers from the administration building, inability of Coy to subdue old Burch, and so on. He knew how important it was for them to get out of the cellhouse and over the yard wall before the escape siren sounded. They were gambling on their ability to quickly eliminate the armed officers in the Main Tower, Model Tower, and Powerhouse Tower after reaching the yard wall.

Thompson learned about the escape date the day before and decided he would not spend his last day on the island at work in the clothing factory. He had pretended to have stomach cramps and, following Sick Call, was allowed to remain in his cell for the afternoon.

At last, his mirror reflected Coy trotting along the tier walkway. "Hurry up, you old squirrel shooter," shouted Thompson.

Coy grinned and waved his rifle as he ran past Thompson's cell to the control box at the east end. In less than a minute, Thompson's cell door slid open and dropped off the hook as Coy reclosed the box saying, "Joe is over in D getting Whitey and Sam. We only got two guns now, but we'll get plenty more when we take the towers."

"Hell, I can wait. What do you want me to do?"

"Get the library ladder and take it down to the west end."

Librarians Cooke and Peabody were rearranging the books on a library bookshelf when Thompson arrived. They were well aware of Coy's intention to escape, although they did not know all the details of the plan. Their illicit kiting of messages to and from the segregation cellhouse had made it possible for Coy and Cretzer to enlist and maintain the assistance of Shockley. They were among the few inmates to be invited to go over the wall with the escapees. When Thompson appeared in the doorway, they knew the plan was in effect.

Thompson looked around until he spotted the library ladder leaning against a bookshelf in the far corner. The aroma of boiling coffee attracted his attention.

"Where's the ja-moke?" he demanded.

"Behind the desk. Help yourself."

"Gotta have some hot coffee. Just took some aspirin for my headache," he said, holding the ladder upright with one hand while emptying the coffee pot into a large stainless steel cup with the other.

"I'm gonna borrow your ladder, too. Bernie says we need it."

"O.K. by us," said Peabody. "Tell Bernie we wish him luck. You too, Buddy. If we weren't so short, we'd go with you."

"Right," agreed Cooke hastily. "We're too short."

"Hell, long or short, what's the difference? You guys gotta like it here to stay when you got a chance to get free."

With the ladder balanced on one shoulder and sipping the steaming coffee, Thompson sauntered down Seedy Street toward the west end.

Cooke heaved a sigh of relief. "Peabody," he said. "Let's you and me find a good place to hide. Before long, this joint is going to be slightly unsafe for us innocent bystanders."

The two men began piling books in the corner close to the wall but with enough room for them to hide behind.

* * *

Thompson set the ladder down near the D-block doorway. He finished his coffee and watched as Cretzer and Shockley examined the control box on the main floor.

"Sam, you still got the 81 key? See if it'll open this damn control box."

With some difficulty, Shockley slid the key into the lock and tried to turn it. The seldom used lock refused to work.

"It won't turn, Joe," said Shockley, handing the key to Cretzer.

Cretzer brushed a strand of hair from his forehead and rubbed his chin. "Fleish," he said, "are you sure you don't know which key opens this goddam control box? We're gonna jam the damn lock if we keep twistin' wrong keys in it. Hell, you're out here on the flats all the time. You must have seen somethin'."

"Joe, I never saw Corwin or any other screw open this box all the time I've been over here. The screw in the gun cage always opens the cells on the flats. The key to this box is probably somewhere up there in the cage."

"Coy gave me the keys he took outta the gun cage. Maybe I didn't get 'em all. Hey, Marv, do you have any D-block keys?"

Hubbard, standing in the doorway where he could watch cell 403, replied, "I don't have any keys, Joe. Coy has the key ring we took from Miller. You got the rest. One of them has got to open that box."

"Try the 81 again," suggested Fleish. "It opened the boxes upstairs. Stands to reason it oughtta open this one, too. This lock don't get used much, so maybe it just sticks or works hard."

"Yeah, Joe," urged Shockley. "Try it. Maybe the lock is rusty or full of paint."

"Cretzer stared at his assortment of keys, selected key 81, slid it into the lock, and worked it in and out a few times to get the feel of it. When he turned it counterclockwise, the key would not turn; clockwise it turned a little. He twisted harder, and the lock clicked. Cretzer quickly grabbed the handle and yanked the box open.

"Guess it just takes a little know how," remarked Fleish.

"Quick, Joe, open Whitey's cell," implored Shockley.

Cretzer stared in dismay at the orderly rows of electrical switches on the panel. "Goddam," he said, "this is worse than the cockpit of an aeroplane. Hey, Fleish, how in hell do these things work?"

"I told you Joe, I don't know. I've heard the screws say if you mess with them and don't know what you're doing, everything gets loused up. Maybe it sets off an alarm. I don't know."

"Corwin knows," snarled Cretzer. "We'll make him open up."

Closely followed by Shockley and Hubbard, Cretzer rushed into the main cellhouse and pulled Corwin from the cell. Pushing him into D-block, Cretzer pointed to the open control box and said, "O.K. you bastard. You're the guy that locks us in the hole. Now get busy 'n let Franklin out 'n don't hand me no crap 'bout not knowin' how to work them goddam switches. I want Franklin outta that hole right now, or you're a dead man."

Because of the way the cell operating controls were positioned in the gun gallery control panel, the electro-mechanically operated cell doors on the flats could not be opened from the control box at the west end of the block. Control could be electrically transferred to the floor from the gallery, but for security reasons, this was rarely done. In case of electrical power failure, a handcrank, which provided a mechanical operation of the locking devices, was concealed inside the control box on the flats. Few people were aware of its existence.

"Go ahead, fink," Cretzer demanded. "Let Whitey out."

Sensing an opportunity to alert the armory officer, Corwin unhesitatingly walked to the open control box and reached for the switches.

"Hold it, Corwin, or I'll blow your head off," bellowed Coy as he came rushing through the entrance door from the main cellhouse. "You hit them switches, they'll ring an alarm out front."

Cretzer stepped up to Corwin and asked, "Is that true about the alarm?" Corwin didn't reply.

"The only place them cells can be opened is from the gun cage," said Coy. "I don't have time to squeeze back in there to do it, so Whitey has gotta stay locked in. We're far enough behind schedule."

Cretzer turned to Shockley. "Sam, go tell Whitey we can't get this damn door open." Reflecting on Coy's statement about the loss of time, he changed his directions to Shockley. "No, forget it, Sam. We better move out." He nudged Corwin with the pistol. "All right, screw. Back into that cell."

Corwin hesitated, then lunged for the switches in the still open control box.

Before he reached them, Cretzer struck him across the head with the heavy pistol. Bleeding profusely from the scalp, Corwin was shoved across the aisle to cell 403. As he stumbled against the cell door, Cretzer moved in closer and sluged him repeatedly. "That's for all your help, screw."

Cretzer pushed him into the cell. "You're lucky we don't kill you, you lousy fink."

Hubbard closed the cell door. "Get down on the goddam floor and stay there," he said. Turning to Cretzer, he asked, "What about them?"

Fleish and the released D-block inmates stood clustered around the cellhouse door. "Those that want to come along can follow us over the wall," said Cretzer. "But don't any of you punks get in our way. We don't want nobody lousin' things up."

Removing his gun belt, Cretzer eased himself into the uniform jacket that Hubbard had discarded earlier. Burch's grease-smeared uniform and the jacket taken from Corwin lay nearby.

"Hey, Marv," Cretzer called as he buckled the belt with its holstered pistol around the ill-fitting jacket, "try one of these on."

Hubbard ignored the invitation. Coy looked across the cellhouse and saw Carnes running towards them. "Someone's coming in the front gate," called Carnes. "I think it's that steward, Bristow."

* * *

Chief Steward Robert Bristow was about to enter the main cellhouse from the administration building. He checked his watch. It was 1:52 p.m. Al Phillips, the Main Gate Officer, had no reason to suspect anything out of the ordinary, and there hadn't been any traffic through the sallyport since Lageson departed to eat his dinner.

"Has Ernie gone back in yet?" asked Bristow.

"Not yet. He's out front, still eating, I guess."

"He never did like my lunch room," laughed the steward, "but it ain't because he don't like to eat."

"Well, your cooking isn't too bad. The price is certainly right."

Bristow entered the cellhouse, and Phillips closed the massive steel gate behind him. In no hurry to return to the kitchen, he strolled leisurely along Broadway. When he neared the dining room gate, he noticed it was partially open, and Miller and Burch were not in sight. Alarmed, he started back toward the main gate. Overtaking him, Thompson grabbed him from behind and held a dagger against his throat. The dagger was improvised from a draftsman's steel dividers. The two arms of the dividers were drawn to a single point, and the upper portion of the instrument was taped to provide a nonslip grip.

Hubbard arrived and helped Thompson subdue Bristow. "Sorry, chief," said Hubbard. "I was hoping you'd stay out front until after we were gone."

Miran Thompson as he appeared in civilian clothes.

Thompson searched the steward and pocketed his wristwatch and wallet. Hubbard growled, "Give them back. This is a real good guy. He ain't like those other finks."

Thompson grudgingly returned the valuables, and Bristow was taken to cell 403. On their way, they passed Cretzer who was walking around fumbling through a handful of keys. "Bernie," he asked, "you got the 107?"

"Hell no. You got it. You got all them fucking keys from the gun cage."

"You gave me a lot of keys, but I can't find no 107."

"Spread them out again so we can see them."

Coy, Cretzer, and Hubbard pawed through the considerable collection of keys.

"Goddammit. It's gotta be here," said Coy. "You got all the keys I took outta the damn cage, and these are all that Miller had on his key ring. That key was here at noon. It's gotta be here now."

"Find it then," snapped Cretzer, stalking away angrily. He stopped when he heard the main gate clang shut. "Dammit. Here comes another one."

Two inmate gardeners, Jack Moyle and Norman Egan, had entered the cellhouse from the administration building. Having worked through their regular lunch hour, they were enroute to the dining room for a late lunch of sandwiches and coffee. Cretzer intercepted them on Broadway and took them, at gun point, to cell 403.

"Why lock us up, Joe?" they asked.

"Why you? Because I don't trust any of you damn trustys."

Still on guard near the west end of C-block, Carnes again heard the metallic clang of the main gate. He called softly to Coy, "It's Lageson."

*   *   *

"Two inmate gardeners, Jack Moyle and Norman Egan, had entered the cellhouse from the administration building."

ALCATRAZ '46

Lageson inspected the cell fronts and the floor of the aisle. He was not pleased. "Coy must be slipping," he thought. "The floor doesn't look any better than it did before I went to lunch."

As he approached the dining room gate, vaguely wondering why Miller wasn't present, Coy, Cretzer, and Carnes sprang into the aisle and quickly subdued and searched the unarmed officer. Coy pocketed his wristwatch, wallet, and cigarette lighter. Cretzer grabbed his keys, hoping that one might be the missing 107. At gunpoint, Lageson was shoved toward cell 403.

Shockley emerged from D-block and saw the cellhouse officer. "That's the dirty son-of-a-bitch I want," yelled Shockley. "Hold him. I'm gonna beat his fink head off. He kicked me when they threw me in the hole last time."

"Shut up," said Hubbard shoving Shockley aside. "You make me nervous."

Shockley leaned against the cellhouse wall and pouted. "He choked me and kicked me," he whined.

"Where's Miller?" asked Lageson calmly.

"He's in the cell here," replied Hubbard. "Get in with him. If you keep quiet, you'll be all right."

The cell door closed. Corwin, battered and bruised, turned to Lageson. "Ernie, there's four of us now. Maybe five counting Burch. From what I've heard, I think Coy killed him in the gallery. They got his guns, so he probably is dead. We'll be dead too, if we don't get out of here."

"That's the dirty son-of-a-bitch I want," yelled Shockley. "Hold him. I'm gonna beat his fink head off."

Bristow pressed against the cell front and looked out.

"Sit down, screw!" bellowed Thompson who was on guard. "It's none of your damn business what we do out here." He stepped forward threateningly. "We oughtta kill all of you," he added.

Bristow retreated to the rear of the cell and seated himself in a corner.

Cretzer brushed a strand of hair from his forehead and looked at Coy. "How many more of these finks are we goin' to have to capture?" he demanded.

"For cri-sakes, shut up," responded Coy.

"How 'bout that damn Stucker in the basement and Pehrson in the hospital? How 'bout Burdette in the kitchen?"

"We'll capture all them screws if we have to," said Coy moving to the dining room gate. He looked through the vision panel in the gate. Burdette was nowhere in sight. There was no sign of the inmate cooks and bakers. Satisfied that the Culinary Department presented no immediate threat, Coy hurried to the screened gate at the head of the basement stairs and listened to the sounds below. As he did, Burdette strolled into the dining room to inspect the recently washed and polished ten-man tables. Surprised to find the gate unlocked, he peered through the vision panel and saw Coy.

"Miller shouldn't leave this gate open," he thought. "He must be having some trouble. I'd better ask Burch what's up."

As Burdette stepped into the cellhouse, Cretzer jammed the cocked pistol into his stomach, and Hubbard pointed the rifle at his head. Carnes threatened with a riot club. Burdette's keys and other valuables were confiscated, and he was rudely herded into cell 403.

After Thompson and Shockley shut the cell door, Bristow said, "Looks like someone else will be serving supper tonight, Joe."

Burdette stared at Miller and Corwin. "What the hell happened to them?" he asked.

Main entrance to Administration Building.

ALCATRAZ '46

"I don't know. Just beat them up to show how tough they are, I guess," replied Lageson. "They probably killed old Burch to get his guns."

"I figured those were the west gallery guns the minute I saw them," said Burdette. "Burch must be dead. He wouldn't give up his guns without a fight."

"What do you suppose they're planning to do?"

"I think they intend to go through the yard and over the wall, but I think something has gone sour for them. When they grabbed my keys, I heard them griping because I didn't have a 107."

* * *

In the basement barbershop, two inmates, who had been held in from work for their regular once-a-month haircut, asked Officer Stucker for permission to go to the recreation yard. Stucker checked to be certain their hair had been cut in the prescribed G.I. style, looked at his watch, and said, "O.K. It's just ten minutes after two. You ought to be able to get out before they lock up for the 2:30 count."

The inmates walked upstairs, knocked on the gate, and waited for the cellhouse officer. Peering through the close-mesh screen which covered the stairwell, they saw no one in the west end of the cellhouse. When the cellhouse officer did not respond to their repeated tappings, they returned to the basement and informed Stucker, "There ain't nobody up there to let us out. Now we're stuck 'til after the count."

Main cellhouse barber shop established after 1946 blastout attempt. There were black barbers for the black inmates and white barbers for the white inmates.

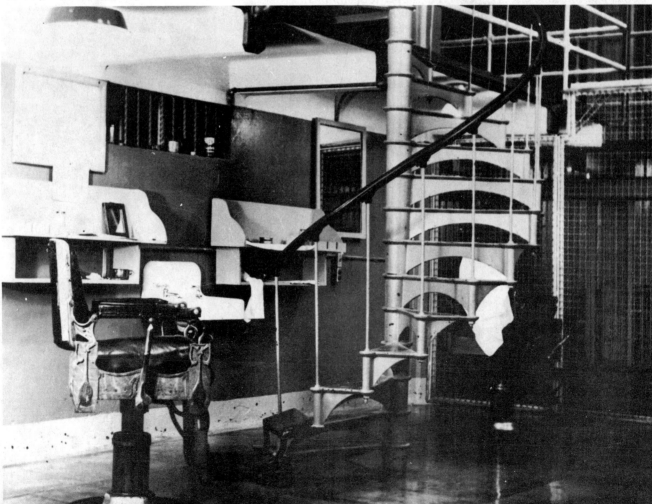

"That's unusual," thought Stucker. "Lageson should be back from lunch, and Miller must be up there somewhere. I'd better take a look."

Stucker climbed the long flight of stairs and peered through the security screen. He did not have a key that would admit him to the cellhouse, however, there was a padlock hasp on his side of the locked gate. This padlock was kept in a locked-open position most of the time. As a security measure, this gate was padlocked every time the basement sallyport gates were opened. Stucker carried the padlock key on his key ring.

Craning his neck to see better through the screen, Stucker saw that the D-block door was standing open and several inmates were milling around it. Cretzer, clothed in an officer's uniform jacket, emerged from the doorway brandishing a pistol.

"My God," thought Stucker. "They must have killed Miller and Corwin. Maybe Lageson and Burch, too. They'll probably be coming after me or Burdette next. I'll delay them by padlocking this gate."

Cretzer, Coy, and Hubbard were halfway across the west end of the cellhouse when Stucker snapped the padlock in the hasp. Cretzer heard the lock snap shut and saw Stucker standing behind the security screen.

"You son-of-a-bitch," he yelled, raising the pistol. "I'm goin' to kill you."

Cretzer raced toward the stairwell. Stucker flew down the stairs, startling the inmates below.

"I'll get you, you fink son-of-a-bitch," he heard Cretzer yell. "I'll get you. I'll come down there and get you."

One of the bathroom orderlies asked, "What's going on up there, Mr. Stucker?"

Stucker, realizing he had to conceal the state of affairs from the inmates under his supervision, said, "It's them damn colored guys again. Demonstrating for equal rights or something. They're throwing their stuff out on Broadway and running around screaming and yelling like a pack of hyenas. I don't want you guys to get messed up in that trouble."

Stucker assembled the inmates and marched them toward his office. Before locking the door which separated the bathroom area from the rest of the basement, he reached for the telephone that was mounted on the bathroom wall near the foot of the cellhouse stairs.

Through the close-mesh security screen covering the gate at the head of the stairs, he could make out the shapes of several inmates including Cretzer. They were trying to force the gate open. He expected them to start shooting at any moment. The telephone, the only one in the entire basement area, was in an exposed location.

Stucker dialed the armory number. Without pausing to identify himself, he spoke almost inaudibly so that his inmate crew could not overhear. He warned the armory officer of the serious trouble in the cellhouse, then hung up the receiver. He retreated with his inmate detail and closed and locked the security door. He was still in a precarious location. In the hallway outside his office was a flight of seldom-used stairs that led to the main dining room. At the extreme north end of the hallway was the sallyport gate. Stucker thought the escapees might use the dining room stairway and might try to exit through the basement gate.

* * *

ALCATRAZ '46

In the narrow confines of the armory, Officer Fish had strained to hear the whispered telephone message. All he could make of it was that there was some trouble in the main cellhouse. Before he could identify his informant or question him, the line went dead.

Fish dialed the west gallery number. "If there is anything wrong in the cellhouse, Burch oughtta know," he thought. "It's probably some damn convict trying to get a rise out of us."

Fish heard the ringing at the other end of the line, but no one answered. In quick succession, he dialed the cellhouse, the kitchen, the clothing room, and D-block. All phones went unanswered.

Alarmed at his inability to reach any of the inside posts, Fish opened the armory issue window and called to Captain Weinhold, "Captain, something is wrong inside. I just had a call saying there was trouble in the cellhouse. Now I can't get through to anybody back there."

"Who called? Burch?"

"No sir, I don't think it was Burch. I didn't recognize the voice. He hung up before I could question him."

"Well, call Burch. See what he knows."

"I did, Captain. He don't answer. Nobody answers."

"Ring all those phones back there. Try the basement and the hospital. Someone is bound to answer. They can't all be in trouble."

Fish continued to dial all the inside telephones. Suddenly, a voice came on the line. Hospital Officer Pehrson was speaking, "Sorry, I was back in the big ward with the doctors and couldn't get to the phone until just now."

"I think we've got trouble in the cellhouse," said Fish. "Have you heard anything suspicious?" "No," Pehrson replied.

"We don't know what it is, so keep locked in and stay away from the entrance gate."

The armory officer continued to dial the other numbers. The basement bathroom phone was answered by Stucker.

"Ed, I've been trying to reach you," said Fish. "What's going on in the cellhouse? Are you having any trouble?"

Stucker, believing he had already told the armory officer all he knew about the trouble, was still anxious to keep the information from his inmate detail; thus he replied in a normal conversational tone, "Cliff, I already told you all I know about it."

Stucker hung up the receiver, relocked the security door, and herded the last few stragglers from the music practice room into his office. He locked his office door and barricaded it with an assortment of boxes and bales from the storeroom. Behind the two locked doors, the telephone rang and rang.

Fish was unable to restore the connection. He turned to Simpson. "Lieutenant, I don't know what to make of it. Stucker finally answered his phone and said he had already told me all he knew. Then he hung up."

"Get him back on the line. I'll talk to him."

"I'm trying, lieutenant. His phone is ringing, but he don't answer. Nobody answers except the hospital, and Pehrson says everything is peaceful and quiet up there."

"Keep trying to raise somebody. Sooner or later, we're gonna get some answers."

* * *

The Marin County shoreline as seen from Road Tower. Freedom—so close, yet so far.

ALCATRAZ '46

A key exactly like No. 107, which Miller hid in gooseneck of cell's toilet, thereby thwarting escape.

In a monotonous succession, the telephones rang at the ends of the cellhouse, in D-block, and in the two sections of the west gun gallery. As they rang, Carnes paraded in front of cell 403, twirling the riot stick. "Look at me," he said. "I'm a cop. A real, goddam, club swingin' cop."

Burdette, sensing Carnes was in a good mood, asked, "Is it O.K. if I untie Miller? He's really hurting."

"Sure," replied Carnes strutting back and forth. "He ain't goin' nowhere."

Miller had regained consciousness. When the gag was removed, he whispered to Burdette, "The key they're hunting for is in my pants pocket. Hide it somewhere."

Burdette found the key and looked for a possible hiding place. The cell contained nothing but a toilet, a washbasin, and an empty electric light socket in the ceiling. While Moyle and Egan were busy watching Carnes' strutting, Burdette shoved the key into the recesses of the toilet gooseneck and felt it slip from his fingers into the soil pipe beyond the water seal.

Realizing what Burdette was doing, Lageson helped divert Carnes' attention by asking, "What I'd like to know is how you guys got those guns."

"Coy got them. I don't know how, but he got them," laughed Carnes. "Hey, you guys are sure calm about all this. Ain't you scared at all? I always heard you screws were cowards."

The telephones continued to ring insistently.

"Listen to those things ring. We don't have much time left," said Hubbard. "Those screws are dumb, but not so dumb they won't get suspicious when those damned telephones aren't answered."

"That guy Stucker saw us," said Thompson. "He'll tell them out front that we're about to bust out of here."

"To hell with him," snarled Cretzer, irritated by his failure to stop Stucker. "That dumb screw don't know nothin'. He thinks there's just some kinda beef up here. Guys fightin' or somethin'."

Coy spread the keys on the cellhouse desk and began to arrange them by types. "Forget Stucker," he said. "The key is our problem."

"Hell, maybe they went and changed the lock on us," suggested Thompson.

"Yeah, maybe they did that," agreed Shockley. "They're real sneaky that way."

Cretzer joined Coy and asked, "Bernie, are you dead sure the 107 is the key we need?"

"Yeah."

"Well, I'm beginnin' to think you went 'n left it up there in the damn cage."

"You ain't thinking very good, Joe. I left nothing in that cage except that little fink I killed. Don't tell me I left him with the key in his pocket because I damn sure didn't leave him no pockets."

"Let's just try all the damn keys," said Thompson. "One of them might fit."

Grabbing a handful of unsorted keys, Thompson walked to the gate and tried them one after another. Coy finished sorting the remaining keys and took them to Thompson.

Thompson tried all the keys without success. Inserting a key into the lock was becoming more difficult because the huge, expensive prison lock was designed to jam when abused.

Pictured together from left to right: E. B. Lageson, E. J. Miller and Bert A. Burch.

Cretzer was seething with frustration. "If Whitey was here, he'd get this door open," he complained. "We shouldda sprung him outta the hole. It's your fault, Bernie. Why the hell didn't you open his cell door while you were in the damn cage?"

Coy did not answer. He was trying to think of other possible places where the key could be. He systematically recalled the events of the past hour, then said, "Miller had to have the key last. It's gotta be on him. Can't be anyplace else. Where's his monkey suit?"

"Hell, I got his coat on," said Cretzer. "There ain't no keys in it. All the keys I had are right here."

"How about his pants?"

"He's still wearing them," said Hubbard.

"Did you frisk him when you threw him into that cell, Marv?"

"Yeah, Bernie. I think so. I think we got all his keys."

"You think so? Damn, you just might have missed the goddam 107."

"That'd be a helluva note," yelled Cretzer, his voice rising in pitch. "Here we waste time with misfit keys, and you didn't even look in that fink's pants."

Cursing, Cretzer ran to cell 403 and shouted to Coy, "Open the goddam cell door."

Miller was yanked into the aisle. Cretzer grabbed the officer's throat and shook him violently. "Where's that key, you fink son-of-a-bitch. Where's that goddam key?" screamed Cretzer.

"What key? You guys took all my keys."

"You know what key. The key to the yard."

"It's kept in the gun gallery."

"You had it, damn you. You used it to let those guys out to the yard."

"Sure I did, but I gave it back to Burch. That's the rule. You guys know that. He's got it up there in the gallery."

Almost berserk with rage and frustration, Cretzer searched the officer with brutal thoroughness. He stripped his clothing and ripped into his shoes. The key was not on him.

"Maybe he passed it to one of these other guys," suggested Hubbard. "If he was cute enough to keep it, he was cute enough to hide it."

"Well, he sure don't have it now unless he swallowed it or rammed it up his ass. Shove the bastard into the next cell, and we'll frisk the other finks." Cretzer called to Coy, "Rack open 402, Bernie."

Coy manipulated the levers and cell 402's door slid open. Two at a time, the other captives were pulled into the aisle, painstakingly searched, and shoved into the cell until all, including the inmate gardeners, had been searched and moved.

"It's gotta be in there somewhere," said Coy staring at the empty cell.

Cretzer and Hubbard examined the cell thoroughly — the light socket, washbasin, toilet, folding steel table and seat, bars, and ledge over the door. They did not find the key. Half-sobbing with frustration, Cretzer snarled, "Well, there goes our last hope."

Moyle and Egan, sensing that Cretzer's anger might explode into violence, asked if they could go back to their cells.

"Joe, we're on your side," Moyle pleaded earnestly. "Let us out of here. We don't belong with these finks."

"O.K.," snapped Cretzer. "Get out. Go on back to your cells. Just keep outta our way."

As they hurried to their cells, Egan muttered, "We're damn lucky to get out of there. Them screws is as good as dead right now."

"How the hell do we get back into our cells? The screws keep them all locked."

"If our's are locked, we'll look for one that's open and hole up there 'til this thing is over. We sure as hell don't want to be loose in the cellhouse when them other screws come blasting in."

* * *

"Keep ringing those phones back there," said the Captain. "I'll go in and find out what's going on."

Lieutenant Simpson, Mail Officer Baker, and Record Clerk Sundstrom watched the captain stride through the main gate into the cellhouse. They knew it was against the rules to go in blind like that, but no one wanted to argue with the captain when he broke one of his own rules.

Weinhold heard the telephones ringing as he entered, but there was no indication of a disturbance and no sign of the cellhouse officers. He hastened toward the west end and was surprised when Coy with a rifle, Hubbard with a dagger, and Carnes with a club surrounded him near the corner of C-block. The three inmates roughly shoved him against a cell front. Handing the rifle to Hubbard, Coy said, "Cover him, Marv. Kill him if he tries anything."

Coy searched Weinhold and pocketed his wristwatch, wallet, and other valuables. "Where's your damn whistle?" Coy demanded. "We don't want you whiffin' that damn pipe on us."

The captain explained that he had no whistle. Coy growled, "Take off that monkey suit. I think it'll just about fit me."

Weinhold slowly unbuttoned his jacket and watched for an opportunity to seize the rifle. Hubbard pointed the cocked weapon at the captain's head and was careful to remain out of reach.

"Where'll we put this guy?" asked Carnes shifting the riot club from one hand to the other.

"Shove him into 402 with the other screws."

Hubbard prodded the captain with the rifle. "Get moving. Over to the other side of the block. We got a whole cage full of you monkeys over there."

"Don't take chances with this old bastard," cautioned Coy. "He's apt to start something if he gets a chance."

The captain was taken to cell 402. Coy, now wearing the captain's jacket, opened the control box.

Spotting the captain, Shockley shrieked, "This is the louse who tried to kill me by putting minerals in my food. He's a no good punk. I oughtta kill him right now. I hate this one."

Shockley swung a wild punch at the captain's head. Weinhold ducked and the punch missed. Carnes maintained a grip on one of the captain's arms. Frustrated, Shockley kicked savagely at the officer's legs. Angered, Weinhold backhanded his attacker across the face with his free hand. Shockley staggered and began to whimper, "He hit me, Joe. That fink hit me."

"We're wasting time with this guy," said Hubbard, still guarding Weinhold with the rifle. "Bernie, this whole goddam jail break is turning into a comedy. The 2:30 count is creeping up on us."

"Conk him. Conk him so he don't bother us no more," whined Shockley. "He got no right hitting me."

103

ALCATRAZ '46

Cretzer stepped in close and swung the heavy pistol against the captain's unprotected head. Carnes released Weinhold's arm as the captain fell. Emboldened by the sight of Weinhold on the floor, Shockley kicked the stunned officer repeatedly.

"If you're gonna kill him, go ahead and do it," said Coy. "You're wasting time beating on him."

"Let up, Sam," said Cretzer, holstering his pistol. "Help Buddy shove Weinhold into the cell."

When the cell door closed, Shockley grabbed Cretzer's arm and pulled on it. "Let's go, Joe. What are we waiting for?"

"Take it easy, Sam. We'll go as soon as we find the key. We still got plenty of time. There's been no siren yet."

Coy was leaning against the cellhouse wall. He had been thinking about the possible hiding places in the cell. "It's got to be in the shitter," he decided.

"Naw, I looked there. I felt all 'round. It ain't there. Besides, them screws been so scared they've been flushin' that thing lots of times."

"The key's too heavy to flush away," said Coy. "I've seen those shitters when the plumber had them apart fixing them. That goddam key could be laying in the gooseneck or in the pipe that hooks up to the back of the bowl where it goes through the wall. It must be in there."

Cretzer sneered, "What makes you so damned sure about it now? Maybe there ain't no goddam 107."

"Damn it, quit stalling around. Let's bust the damn thing apart," said Hubbard.

"Wait, Marv," said Coy. "Let me see if I can reach it. I've got the skinniest arms and the longest fingers." Rolling up his overlong coat sleeve, he thrust his arm into the toilet, through the water seal of the gooseneck, and beyond. His straining, groping fingers barely reached the joint where the soil pipe connected to the toilet. "Goddam. I got it!" he exclaimed. His scratched hand emerged dripping wet and holding the 107 key.

Building 64, dock, and tower in early 1946 before the blastout.

Lieutenant Simpson and Baker, the mail censor, anxiously waited for some word from Weinhold. Becoming certain that the captain needed assistance, they entered the cellhouse and hurried down Broadway. When they reached the west end, they found the inmates waiting for them. Coy stepped from behind the shelter of the cellblock and pointed his rifle. Cretzer threatened with the pistol. Thompson, Carnes, and Hubbard stepped forward, searched the two officers, and shoved them into cell 403.

Cretzer snapped, "How many more of you guys comin' in here, anyhow? You're interferin' with our work. Why the hell can't you stay out front where you belong?"

Shockley stood guard at the cell as Cretzer took the 107 key from Coy and went to the recreation yard door. Several of the freed D-block inmates crowded around, eager to rush out into the fresh air and sunshine. Cretzer turned to them and growled, "Look, you guys. We've got things to do 'n don't want nobody gettin' in our way. You can follow us outta here, if you want, but stay back, way back outta our way."

"Don't go out yet," said Coy. "Wait'll I pick off those screws in the towers."

Coy trotted off with the rifle toward the Culinary Department. Hubbard followed carrying the extra ammunition in a webbed belt draped across his shoulder. With Bristow and Burdette held captive, there was no one in the Culinary Department to interfere with their movements. The six inmate workers quietly stayed out of their way.

* * *

Except for several civilian clerks and the warden's secretary, the administrative offices were drained of reserves. Two officials and one officer had disappeared into the cellhouse as if they had been swallowed by quicksand. Fish kept the telephones ringing constantly and discussed the problem with Sundstrom.

"I'll go take a quick look, and let you know what's going on," decided Sundstrom. "We can't stand here doing nothing."

"Go ahead, Sunny, but be careful. Don't go in any further than necessary, and get out as fast as possible if you see anything sour. In the meantime, I'll call the warden."

Like the several officers who had preceded him into the cellhouse, Sundstrom hurried along Broadway and into the hands of the escapees. Thompson frisked him. "You do like we say, and we won't hurt you. Hell, you been good to me, and I don't want to see you get hurt," said Thompson remembering how Sundstrom had recently helped him challenge the legality of his sentences by suggesting that he petition for a court-appointed attorney and a retrial.

Cretzer approached. Brandishing his .45, he shoved the officer into the cell with Simpson and Baker.

"Don't hurt him, Joe. He's a right guy," said Thompson. "I owe him."

"Forget that owin' stuff, Buddy. We don't owe none of these finks anythin'."

Before Thompson could close the cell door, Shockley sneaked up and punched Lageson who was leaning against the cell front listening to Cretzer. Lageson fell to the floor. Shockley then ran into cell 402 and slammed his fists into Sundstrom's side. As the officer buckled from the unexpected blows, his wallet fell from his hip pocket. Shockley's final punch grazed Sundstrom's chin. Simpson and Baker dragged Sundstrom to the rear of the cell away from Shockley.

Cretzer, whose pistol covered the officers during Shockley's attack, reached into the cell and picked up Sunstrom's wallet. Holstering the pistol, he examined the contents as Shockley stumbled back into the aisle, and Thompson closed the cell door.

"Ninety bucks," Cretzer announced after counting the currency. "Now you can call this a heist, screw. Highway robbery in the cellhouse."

Shockley, still excited and angry, turned on Fleish who was standing with other D-block inmates near the door to the segregation cellhouse. "This is one mean bastard," screamed Shockley as he clawed at the surprised orderly. "He's a real no good, lousy, crummy screw-lover."

Fleish, who was twice Shockley's size, caught most of the frantic blows on his arms and shoulders.

Cretzer intervened and yanked Shockley away. "Sam, calm down. You know he ain't no fink. Leave him be. Just stay here and guard the cells while I open the yard door."

* * *

Resting the rifle on the concrete sill of a window in the west wall of the deserted bakery shop, Coy sighted it on Hill Tower. Officer Besk was relaxing at his post, smoking a cigarette. Coy's first two bullets bored neat round holes through the glass wall of the tower a few inches from the officer's head. His third bullet ricochetted off a steel pillar and lodged in Besk's leg. Immediately, Besk dropped to the tower floor and grasped his bleeding leg. Slowly he made his way across the floor and took a weapon from the gun rack. The bullet holes in the glass and the scarred pillar indicated that the three shots had come from the prison building. Stuffing several ammunition clips into his pockets, Besk cocked the Thompson submachine gun and crawled eastward along the catwalk. He stopped when he was half way to the yard wall. A trail of blood was left on the rusty steel desk behind him, and his leg throbbed. Hunched against the railing on the swaying steel trestle, he tried to ignore the pain as he scanned the area in front of him for some sign of his assailant. He could see the top of the yard wall with Officer Barker patrolling slowly along the south parapet and a score or more inmates sunbathing on the concrete bleachers north of the baseball diamond. Further along the wall to the southeast, Officer Levinson was standing just inside the Road Tower door, casually watching an inmate clean the trash incinerator in the area below. Everything seemed normal. Bewildered, Besk remained crouched on the catwalk, carefully scrutinizing the area from which the shots must have come. His injured leg rested in an enlarging pool of blood.

Thinking they had slain the Hill Tower officer, Coy and Hubbard hurried from the bakery shop window into the adjacent kitchen. Ignoring the kitchen workers who had holed up in the officer's dining room, they ran toward the windows in the south wall, and selected a window that provided a clear line of fire at the officers on the yard wall and in the nearby Road Tower. Neither post was more than 50 yards away, and the unsuspecting officers were standing in the open. Coy punched out one of the small window panes and listened to the broken glass as it tinkled on the concrete bleachers below. He calmly sighted his rifle through the opening. "I'll get the tower screw first," said Coy. "He's the backup man for that guy on the wall."

Levinson in the Road Tower had been alerted about the possibility of trouble in the cellhouse by the armory officer. Deciding to take a few precautionary steps just in case the trouble proved to be serious, Levinson set his rifle in the gun rack and stooped to remove the wooden chock which held the tower door open.

Coy's shot whizzed through the open tower door, narrowly missed the stooping officer, bored through the glass wall, and whined out the other side. Levinson, recognizing the sound, sprawled flat on the tower floor. He carefully eased his Thompson submachine gun from the rack, cocked it, and pointed it toward the prison building. Looking around, he saw Barker drop flat on the catwalk behind the yard wall, and he knew that Barker was also under fire. Levinson expected the convicts in the yard to come swarming over the wall to attack his tower at any moment.

In the exercise yard, the inmate sunbathers heard the rifle blasts and hurried away from the exposed bleachers to a sheltered corner of the yard where the domino-bridge players were congregated.

Coy was jubilant at his apparent success. With the gun towers knocked out, the inmates would have a clear run to the island dock and the prison launch. "O.K., Marv. That's three down and one to go."

View from the prison launch.

ALCATRAZ '46

Hubbard's hopes began to rise. He had been worried about the endless delays, but now luck seemed to be with them.

Coy and Hubbard ran across the dining room to a window in the north wall, punched out a pane of glass just above the concrete sill, and stared down at the gun tower above the island dock. Dock Tower Officer Comerford was standing on the catwalk on the near side of the tower talking to someone on the roadway below.

Resting the rifle on the window sill, Coy sighted carefully and squeezed the trigger. His bullet whizzed past the officer's head and bored through the glass wall of the tower. Comerford dropped to the catwalk and cautiously inched his rifle into firing position. He studied the side of the prison building, window by window, for some sign of the unknown gunman.

Below the tower, at the curve in the single lane road, Associate Warden Miller had been chatting with the tower officer. He was on his way to the administration building following an inspection tour of the beaches and the island dock. Hearing the bullet hit the tower and the sharp crack of the rifle, he shouted, "Don't move, Jim. Stay flat. Let him think he killed you. I'll get to the top as fast as I can and see what's going on."

All of Coy's shots missed their targets, and each officer, realizing he was under fire, dropped to the floor of his post, thereby convincing the gunman that each had been hit.

Turn of the road, near officers' clubhouse (not shown). Tunnel under bachelor officer quarters leads to dock.

"Good shot, Bernie," applauded Hubbard. "That's another screw who won't be bothering us. You sure are a dead shot."

"Well, I got lots of practice back home in the hills. A man has to be good to bark squirrels off a tree without spoiling them for skinning or eating."

Smiling, the two men headed back toward the cellhouse. Carnes met their approach with a shout, "We can't open the gate. That damn 107 won't work. It jammed the lock."

"What do you mean you can't get the damn gate open? You got the 107 key, don't you? What the hell more do you guys need — someone to twist it for you?" asked Coy.

"We used the right key. It goes into the lock O.K., but it won't turn, no matter how hard we twist it."

"You dumb bastards just don't know how to do it. Some of these jailhouse locks are old and cranky. You gotta be careful with them. They're bound to jam if you don't turn them just right."

Coy and Hubbard rushed from the dining room to the yard gate where Cretzer, Thompson, and Shockley were huddled around the unyielding lock. Cretzer complained, "Bernie, we can't get the damn thing open. I think the lock is jammed for keeps."

He dropped the 107 key into Coy's outstretched hand.

* * *

View from prison building of Chief Medical Officer's residence.

ALCATRAZ '46

The Armory was the prison's control center as well as its arsenal. Adjacent to the main gate and the offices of the record clerk and the captain, the armory was a miniature fortress five feet wide and ten feet long. Its walls, floor, and ceiling were constructed of reinforced concrete, hardened steel, and bulletproof glass. Most of the area within its walls was used for storage of ammunition, keys, firearms, and other defensive equipment. Located in the armory was the switch that activated the escape siren.

The armory was manned 24 hours a day, every day of the year. The officers assigned to the post controlled the two-way shortwave radio, the PBX switchboard which handled the two telephone trunk lines to mainland San Francisco, and the island's private telephone system which linked the watch towers and other duty stations with the armory. When reports of trouble reached the officer on duty, it was his responsibility to relay the information to the captain or to other responsible officials.

Armory Officer Fish was faced with a crisis. He had tried desperately to determine the nature of the trouble in the cellhouse. No one in a position of authority was available to offer advice or assistance. Although he was still not certain about the extent of the trouble, Fish decided to contact the warden.

Bertrand, the warden's secretary, told Fish, "The warden hasn't been feeling well for several days. He's pushing 70, you know. He was in earlier, but returned to his residence before noon."

Fish said, "I know he hasn't been feeling well, and I certainly wouldn't bother him if I didn't think it was urgent."

Warden Johnston had an enviable reputation. More than 34 years as a penologist in the service of the State of California had brought him national prominence. Born in Brooklyn, New York, in 1876, he came to San Francisco at the age of six, grew up in the Fillmore section of the city, and later served as city supervisor in the Taylor administration. In 1910, he was elected President of the State Board of Control, and in 1912, Governor Hiram Johnston appointed him Warden of Folsom Prison in order to "correct that volcano of raw emotions where riots and attempted escapes are out of hand."

Quickly and quietly, Johnston went to work. He abolished corporal punishment and indiscriminate use of the straight jacket. He installed showerbaths for the prisoners and improved their food, clothing, and housing. No longer could guards truss up the prisoners or freely indulge in practices considered inhumane. After a dramatic and innovative two years at Folsom, Johnston was appointed Warden of the State Prison at San Quentin, near San Rafael, California. During the following 12 years he became the one man most responsible for the emergence of an enlightened prison system that was later regarded as a model for the nation.

During these years, Johnston studied law in the evenings, and in 1919, he passed the Bar Examination. In 1926, he resigned his wardenship to become vice-president of the American Bank in San Francisco, but in 1929, he returned to his career in prison administration when Governor C. C. Young appointed him to the California

Warden Johnston explains purpose of a prison security door.

ALCATRAZ '46

Crime Commission and named him State Director of Penology. On November 24, 1933, he was appointed warden of the newly created federal civil prison on Alcatraz Island.

There was no question about his competence. At 57 years of age, Johnston was one of the nation's most outstanding prison administrators. He frequently walked unarmed and unguarded among the most violent men in Folsom, San Quentin, and Alcatraz. He was never assaulted. Inmates and officers admired his inner strength, commitment, and conviction.

But at age 61, as he stood in the prison dining room, Johnston was viciously slugged, knocked to the floor, and repeatedly kicked about the head and body by Alcatraz inmate, Burton E. Phillips. Johnston escaped serious injury by the intervention of a prison officer. The incident, however, left its psychological scars. According to some officers who continued working with him, Johnston seldom entered the cellhouse or dining room following the incident. As he grew somewhat distant from the inmates, they called him Old Saltwater, a nickname that inexplicably stuck.

In 1940, Johnston received his highest formal recognition. He was elected President of the American Prison Congress by wardens and other prison officials throughout the nation.

The warden's telephone rang four times before it was answered.

"Warden," said Fish, "I'm sorry to have to disturb you, but we have some serious trouble in the cellhouse. I don't know exactly what it is, but it looks bad. Captain Weinhold and Lieutenant Simpson went in there, and now I can't contact them. Burch doesn't answer his telephone. Associate Warden Miller doesn't answer his residence phone. I thought I'd better let you know."

"All right, Mr. Fish," answered Johnston calmly. "Alert the gun towers and kick on the siren. I'll get over there as fast as I can."

Fish flipped the switch that activated the escape siren. Slowly at first, then picking up speed, the siren's low, whining moans grew into an eardrum-splitting, nerve-shattering crescendo. The sound flooded the entire island and the surrounding Bay Area with its unmistakable warning.

"That's it," said Coy pulling the 107 key from the unyielding lock. "Our luck just ran out. We ain't going nowhere now."

* * *

Associate Warden Miller was trotting along the walkway behind the chief medical officer's residence when he heard the siren. Moments later, he burst into the administration building and demanded, "What the hell is going on?"

Fish swung the service window open. "Mr. Miller, there's trouble in the cellhouse."

"I know damn well there is. Some son-of-a-bitch fired a shot at Comerford while I was standing below his tower talking to him."

"I didn't know there had been any shooting. Was Comerford hit? He doesn't answer his phone."

"Came close, but he wasn't hit. He's laying flat on the tower cat-walk playing possum. Give me a gas billy. I'm going in and see what's happening."

"Better wait, Mr. Miller. Nobody answers their phones in there except Pehrson in the hospital, and he doesn't know anything. Stucker answered once. He hung up before I could question him."

"Call him again."

"I've been trying. He doesn't answer his phone now."

Miller took the gas billy from Fish's hand and glanced around the office. "Where the hell is everyone?"

"All in the cellhouse. They went in when I got the first warning. None have come out again."

"Have you alerted the towers?"

"Yes, sir. As soon as I got the warning. Since then, some of them don't answer their phones."

"They've probably been shot at and hit the deck too. They'd have to expose themselves to answer the damn phones. Too bad we don't have intercoms in those towers." Turning to leave, Miller asked, "Did you notify the warden?"

"Yes, sir. He ordered me to kick on the siren. Said he'd be right over."

"Well, when he gets here, tell him I went in to find out what's going on."

Gas billy in hand, Miller approached the main entrance into the cellhouse. Gate Officer Phillips asked, "What's happening in there, Mr. Miller, a riot?"

"Don't know yet. That's what I intend to find out. Keep this gate closed. Don't let anyone in or out except officers. I may be coming back out in a hurry, so be ready to open up for me."

As the heavy steel gate clanged shut behind him, the sound echoed throughout the building. Miller's eyes swept the east end of the big room from the locked entrance of inactivated A-block to the south wall of the C-D aisle. It seemed abnormally quiet, but everything appeared to be in order. Miller knew he was taking a risk, entering alone and virtually unarmed, but he thought, "Somebody's got to find out what's going on. If I don't do it, I'd have to send somebody in to do it for me."

He moved quietly to the southeast corner of B-block and cautiously peered down Broadway toward the west end. The long aisle was clear.

When he came abreast Bitsy Durnell's cell, he found the inmate perched on the end of his bunk, an unlighted cigarette dangling from the corner of his mouth. Durnell was Miller's most dependable informer, but at this moment he looked frightened. Miller asked, "What's going on in here?"

Durnell nervously lit a match and raised it to his cigarette. Shrugging his narrow shoulders, he quavered in a low voice, "Don't know, boss. Cap'n Weinhold and some other guards went down there a while back, but I ain't seen nor heard nothing since. Everything's quiet and peaceful in here."

Somewhat reassured, the associate warden continued down the aisle. As he reached the cut-off, half-way along the cellblock, he again paused to look and listen. "I wish I had brought the cellhouse keys," he thought. "I'd cut through here into the A-B aisle."

Coy and Hubbard planned to jump the associate warden when

he reached the west end, but now it appeared that he was about to retrace his steps. Deciding not to wait, Coy grabbed the rifle from Hubbard. "I'm going after old jughead," he said. "I'm going to kill him here and now."

Miller saw the tall, thin man dressed in an officer's uniform come around the end of C-block. At first glance, he thought the man was Captain Weinhold. Holding one hand behind his back, the figure approached with his head inclined forward so that it was difficult to discern his features. When the two men were within 20 yards of each other, Miller halted in mid-stride. "Coy," he said with surprise, "What the hell . . .?"

Coy raised his head, brought the rifle from behind his back, and leveled it. "Jughead," he said, his blue eyes glaring in a fixed gaze, "You're a dead man. I'm going to blow your head off."

Miller whirled and ran down the empty aisle. The forgotten gas billy swung from his wrist as he pumped his arms. The long line of locked cell fronts on either side offered no shelter. Inmates watched from behind their bars as Coy grinned and sighted the rifle. "I said I'd blow his fat head off, and I'm going to do just that."

The sharp report of his rifle echoed and reechoed throughout the cellhouse. The bullet whizzed past Miller's head, two inches to his right, and smashed into the east wall of the cellhouse. Cretzer and Hubbard stood at Broadway and Times Square and grinned. They thought Coy was playing with his victim because Miller was still running. Coy sighted the rifle again and squeezed the trigger. Nothing happened.

"The sharp report of his rifle echoed and reechoed throughout the cellhouse."

Coy quickly lowered the rifle and cursed as he ejected the spent round and loaded a live cartridge into the firing chamber. In his eagerness, he had forgotten to reload. Again he raised the weapon and sighted on the rapidly diminishing target.

Fully expecting a second shot to cut him down, Miller raced on. Ten feet from the corner of the block, the gas billy, swinging wildly from his pumping arm, struck the concrete overhang and exploded downward along the side of his sweat-streaked face. For a moment, he thought Coy had shot him, but he instinctively kept running. As he turned the corner of the cellblock, Coy's hurriedly aimed second shot whined past him and smashed into the wall of the visiting area.

Officer Phillips, waiting with his eyes to the vision panel and the key in the gate lock, saw Miller running toward him. With precision and speed, he opened the massive steel gate, then closed it behind the panting associate warden.

"Thanks, Al," gasped Miller. "I think you just saved my life."

"My God, Mr. Miller. What happened to your face?"

"My gas billy exploded," he said leaning against the wall and wiping his brow. "Coy is loose in there with a rifle. Keep the gate closed, and stay out of sight behind the concrete. He might try to shoot the lock off the gate."

"What happened to the captain and all those other officers?" asked Phillips as he passed the associate warden through the sally-port into the administration building.

"I don't know, Al. They may all be dead."

* * *

Miller shows face wound caused by exploding gas billy.

Coy did not pursue Miller. He returned to the west end of the cellhouse and was met by a sneering Cretzer. "How in hell did you miss him? You were almost on top of him."

Coy stared glumly at the rifle. "This goddam old bolt action army gun is for the birds. You'd think the screws could afford something better than this thing."

"Hell, we'd better be glad their guns don't shoot straight, since they're gonna be shooting at us soon," said Hubbard.

"Guess I'm out of practice. Can't shoot offhand anymore. I need a rifle rest, like them window sills. I sure did nail them tower screws from the windows."

Cretzer caressed the grip of his holstered pistol and said, "I shoulda blasted old jughead with a couple of these .45's. I know we ain't gonna get 'nother chance at that bastard."

On the cold steel deck of the gun gallery, Burch slowly regained consciousness. Hearing the rifle shots and the turmoil in the cellhouse, he dragged himself to his knees and peered cautiously over the half-wall of the gallery.

Cretzer heard the movement above him and spotted Burch. Angered by the accumulated frustration of the past hour, he unholstered the .45 and fired two quick shots at the officer. The bullets dimpled the steel wall below Burch's startled face. Cretzer shouted, "Lay down, you dumb son-of-a-bitch. How many times do we have to kill you?"

Burch ducked behind the gallery wall and stayed out of sight. Stretched out on the cold steel deck, the nearly naked officer took stock of the situation. "Damn," he muttered. "Why did those dirty rats have to take my cigarettes?"

Warden Johnston reached the administrative office area a few minutes after Associate Warden Miller came rushing in with his face blackened and burned. Miller reeked of the sharp, unpleasant odor of the exploded gas billy. Still panting for breath, words tumbled out of him when he saw Johnston.

"Warden, that damn Coy is on the loose with a gun in the cellhouse. He shot at me two times."

"With a machine gun?" asked the warden in his customary steady, calm voice.

Miller did not hear the warden's question, but excitedly continued his story until the warden interrupted him, "What happened to your face? Were you hit?"

"No. Just burned with teargas. Damned gas billy exploded."

"Are you sure it was Coy who shot at you?"

"I know it was Coy. He's wearing a uniform that looked like Weinhold's. The uniform fooled me for a minute, but I saw his face."

"Did you see any sign of Mr. Burch or the others?"

"No, warden, Coy is the only one I saw. There's nearly a dozen of our officers in there somewhere. They're dead or taken prisoner."

Warden Johnston attempted to evaluate the information. It didn't seem possible with all the security precautions, searches, and shakedowns to now have armed convicts at large in the cellhouse. However, since Burch did not answer his telephone, Johnston realized that the inmates must have found a way to prevent him from doing so and had probably taken his weapons. Firearms in the hands of Alcatraz inmates meant only one thing — a blastout was taking place in the most escape proof prison in the world.

The prison dock area.

ALCATRAZ '46

The Siege

The siren's nerve-wracking wail continued monotonously without interruption. Knowing that the siren would alert law enforcement officers throughout the Bay Area, the six escapees and the several freed inmates from D-block gathered at the west end of Seedy Street to decide what to do next.

"We have all these guys for hostages," said an inmate. "Maybe we can deal. Do you think the warden will deal?"

"Not with all them screws laying dead around them towers. Nobody's going to deal with us no more," said Hubbard.

"We could give up," suggested another inmate.

"That means the gas chamber at San Quentin," came a reply.

Coy rubbed the white stubble of a beard that was beginning to grow on his chin. "No gas for me," he announced. "I'm going to go out in style, and I'm taking as many of them screws with me as I can."

Cretzer nodded, "I'm with you."

"I don't like cyanide any better than you do," said Hubbard. "Count me in. I only wish I had a gun."

Cretzer and Hubbard took stock of the weapons — one rifle, one pistol, one butcher knife, an improvised dagger, several riot clubs, gas grenades, gas masks, and 61 rounds of ammunition — 19 cartridges for the pistol and 42 for the rifle.

Carnes turned to Coy. "Can't we just slip through the Spanish tunnels?" he asked. "You said you knew the passageways to the docks."

Coy's taut features smiled at Carnes. His expression conveyed that he knew nothing of the tunnels. Carnes felt a deep depression well within him. He had been naive to believe Coy's story of tunnels and had followed him with complete trust. It saddened Carnes to discover that his friend had deceived him.

"Well, since we ain't goin' nowhere, let's make it last as long as we can," said Cretzer.

The freed D-block inmates seemed unsure about what to do. Noticing this indecision, Coy said, "It's all down the sewer now. Go on back to your holes unless you want to stick around and watch us shoot it out with the screws. You too, Fleish. There's nothing here for you. They'll come busting in before sundown. Some of those guys may be lucky to get out of this alive."

Fleish and the others from D straggled silently back to their cells. When the last man was out of sight, Coy said, "By now, the screws are all around us. They may try to come in from the yard, the gun cages, or the basement gates. The front gate is the likeliest, so I'll cover it. You other guys watch this end, and keep an eye on the screws in the cells. Don't let them start nothing."

Coy headed toward Michigan Boulevard to keep watch.

118

* * *

Carefully picked San Quentin sharp-shooting reinforcements boarding prison launch on route to join battle.

ALCATRAZ '46

Lying on the cold floor of cell 402, Captain Weinhold thought he might reason with Cretzer who stood nearby. "If you try to shoot it out, you'll all be killed, Joe," he said quietly. "You haven't a chance. Just think about it for a while. Don't throw your life away."

"Shut up, you lousy screw," yelled Shockley. "You beat me up when I burned my cell last time. I hate you."

"You think we'll all be killed, Cap'n?" asked Cretzer, moving closer to the cell where Weinhold had risen to his feet.

"Joe, you hear the siren. So does everybody else for miles around. You know what that means. By this time, there's a double ring of guns around this prison. What can you do with a pistol?"

"We can do it, Joe," pleaded Shockley. "We can hold them off."

"Don't listen to that screwball," said the captain. "Think for yourself, Joe."

"I'm thinkin', Cap'n. I'm thinkin' there'll be lots more killed here today besides us."

Angered by Weinhold's remark, Shockley screamed, "Kill 'em all, Joe. Especially him. He took my shoes. He made me go without shoes, Joe." Nearly convulsing with rage, Shockley yanked off his shoes and socks and threw them at the captain.

Sensing that Cretzer's judgment was being influenced by Shockley's screams and antics, Carnes quietly urged, "Don't hurt them, Joe. They didn't give us any trouble."

"Hell, go on and kill every goddam son-of-a-bitch in there," advised Thompson. "We don't want no witnesses. They'll put us all in the gas chamber."

Cretzer stared at the worried faces within the cells. "It's funny as hell, us arguin' what to do with you screws," he smiled wryly. "Yesterday you was arguin' 'bout how to handle us."

"They'd hang us if they got a chance," screamed Shockley hysterically. "They'd hang us, hang us, hang us. Kill them, Joe. Kill them."

Cretzer wavered. His temper was rising with his inability to reach a clear decision.

"We don't need no hostages, right Marv?" asked Cretzer, seeking support for a possible decision.

"Wrong, Joe. A deal is always possible if you got something to bargain with," replied Hubbard.

"They're pretty good guys, Joe, why kill them?" supported Carnes.

Shockley wildly grabbed for Cretzer's pistol. "Gimme that iron. If you ain't got the guts to do it, I'll show you how easy it is."

Cretzer became incensed and shoved Shockley aside. Breathing heavily, he moved closer to cell 402 and stared past Weinhold at Miller. For a full thirty seconds, he glared at the cellhouse officer. Shockley chanted behind Cretzer, "Kill him, kill him."

"You sank our goddam boat, Miller," said Cretzer, his voice sounding higher than usual. "You hid that damn key."

Shockley continued to scream in a sing-song pattern, "Kill him! Shoot! Shoot! Kill them all! Shoot! Shoot!"

"Weinhold," cried Cretzer. "You said your goons are gonna kill us. That ain't nothin' new. You put the tag on other convicts — Bowers, Cole and Roe, Limerick, Barker, Boarman. You rotten old mudder-fugger. You ain't gonna be here to see it happen to us!"

Weinhold backed away. Cretzer's voice sounded unnatural as he stepped closer to the cellfront and rested the pistol on one of the crossbars. Shockley's voice was a distant song in the back of his mind. He aimed carefully and pulled the trigger.

The bullet struck the captain in the chest, slamming him backward and half under the cot. The heavy .45 roared again and again. Miller was hit in the right arm, spun around, and flung into the huddle of captives at the back of the cell. Bristow and Burdette fell to the floor with him. In quick succession, Cretzer fired two more shots. Corwin and Lageson fell together.

Still breathing heavily, Cretzer ejected the spent clip, inserted a loaded one, and walked to cell 403 where Simpson, Baker, and Sundstrom huddled in a corner. The released slide of the pistol snapped forward with a metallic click, seating a live round in the firing chamber. Again resting the pistol on the bars to steady his aim, he pulled the trigger. One of the bullets tore into Simpson's abdomen, slamming him violently against the wall. As he fell, a second bullet ripped into Baker's leg and toppled him against Sundstrom who fell to the floor with Baker on top of him. A third bullet, intended for Sundstrom, smashed harmlessly into the cell wall.

Cretzer stared at what he had done, then turned to Thompson and said, "Well, Buddy, I figure things are about even up. Now we better get ourselves ready to greet the other screws as they come in."

Thompson and Shockley stared through the cell fronts. An officer's arm reached out from under the bodies. Shockley, seeing the hand, cried, "Joe, here's one screw that ain't dead yet."

Shown here is James Boarman, a close friend of Cretzer's, who was killed in another escape attempt. He died in the fog-shrouded waters off Alcatraz.

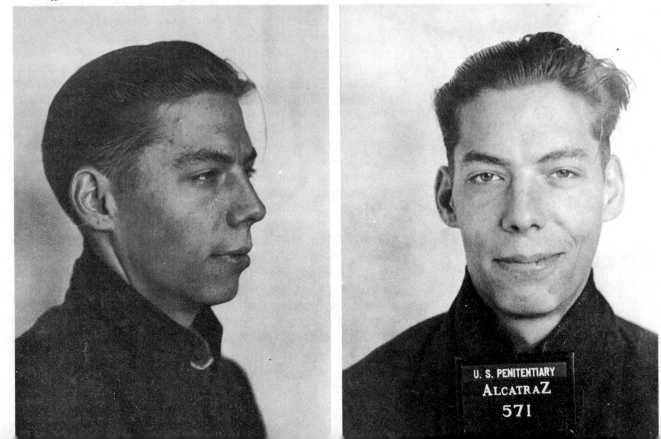

ALCATRAZ '46

Squinting his dark brown eyes, Cretzer peered into the dimly lit cell and exclaimed, "Why, it's my friend, Mr. Lageson."

"Friend, hell," wailed Shockley. "He's gonna go to court and squeal like the others."

"Take it easy, Joe. I'm not your enemy," pleaded Lageson. "Sam knows I never did anything to hurt him."

"Take it easy?" echoed Shockley. "How easy did you go when you beat my head open over in D-block? Kill him, Joe. Kill him."

Pointing the pistol at the officer, Cretzer said regretfully, "I'm truly sorry to do this, Mr. Lageson. You ain't so bad a guy, but like Sam says, we can't have nobody alive to put the finger on us."

Cretzer aimed at Lageson's head and squeezed the trigger. The bullet creased the side of the officer's face, and Lageson slumped helplessly among the other bodies.

Pleased at the sight of the motionless forms, Cretzer strolled away. He was followed by Hubbard, Thompson, and the still chattering Shockley. Carnes remained behind, shocked and bewildered at the carnage. He hadn't counted on this when he accepted Coy's invitation to escape.

Thompson paused in front of the recreation yard gate. "Do you think they'll try to come through here?" he asked.

"Hell, no," replied Cretzer. "How the hell can they get in? That lock don't have no keyhole on the outside. It kept us in. It'll keep them out."

"How about that outside entrance to the gun cage over there by D-block?"

"Yeah, that's one way in. We'll have to watch it."

Shockley leaned against the cellhouse wall muttering to himself. Cretzer looked at him appraisingly. He knew that Sam was not going to be any good to them now. In fact, Sam would probably get in their way when things got rough.

Cretzer decided that there was no point in Shockley hanging around any longer, so he reached into his pocket and brought out the wad of currency he had taken from Sundstrom. "Sam, run this dough over to Whitey. It ain't gonna do us no good, now. Maybe Whitey can find a way to use it."

"O.K., Joe. I'll take it to him and be right back."

Hastening into D-block, Shockley quietly climbed the steel stairs to his own cell on the middle tier and thrust the money into his pocket. Looking around, he muttered, "I gotta find me a place to hide. I'll split this dough with Whitey, later."

* * *

In the crowded cells, the bleeding officers remained silent and motionless. They hoped that with a little luck, the inmates might think they were dead.

In cell 402, Captain Weinhold was unconscious from his wound. The bullet had torn into his chest and emerged through his back, leaving a gaping hole as big as a man's fist. Corwin was also unconscious. His lower jaw had been torn away by a bullet. Miller's wounded right arm continued to bleed. Lageson lay motionless in a spreading pool of blood. Somehow Cretzer's bullets missed Burdette and Bristow. In great peril every time they moved, the two uninjured officers did all they could to help the others without attracting attention.

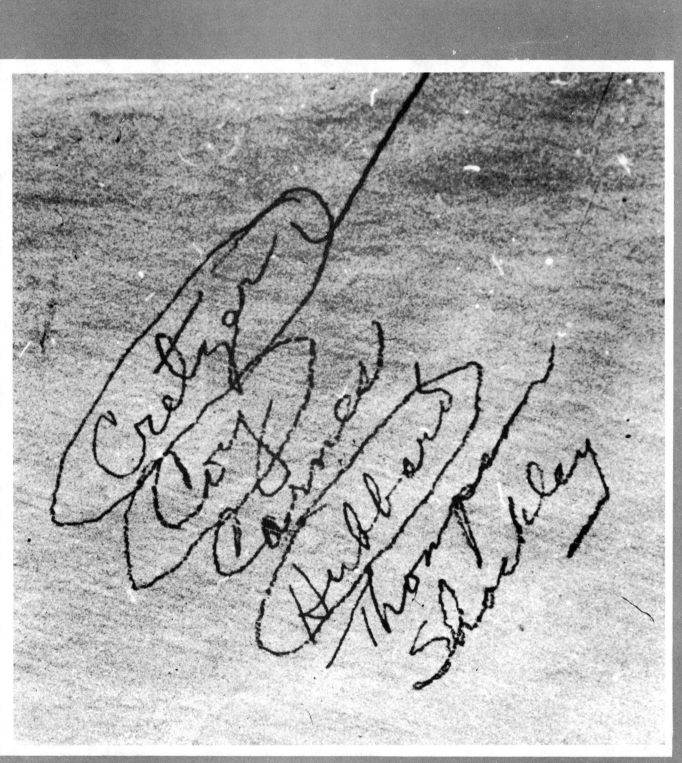

The names of the mutineers scrawled onto cell wall by Officer Lageson.

ALCATRAZ '46

In cell 403, Simpson and Baker were severely wounded. Simpson was unconscious. Sundstrom had escaped injury. Miraculously, none of the officers were dead, however, the wounded were in critical condition and needed attention. As Simpson regained consciousness, the pain in his stomach became unbearable, and involuntary moans escaped his lips.

Hearing the moans, Cretzer ran back to the cellfront. At the back of the dimly lit cell, he could see Baker and Sundstrom lying motionless on the floor. Simpson was obviously alive. Cretzer shouted, "Goddam it. How much does it take to kill you bastards?"

Again at point blank range, he fired three times into the cell, pulling the trigger in quick succession until the pistol was empty. Baker and the lieutenant were hit again and again. Their battered bodies bounced with each impact. For the second time, Cretzer's bullets missed Sundstrom completely.

Simpson relapsed into unconsciousness from the pain and shock. Now sprawled face down on the floor, he appeared dead. Sundstrom and Baker remained mute and motionless, just barely breathing. Silently they prayed that the gunman would be deceived.

Coy, who had been watching the front entrance, heard the last volley of shots and rushed back to the west end. He thought the anticipated attack had come through the back of the cellhouse instead of through the main gate. When he reached Times Square and learned what had happened, he was disgusted. "Joe, you've wasted bullets. How many you got left?"

"Seven shots. That's enough to kill seven men."

"Don't go wasting no more bullets. Killing them screws is O.K. with me, but you should have cut their throats with the butcher knife. It'd save ammunition."

"Sorry, Bernie. I guess I got excited. The guys wanted these finks dead, and I figured they was right. These automatics use up lead faster than you'd expect."

"Now we have to make sure they're all dead. Kid, you Injuns know how to use a pig-sticker. Take Marv's knife and cut their damn throats. Then we'll know they won't talk."

The gloomy cells reeked with the stench of burned cordite and the smell of human blood. Carnes didn't like the assignment, but he felt he couldn't argue with Coy and Cretzer. They watched and waited just a few feet behind him in the aisle outside the cells.

Leaning over the gory tangles of motionless bodies, Carnes realized that some of the officers were not dead. Although he knew he might be killed if Coy or Cretzer suspected he was not obeying orders, he could not bring himself to murder the helpless men.

"Looks like they're all dead," he reported after a few moments. "Those last bullets ended them." Carnes checked the second cell and reported the same findings.

Satisfied that no officer witnesses were alive to testify against him, Thompson wanted to return to the relative security of his cell. He knew that retribution by prison personnel would be swift and merciless, therefore he desperately wanted to get back to his cell and develop an alibi. He glanced furtively at Cretzer, then said, "Joe, if I just had a .45, I'd stay here and shoot it out with them, but what good am I without a gun? It's better if I cut out."

Cretzer expressed his contempt by ignoring Thompson. Hubbard watched Thompson as he hurried toward the C-block stairs. Thompson's actions reminded him of his friend who ran out during the cabin shoot-out many years before. Hubbard sighed, then said in a soft, low voice, "I'm going to check out. This is all of it for me." The tone of his statements made it clear to Carnes that Hubbard intended to die fighting.

"I'm checking out too," said Coy.

"We'll save enough bullets for ourselves in case we need them," said Cretzer.

Carnes thought the conversation was odd. It was clear to him that each man intended to die fighting, but it was strange to find them speaking so calmly. It was much like the discussing of an ordinary event.

The few moments of silence which followed seemed very long. Carnes broke the silence by telling Coy that he had decided to return to his cell.

"All right, old man," Coy said. "I left your cell door unlocked when I opened it earlier. Good luck to you."

Carnes asked what Coy wanted him to do with the Life Route book. Coy replied, "Burn it."

Carnes turned to cross Broadway, but before he did, he looked back at the men watching him.

"Sorry it turned out this way, old man," said Coy. Carnes lifted his hand in acknowledgement, then ran into his cell.

* * *

When Weinhold and the other officers dashed into the cellhouse to investigate the anonymously reported trouble, they exhausted the prison's first line of reserves. The clerical staff, shop foremen, launch operators, and other non-custodial personnel had not been trained in defensive tactics or the use of weapons. They were classified as non-combatants. Because of this, further official reaction had to be delayed until a sufficient number of off-duty officers responded to the siren's call.

Warden Johnston leafed through the Alcatraz Escape Procedures Manual on a desk in the captain's office. Assembled with him were Associate Warden Miller, Chief Clerk Mills, Secretary Bertrand, and civilian clerks Gaynor, Ballard, and Washington. The escape procedures in the manual had been devised by experts, and careful planning had gone into their preparation, however, none were designed to solve the problem that now confronted the depleted staff. The planners had not foreseen that inmates might get their hands on firearms.

"I think we should use Plan 3: Procedures for the Control of Rioting and Inmate Take-over of the Cellhouse," Miller said. Miller was a veteran of the federal prison service and had come up through the ranks. He had little formal education but had accumulated a common sense store of know-how about prisons and prisoners. He was skeptical about some of the provisions in the manual but decided that Plan 3 was perhaps the best at this time.

"Fine," said the warden. "Let's get started with it."

The warden turned to the armory officer. "Mr. Fish, you have a copy of Plan 3 in the armory. I suggest you commence calling all the police agencies listed and the Coast Guard. We must anticipate the possibility of an attempted mass escape from the island and be ready to stop it."

"I'll call the dock and get Lieutenant Faulk started rounding up the work details," said Miller picking up the receiver of the desk telephone. "We can hold all the outside crews in the Hill Tower sallyport. Faulk has a few extra officers. We can use them up here. Lieutenant Rychner can take charge of the dock and get the launch patrolling around the island."

"We'll want to put several officers into the east gun gallery as soon as possible and at least one observer in the visiting room," added Johnston. "Mr. Fish should have someone in the armory to help him handle the communications."

With his eyes on the manual, Johnston continued talking but to no one in particular. "In an emergency of this kind, it is usually the first few minutes that count most," he lectured. "Our objective is to regain control of the situation in the shortest possible time. Prompt and proper action may mean the difference between success and disaster."

Miller dialed the dock office number. "We'll have this thing under control before long," he thought. "Teamwork is our big advantage. Convicts don't work together very good."

"The objective of our plan," continued Johnston, "is to regain control of the prison and stop any attempt to break out and escape. It appears that the inmates, we don't know how many of them, control everything except the hospital. We must wrest that control from them as swiftly as possible."

"Right," agreed Miller breaking into the monologue and returning the receiver to its cradle. "Faulk has things rolling in the dock area. He swung into action as soon as he heard the siren. The launch will be manned and underway in a few minutes. When everything is squared away there, he'll come up here with all the officers he can find."

"Warden," called the armory officer, "Mr. Pehrson says everything is O.K. in the hospital. He heard the gunshots but hasn't seen anything of the escapees. He says the inmates up there are too sick to cause trouble. They have the gate locked and will stay well away from it."

"Have you heard anymore from Mr. Stucker?"

"I still can't raise him, warden."

"Mr. Stucker must be unable to get to the phone. Perhaps his men have joined the escapees. Keep ringing his phone, Mr. Fish."

"Yes, sir. I'll keep on all the inside phones. What about the outside phones. You know I can't get in touch with most of the tower guards."

"They probably got shot at like Comerford," explained Miller. "Maybe they're flat on the catwalk and can't answer the phone because they'd expose themselves to gunfire."

"If they have been fired upon, I pray they escaped injury," said the warden. "I hope none have been killed. We'll have to get someone out there to them as soon as possible. Those towers are vital to our plan."

"I wished all along we had intercoms in those towers," complained Fish. "I feel helpless when they don't answer their phones."

Johnson moved across the office and stared thoughtfully at the floor. "I've been considering the installation of an intercom system for all the armed posts, including the gun galleries. I think this emergency points up the need for it."

* * *

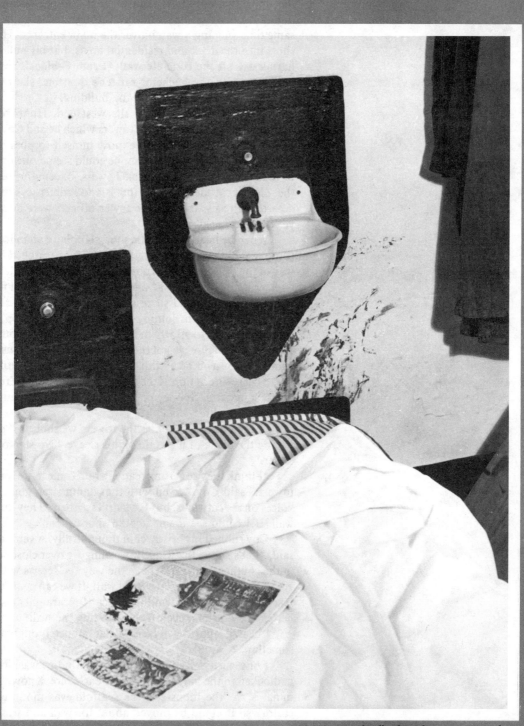

Blood-stained cell where hostages were shot.

ALCATRAZ '46

Cretzer and Hubbard stood alone at the west end of the cell-house. They waited, hoping to ambush officers who might attempt to enter the west gun gallery from the catwalk outside D-block. Along the upper tiers of A, B, and C-blocks, Coy searched for vantage points from which he could fire through the windows while at the same time keeping a watch over the main entrance. He fired several shots into the dock and residential areas, but his bullets ricochetted harmlessly off the concrete walls. From C-block's top tier, he fired two shots into the bachelor officer's quarters, shattering a pair of windows in the north wall of the building.

Bored with inactivity at the west end, Hubbard went to the dining room to check the gun towers which he and Coy had fired into earlier. Being careful not to expose himself to possible gunfire, he watched for armed officers, but he could see no one on the yard wall or in the Hill, Road, and Dock Towers. Except for the tiny figure in the distant Model Tower, the island's defenses appeared to be deserted. Presumably, all the tower officers were dead and had not yet been replaced.

When he heard Coy's rifle shots, Hubbard abandoned the dining room without a word to the six inmates who watched from the door-way of the officer's dining room. As he passed through Times Square, Cretzer left his position at the D-block entrance and followed. Both men thought Coy had surprised some officers near the main gate.

Coy heard them coming and leaned over the top tier railing. "I just been trying to stir them up but can't get a rise out of them," he explained. "I figure we got them stopped cold. They just ain't got guts enough to bust in here with us waiting for them with these guns."

"There's no action at the other end either," said Cretzer. "They're up to somethin'. Sooner or later they gotta come in here after us. Then we'll clobber 'em."

"I took a quick look at the towers we shot up," said Hubbard, wiping the blade of his knife on his sleeve. "No sign of life out there either."

"I think they're getting ready to ram some more screws into them towers," said Coy. "Even with that damn siren going, I could hear voices on the catwalks, but I couldn't see them. They hung close to the wall. If I could see them, I could shoot them."

Coy rubbed his bristly chin thoughtfully. A smile appeared as he said, "Let's shove the window washing rig over close to the windows in the southeast corner. That's the way the screws will have to go to get to the Road Tower and yard wall. If we can get high enough and reach out through the window, we can fire straight down. It gives us a better line on them even if they do hug the wall."

"Yeah," agreed Cretzer. "That monster oughta be good for somethin'."

For security reasons, the portable window washing scaffold was padlocked to the bars of the library enclosure. Known to officers and inmates as "the monster", the scaffold was mounted on oversize castors so it could be moved about for wall and window washing, painting, and routine inspections of the tool-resistant window bars.

"We'll move the thing to where it'll be useful," said Cretzer. "Bernie, you got Miller's keys. Unlock the damn padlock. Me and Marv'll jam this thing right up close to the windows."

With Coy covering the main gate, Cretzer and Hubbard laboriously wheeled the scaffold into position. Although Miller's uniform jacket and the gun belt with its holstered pistol made climbing awkward, Cretzer quickly managed to scale the framework to the top platform high above the cellhouse floor. From there he had a commanding view of a broad area below. He punched out several panes of detention sash glass and began experimenting with a number of possible firing positions. He could see no officers anywhere.

"Bernie," he called, "this job is right down my alley. When the screws show up, I can stick my pistol through the window and shoot at their goddam heads. I just wish I hadn't used up so many bullets."

After telling Hubbard to watch the main gate, Coy trotted down Seedy Street toward the west end. The library gate was open, but there was no sign of Cooke or Peabody.

"They're probably holed up in a wastebasket," he said. "This place is full of lifers with no guts."

Coy paused indecisively at the D-block door. He intended to enter the Culinary Department for another look at the gun towers, but the outside entrance to the gun cage had to be watched. The prison assault squad might come busting through that entrance, and he wanted to be there to greet them with a hail of lead. Finally, he strolled to the cellblock officer's desk and looked at the upper tiers with their unlocked cell doors. "Might be a good place to shoot from later on," he thought. His mind explored the possibilities of keeping the gun cage entrance covered without exposing himself to the fire of invading officers. "If I play it right, I can kill a lot of them from here. They gotta come in this way or through the front gate. It figures they'll try this way first because it ain't so exposed. I'll be here, waiting."

* * *

Unaware of the trouble in the cellhouse until the armory officer called to ask Officer Pehrson what he knew about it, the medical staff and the custodial officer were now concerned about the safety of their inmate patients, many of whom were very ill. James Sweet, medical technical assistant, Dr. John Farr, dentist, Dr. Stuart Clark, relief medical officer, eight inmate patients, and one inmate orderly were isolated above the Culinary Department in a vulnerable location.

"Can those escapees get in here?" asked Dr. Clark.

"I don't know," Dr. Farr answered. "My office is one place that isn't safe. It's too close to the entrance. They could shoot right into it through the grille."

"Doesn't the cellhouse officer carry a key to the hospital gate?" asked Sweet.

"Only to the gate at the foot of the stairs going into the dining room. But there is a key to this upper gate in the gun gallery. The lieutenants use it when they come around to check on us. I don't see how the cons could get at it without breaking into the gun gallery," said Pehrson. "If they have guns, they might have the key, too. It wouldn't do much good to just lock the gate."

"Maybe we can barricade it," came a suggestion.

"I got a better idea," said Dr. Farr. "I can fix the lock so it won't open with a key. I have plaster of Paris in my laboratory. Plaster in the lock mechanism might jam the lock."

Pehrson cautioned, "What if they set fire to the building?"

"I don't think we have to worry about that. The building is solid reinforced concrete and so is the roof," said Dr. Clark. "The only

129

ALCATRAZ '46

things that can burn are the tables, benches, and mattresses. I think we should use the plaster."

The other men agreed, and Dr. Farr mixed the plaster, then tamped it into the keyway. It hardened quickly, and the lock became inoperable.

When the telephone rang again, Dr. Farr told Fish what had been done to insure the safety of the hospital. "Just come and get us when you can," he said. "We'll be waiting for you."

The medical staff resumed caring for the medical needs of the prisoner patients, knowing that a rescue party would eventually arrive.

* * *

The persistent wail of the siren continued to resound throughout the island. Added to the wail was the incessant shrieking of the powerhouse whistle which also served as a warning signal. In the residential area, off-duty officers put on their uniforms then rushed uphill to the armory.

Warden Johnston, the associate warden, the chief clerk, and the warden's secretary were clustered around the captain's desk discussing the implementation of Plan 3 when Lieutenant George Boatman arrived. Boatman, a Marine Corps veteran with many years of federal prison experience, was given a description of what had happened.

View of interior of powerhouse.

Johnston said, "Lieutenant, we must assume that Coy is not alone in this and that there will be an attempt to blast out of the cellhouse to effect a mass escape from the prison. I want you to take over the coordination of our anti-escape plan. Mr. Miller will assign the reserve officers as they arrive. You keep a record of the assignments so we will know where each man is stationed."

As Boatman took Miller's place behind the captain's desk, Lieutenant Ike Faulk and two officers from the dock area rushed into the office. Boatman entered their names on the roster.

"Did you get the outside details rounded up?" asked Miller.

"Yes, sir. The garbage and cleanup crews came to the dock as soon as they heard the siren. I sent them and my dock crew in the garbage truck to the Hill Tower sallyport."

"Who's left on the dock?"

"Lieutenant Rychner is in charge. The launch was just getting underway when we left to come up here."

Fish opened the armory issue window and announced, "The launch operator checked in on the radio. They're away from the dock and are starting the patrol around the island."

"Faulk," said Miller, "I think you better help Fish take care of the armory. You handle communications. There will be a flood of calls from the mainland — probably from everywhere the siren is heard."

"What do you want me to tell them?"

"That depends on who is calling. If it's the police or the military, tell them we have an emergency situation and need their assistance. If it's one of our officers, tell him to get down to Dock 4 at Fort Mason as fast as he can. We'll use that dock as our rallying point for all our men on the mainland."

Fish admitted Faulk to the armory as Miller said, "Issue a .45 to these other officers. One can support Mr. Phillips in the main gate. The other can be our escort to cover the men we send to the emergency posts around the cellhouse."

As Fish armed the two officers, Faulk said, "Mr. Miller, Besk just called in from the Hill Tower. He has the outside crews and their officers in the sallyport. He's wounded. Bullet in his leg. Thinks the inmates were shooting at him from the kitchen bakeshop."

"Is he hurt bad?"

"He's lost a lot of blood. Says he can hold out until we send someone to relieve him."

"Get some men out there to relieve Mr. Besk right away," directed the warden. "The Hill Tower is one of our most important posts. Lieutenant Boatman, put at least two armed officers out there, and send an escort officer to bring in Mr. Besk. My secretary has some first aid things. We can put some sort of a bandage on his leg temporarily."

Officers began arriving at the captain's office from the residential area, and Boatman methodically recorded the assignments and handed each man his typewritten post instructions as the associate warden told the officer where to post himself.

Warden Johnston greeted the men as they entered, and as Fish issued firearms, tear gas grenades, and other defensive equipment, the warden warned the men of the dangers they might face.

"Don't expose yourselves unnecessarily," he cautioned. "The escapees have firearms and have been shooting at us through the cell-

ALCATRAZ '46

house and kitchen windows. If they fire at you, fire back. If you are close to a window through which shots are fired, throw your tear gas grenades into the cellhouse. The gas will drive them away from the windows, and it won't seriously hurt anyone."

The heavily armed officers proceeded to their assigned posts. At the entrance to the west gun gallery, Lieutenant Faulk narrowly escaped death when Coy fired at him from the west end of D-block. The officers immediately returned the fire and hurled tear gas grenades into the library, D-block, and the main cellhouse.

* * *

Within 15 minutes of the first sounding of the siren, all the off-duty officers on the island had arrived at the administration building to assist in the defense of the institution. Although a tightly knit cordon of armed men was set up around the prison to repel any attempt to blastout, the number available for duty was not enough to implement Plan 3 completely. An assault upon the cellhouse was not feasible until additional officers from the mainland arrived.

After the last available man had been assigned a post, Boatman stepped into the armory where Fish was checking the count figures. "How many cons are apt to be in on this thing?" he asked.

"Our count was 280 men at noon. Right now there are 114 in the work area, 13 in the Hill Tower sallyport, 50 in the yard, and a couple under the Road Tower. I figure none of these are in on the escape, but if the guys inside bust out, most of those in the yard will probably join them. The prison building has 26 in D-block, 9 in the hospital who we know aren't in on it, 18 in the basement, a few in the kitchen and library, and about 30 who are idle in the cellhouse. They could all be in on it."

"Then there may be as.many as 75 or 100 inmates ready to break out," surmised Boatman.

Guard giving instructions during siege.

Outside the armory, Associate Warden Miller paused at the warden's office doorway and waited for Johnston to notice him. The warden sat alone and seemed lost in thought. His responsibilities at the moment were awesome. He was concerned for the captive officers, for the inmates who were attempting to break out, and for the officers who must soon be ordered to charge into the cellhouse. The warden, although old and ill, was a proud, decisive man with one standard — perfection. He seldom raised his voice and never lost either his temper or his self-control. Though not a large man physically, his personality dominated every officer, every inmate, and every inch of the penitentiary.

After a long period of silent waiting, Miller finally moved from the doorway and returned to his own office to restudy the anti-escape plan. A few minutes later, Johnston sighed, stood up, squared his frail shoulders, and walked toward the armory. His smoothly operating prison was not working to perfection.

ALCATRAZ '46

Coast Guard cutter cruising around the island during the siege.

* * *

After being contacted by shortwave radio, the U.S. Coast Guard assigned several armed vessels to patrol the waters around the island. The San Francisco Police Department stationed police officers on wharves and docks along the city's waterfront to intercept any escapees who might reach the mainland. The Alcatraz launch patrolled offshore inside the 200-yard buoys. All possible avenues of escape from the island were methodically blocked.

Orders were relayed to gun tower officers and Army, Navy, and Coast Guard personnel to shoot any escaping prisoner who refused to surrender. A call was sent to Bay Area doctors and nurses, requesting assistance in handling the expected casualties. The American Red Cross offered to send food, hot coffee, and cigarettes to the fighting men on the island.

Hollywood-style photo showing members of San Francisco Police Force who were alerted shortly after the battle broke out.

ALCATRAZ '46

The FBI and the Bureau of Prisons in Washington, D.C. were alerted. Johnston urged prison bureau officials to rush experienced officers from other federal prisons. He also asked his old friend, Warden Clinton Duffy at San Quentin, for all the officers he could spare.

When all available off-duty officers were assigned to strategic positions as outlined in the escape-prevention procedure, Johnston called Miller, Faulk, Boatman, and Mills to his office. With their assistance, he tried to analyze the breakdowns in the prison security system.

"I don't see how anyone could get into that gun gallery from inside the building," he said. "A lieutenant always accompanies the officer to the outside entrance, and he carries the keys. He passes the officer into the gallery through a solid steel door which has a pick-proof security lock on it. No inmate ever gets anywhere near that lock, and the key is always kept in the armory except when a lieutenant takes it out to pass officers in or out through that security door."

"Still, it seems Coy and other inmates managed to assault Mr. Burch and seize his weapons," said Faulk.

"We know there were two guns in the west gallery — a rifle and a pistol," continued the warden, "but how could the inmates get their hands on those guns, let alone a machine gun? No machine gun is ever allowed in the cellhouse, not even in the hands of an officer. How did they get a machine gun into the cellhouse?"

The associate warden said, hesitantly, "Warden, I don't believe they have a machine gun in there. I think that all they have is one rifle and one pistol, the guns from the west gallery."

"And how do you think they got them?"

Some Alcatraz officers pose for a photo during happier days.

"I don't know, warden. Maybe Coy conned Mr. Burch into letting him get close to the gallery to show him a book or a magazine or something so he could grab him. Inmates from the kitchen crew might have helped Coy. If they once got their hands on the officer, they could hold him against the bars long enough to take his guns and keys."

"We won't really know what happened until we get back in there," said Faulk. "I only saw Coy, but there must be more cons than Coy in on it."

"Well, that may be," said Johnston. "One thing is certain, they do have firearms, and one is probably a machine gun. Yes, after thinking through the events, I am absolutely convinced that an inmate has a machine gun in the cellhouse. Our situation is desperate."

Like Miller, the two lieutenants knew it was unlikely the escapees had a machine gun. If they had, they certainly hadn't fired it. The characteristic bursts of machine gun fire were easily recognized, and only rifle and pistol shots had been reported. But the warden seemed positive, and the lieutenants knew from past experiences that once he had made a statement, he would cling to it tenaciously.

Following a long, silent pause in the conversation, Johnston took a deep breath and said slowly, "Gentlemen, the tradition of secrecy which has enveloped us all these years will now have to end. As much as I hate to do it, I've got to tell the nation what has happened. Mr. Bertrand, call Western Union and have them deliver immediately and simultaneously to all newspapers, radio broadcasters, and press associations in the San Francisco Bay Area, this telegram:

'Serious trouble. Convict has machine gun in cellhouse. Have issued riot call. Placed armed guards at strategic locations. Many of our officers are imprisoned in the cellhouse. Cannot tell extent of injuries suffered by our officers or amount of damage done. Will give you more information later in the day when we regain control.'

* * *

When the call went out asking Bay Area hospitals, physicians, and nurses to stand by, Warden Johnston was unexpectedly called by General Joseph Stillwell from his office on Treasure Island.

"Can we be of any assistance, warden?" asked Stillwell.

"Yes, general, most certainly," replied the warden. "We are very shorthanded. If you could send us ten or fifteen good men to help guard the prisoners who have not become involved in the escape, I would appreciate it very much."

"The admiral has marines available. They'll be over there within the hour, and we'll come by tomorrow to see if we can be of further assistance," Stillwell replied.

* * *

In Bay Area newspaper city rooms, reporters, rewrite men, and editors were busy preparing news stories for publication. The Harold Ickes story and a recent recall movement in San Francisco were the top priority headlines.

At the San Francisco Chronicle, copy had been submitted for the first edition deadline when the city desk telephone rang and an

ALCATRAZ '46

excited reporter from the Oakland beat exclaimed, "The highway patrol on the Bay Bridge tells me that gun shots can be heard from Alcatraz. And you can hear the escape siren. Coast Guard patrol boats are said to be circling the island. You better check it out."

An editor immediately dialed the Alcatraz number, but a busy signal was the only answer.

A second call was answered by the city editor who turned to his reporters and yelled, "Check Alcatraz. There's a big break on the Rock. A Marin County correspondent just called to report that residents on Tiburon Island and dockside workers in Sausalito heard explosions and gunfire from the Rock."

Checking the FBI office in San Francisco, one reporter received the cautious statement, "All we can say at this time is that there might possibly be an attempt to escape from the island."

A copy woman ran in to the city room with a telegram. It began, "Serious trouble . . ."

The city room sprang into action. Reporters and cameramen raced to docks and yacht harbors to rent any available craft. For 12 years they had been barred from the island. They were now determined to let no one prevent them from coming within camera range of what might well be the biggest story of the decade.

* * *

Another view of the island dock.

Members of the Press cruising around off Alcatraz during siege.

ALCATRAZ '46

Non-combatant clerks, storekeepers, and shop foremen continued to arrive at the administration building. Each was given an assignment.

"Warden, all the gun towers have checked in," said Fish. "Some of the reinforcements we sent out were fired upon as they ran along the catwalks on the south side of the cellhouse. They returned the fire with bullets and tear gas grenades. None of them were hit, and they don't know if they hit any of the escapees. It's impossible to see anything inside the cellhouse."

Boatman asked, "What are we going to do about the inmates in the work area? They can hear the siren down there. They know that we have trouble up here."

The warden directed, "I think we can dispense with the siren now. It has served its purpose. Mr. Fish, call the powerhouse and tell the engineer to turn off his steam whistle."

Fish switched off the siren and dialed the powerhouse number.

"Mr. Faulk," said Miller, "you better get the inmates from the industries shops into the yard. Start them in the same as always with the outside details heading the line. It'll be safe enough to move them with all those extra guns in the towers."

"Start them in," agreed Johnston. "When they are safely in the yard, we'll have additional officers available for guard duty around the cellhouse or wherever else they are needed."

"Warden, we must put an assault team together and get back into the cellhouse as quickly as possible. Some of those officers in there may still be alive."

"I'm afraid there's not much possibility of that," hesitated Johnston, "And we don't want to lose any more officers. We must get this thing organized sensibly. The right officers must first be chosen for the assault team. Who is available at this time?"

Alcatraz from the air.

Miller looked down a list of names. "Several of the lieutenants could be used: Boatman, Faulk, Johnson, Klein, Roberts, and Rychner. Morrison and Robertson are on annual leave. Then there are the men on the rifle-pistol team: Bergen, Cochenour, Fish, Mahan, and Mowery. They can be ready to go in when you give the word."

"Where is Lieutenant Bergen? Why isn't he here?" asked Johnston.

"He's off the island. Faulk said he went over to town on the Coxe at 10:00 a.m. Took his wife to the hospital. He'll call in as soon as he hears the news flash on the radio."

"There must be more than 20 of our men over there on the mainland. They should all be here on the island when emergencies like this arise," said the warden. "It has long been a sore point with me that we don't have accommodations for all our people on the island. We will have to send a boat for them."

"What about the school kids?"

"They will have to stay in the city until this is over. It would be too dangerous to bring them to the island."

Fish interrupted, "Warden, all the inmates from the work area are marching to the yard. The shop foremen are searching the shops for stragglers, just in case some tried to hide out."

"Thank you, Mr. Fish. Instruct all unassigned officers to report up here as soon as possible. All officers who call in from the mainland should rendevous at Dock 4. Let me know when they call, and I'll arrange for transportation."

"What shall I say about the women and children?"

"Tell them they can't come home for a while."

"Calls are coming in from the newspapers and the radio stations asking for more details about the trouble. What shall I tell them?"

"Say only that we are getting the situation under control and that we will issue news bulletins as soon as we have anything of consequence to report. We must be careful to avoid giving out unsubstantiated information which might get rumors started."

* * *

"The shop foremen are searching the shops for stragglers, just in case some tried to hide out."

ALCATRAZ '46

Sam's Pharmacy, on Van Ness Avenue near Green Street, was exceptionally busy at 2:40 p.m. Lieutenant Philip Bergen and his wife sat quietly in their 1939 Ford waiting for the pharmacist to fill a prescription. It was a warm mid-afternoon, and traffic was light on the avenue.

As the two waited, Sam rushed from the drug store. "Mr. Bergen," he shouted. "I just heard the news flash. A big escape from Alcatraz. Turn on your radio. It's on KGO."

Bergen switched on the car radio. As it slowly warmed up, he turned the dial through the usual discordant jangle of music and commercials and stopped at a newscaster's excited voice, ". . . and I repeat, a bloody uprising is underway on Alcatraz Island. Rampaging convicts have stormed and captured the prison arsenal. Prison officers have been slaughtered. Armed prisoners are over-running the island. Women and children, families of the prison employees, are in desperate peril. The warden has sent out a call for help to all military and police agencies. A desperate emergency confronts everyone in the San Francisco Bay Area."

"That's not possible," Bergen exclaimed. "Nobody, especially no dog-eared convicts, could take that arsenal. They might capture an officer or two. They might even surprise and capture one of the gun towers as they almost did in '38, but capture the arsenal? That just couldn't happen."

Mrs. Bergen became worried and anxious. "I hope Aunt Mary is all right. She's all alone in the apartment and probably half scared to death. I wish there was some way we could talk to her, to reassure her that everything will be all right. Cliff Fish is in the armory, isn't he? Why don't you call him, Phil."

"Sam, you have a phone in the store? I've got to find out what is really going on over there."

Behind Sam's prescription counter, the store radio was still blaring. Bergen turned down the volume and dialed the Alcatraz number. Incredibly, the call was completed on the first try.

"Cliff, this is Phil Bergen. I just heard the news. What's going on over there? The radio says the cons have captured the arsenal and have taken over the island."

"It's bad enough, but not that bad," replied Fish. "We think it's an attempted blastout. The cons have guns. They've been shooting at us, and they may have killed some of the officers in the cellhouse. But they haven't captured the arsenal, and they aren't going to capture it. We have them contained. Where are you calling from?"

"I'm in a drug store on Van Ness. How can I get over?"

"Just a second, Phil . . ." There was a break in the conversation, then Fish continued, "Associate warden Miller says to tell you to gather all the officers you can find and wait at Dock 4. He'll send a boat to pick you up."

"We'll be there."

Evelyn Bergen stood nearby, listening. Sam handed her the filled prescription and commented, "Mrs. Bergen, you look like a lady pirate with that black patch over your eye."

"I probably should have one on the other eye, too. This Iritis is almost too much. I can hardly see. All I could think of before we heard the news was to get home to lay down and rest. Now, I'm afraid none of us will get much rest."

Phil Bergen paid for the medicine and advised the pharmacist,

"That news broadcast exaggerated the situation. It seems that some of the prisoners have guns, and they're shooting up the place. They may have killed some of our officers, but no prisoner has escaped yet. I'm going to get over there as quick as I can."

The drive to the dock at the foot of Van Ness took just a few minutes. As they neared the parking area adjacent to the grassy slopes of Aquatic Park, the Bergens saw the Army steamer, General Frank M. Coxe, loading passengers.

"That old tub will be departing for Angel Island in a few minutes. Maybe they'll consider a special stop at Alcatraz. That would be the quickest way for me to get over there."

Locking the car, the Bergens hurried onto the dock just as the dock officers were detaching the steamer's gangplank.

"Sorry," said an elderly deckhand. "We've orders not to take anyone to Alcatraz. It ain't safe to cruise near the island. We probably won't be stopping there until the trouble is over."

As the steamer cast off its lines and departed for Angel Island, Bergen stared across the mile and a quarter of mirror-smooth water and saw occasional puffs of white smoke in the vicinity of the cellhouse. He could hear the distant popping of rifle and pistol shots. Scanning the island carefully, he was relieved to observe that the trouble had not spread to the residential area at the east end where his aged aunt, several other women, and a number of pre-school children were isolated.

"Scanning the island carefully, he was relieved to observe that the trouble had not spread to the residential area at the east end where his aged aunt, several other women, and a number of pre-school children were isolated."

ALCATRAZ '46

He turned to his wife and said, "Evelyn, it looks like we're holding them inside the walls. The most important thing will be to keep them from breaking out and taking over the island. God help any woman or child who falls into their hands."

"Do you think they might get out of the prison?"

"No, but then I never figured they could get their hands on guns and ammunition either. A lot depends upon how many of our officers are still alive and available for duty. If the gun tower officers are dead, anything can happen." Bergen watched the launch as it patrolled around the island and said, "Damn it. There must be some way to get over there."

"You're in a dreadful hurry to get yourself shot at."

"Not really. I know I'm not bullet-proof, but the department spent fourteen years and God knows how many thousands of dollars preparing me to meet challenges like this. I'd better not let all that go down the drain."

"Especially on your anniversary."

"What anniversary?"

"Yours. Fourteen years ago today, May 2, 1932, was the day you were sworn in, in New York City."

"I had forgotten about that. It seems so long ago."

Officer Harry Cochrane and his wife, Betty, arrived at the dock. They had been returning to San Francisco from a leisurely drive through the wooded areas of Marin County when they heard the news on their car radio.

"The most important thing will be to keep them from breaking out and taking over the island. God help any woman or child who falls into their hands."

"How bad is it, Phil?" asked Cochrane.

"It's bad enough, I guess, but not as bad as they make it sound on the news."

"Have you talked to anyone over there recently?"

"With Cliff Fish. He said they'd send for us."

"Isn't that the Johnston swinging around the island? Do you think they'll send her over to get us?"

"Probably, to pick us up along with the 3:35 p.m. crew."

"By then it'll be over. I didn't come rushing across the bridge and through that Marina traffic just to get a grandstand seat here on Dock 4. You're a lieutenant, Phil. Pull some rank to get us over there."

Bergen entered the pay telephone booth outside the dock waiting room. After several attempts, he finally heard Fish's voice. The lieutenant identified himself, and Fish said, "The Coast Guard has been contacted. A vessel should pick you up within minutes. Has anyone else shown up?"

"Harry Cochrane and his wife just got here. Otherwise, the dock is empty."

"The warden says for you, Harry, and any other officers that show up, to come right over on the Coast Guard boat. Don't wait for stragglers, and don't bring any women or children."

"O.K., Cliff. I can see the vessel coming now. See you in a few minutes."

By the time the Coast Guard cutter arrived, off-duty officers Norman Anthony and John Wright had joined Bergen and Cochrane. Upon hearing the news bulletin, both had rushed to the dock, but Anthony, who had been enjoying the day in the bars on Chestnut Street, was intoxicated.

"He should go lay down on a bench and sleep it off," said Cochrane. "He's in no shape to go over to the island."

"I'll steer him into the waiting room, Harry," said Bergen turning to Anthony who staggered close to the edge of the dock. "Norman, get into the waiting room and stay there until you sober up. You're in no shape to go to work."

"Awright, awright. If you shay so, sir. But I ain't drunk, lieutenant, sir."

Bergen grabbed Anthony's arms, swung him around, and pushed him into the waiting room. Muttering and grumbling, the disgruntled officer seated himself. Turning to his wife, Bergen said, "Evelyn, keep an eye on this fool. He's apt to fall into the bay if he keeps staggering around the dock. Too bad he's so damned drunk. He's an excellent shot with a rifle."

Cochrane called from outside the waiting room, "Phil, the skipper is asking for you."

Bergen hurried to where the lean, grey vessel lay alongside the dock. The young Coast Guard officer asked, "Are you Lieutenant Bergen?"

"I'm Bergen. Are you taking us to the island?"

"My orders are to bring you and any others you O.K. You guys must be pretty important for this special ride."

"Not important, just needed," shrugged Bergen, looking down upon the deck below the dock. "Say, how do we come aboard? It's quite a drop to your deck. Can't you come alongside the landing float?"

ALCATRAZ '46

"There's not enough clearance, I'm afraid. You guys will have to jump down from up there. My men will assist when you hit the deck."

In quick succession, Bergen, Cochrane, and Wright jumped from the dock to the gently heaving deck of the Coast Guard vessel.

"Let's go, skipper," shouted Bergen, but as he spoke, Anthony appeared on the dock above and contemplated the ten foot gap between him and the vessel. He jumped recklessly to the deck, and the impact staggered him backward. Wright and Cochrane reached out and grabbed the unwanted officer, thus preventing him from toppling into the water.

"Now what do we do with him?" asked Cochrane.

"Well, we can't throw him back up on the dock," replied Bergen. "We'll just have to take the idiot along with us."

Alone on the dock, the two wives watched the vessel carrying their husbands depart.

"Evelyn, what in the world do you suppose they'll do with that drunken officer?" asked Betty Cochrane.

"They'll probably send him back here on the next trip of the Johnston or put him to sleep in his room. I believe he lives in the bachelor quarters on the island dock."

"We would probably have had a terrible time with him if he had stayed here. Imagine us trying to keep him penned up in that waiting room."

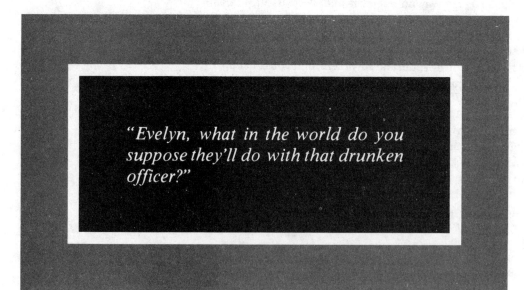

"Evelyn, what in the world do you suppose they'll do with that drunken officer?"

"I'm afraid he will give our men a lot of trouble, Betty. They'll probably have to sit on him all the way to the island."

Everlyn looked uphill along Van Ness Avenue. It was almost 3:00 p.m. and she saw the first wave of young school children, dressed in light summer clothing with textbooks and empty lunch boxes under their arms, straggling along the sidewalk toward the dock. Some 50 Alcatraz children, who attended San Francisco public and parochial schools, were within walking distance of the dock. Half of them were in the primary grades. The others were in high school or college and would not arrive until after 4:00 p.m.

For most of the young children, the trips on the Johnston were an enjoyable interlude in the well-ordered but somewhat restrictive routine of life on the island. Rain, fog, or wind-whipped waves failed to prevent the launch from making its scheduled round trips.

Awaiting the youngsters, Mrs. Bergen and Mrs. Cochrane watched anxiously as the Coast Guard vessel disappeared behind the easternmost point of the island.

* * *

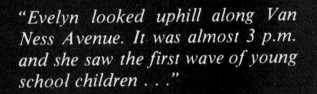

"Evelyn looked uphill along Van Ness Avenue. It was almost 3 p.m. and she saw the first wave of young school children . . ."

ALCATRAZ '46

As the vessel slowed alongside the face of the dock, the Coast Guard skipper said, "I have orders to patrol around the island as soon as you go ashore. Good luck to you guys."

Bergen smiled his appreciation and looked around. No inmates were in sight, and no one was shooting at them. All dock activity had ceased. The boat slip below the tower was empty because the Johnston was out patrolling. Bergen looked up and waved to Comerford who was hunched down in a sheltered corner of the Dock Tower.

Lieutenant Emil Rychner stepped out of the dock office to help the officers move Anthony from the vessel's deck to the dock.

"Why did you bring this drunk over here?" asked Rychner as the vessel eased away from them. "He'll be of no use to us."

"Hell, we know that. We just couldn't stop him. Maybe you can," said Bergen. "Dump him in his room in the bachelor's quarters, and let him sleep it off."

"All right, I'll handle him. You guys be careful when you hike up to the armory. Any time you can see the windows up there, a con with a gun may be behind that window ready to shoot at you."

"Thanks, Rych, we'll be careful."

Leaving the unhappy Anthony with Rychner, the three officers passed through the security gates and trotted up the back stairs to the residential area. By avoiding the island roadways and staying close to the buildings, they were able to reach their respective apartments without incident.

Knocking on his apartment door, Bergen had difficulty persuading his aunt to open it. She and several other women, including Bill Miller's wife, had been hiding in the barricaded apartment. None of them knew anything about what was happening in the prison.

Bergen changed into his dark grey uniform and gulped a cup of hot coffee. Before departing, he reassured the anxious women, "The children will be looked after in town. Evelyn and Mrs. Cochrane were getting things organized over there when we left. I'll call you from my office, and let you know how things are going up top."

The fastest way to the administration building was along a trail through 'Windy Gulch'. This trail wound uphill and merged with the single lane road below the lighthouse. Because the rugged path hugged the precipitous cliffs and was hidden from view of the cellhouse windows, the fastest way to the administration building was also the safest. Moving uphill, Bergen glanced at his watch. It was 3:30 p.m.

* * *

"Why did you bring this drunk over here?"

The cellhouse telephones continued to ring persistently. "They got all those phones covered," Hubbard told himself. "If I was dumb enough to answer one, I'd be dead in a hurry."

Hearing keys rattle against the steel door in the east gun gallery, Hubbard got up from his perch on the C-block stairs, shouting, "Joe, they're coming into the east gun cage."

Cretzer whirled atop the window washing scaffold and lined his pistol sights on the doorway, however, the long row of closely spaced bars obstructed his line of fire. To shoot between the bars was nearly impossible, so he scrambled down the far side of the scaffold and joined Hubbard behind the southeast corner of C-block. Glancing down the aisle, he noted that Coy had abandoned his lookout position at the D-block entrance.

"Joe," hissed Hubbard. "Look at those finks coming in there. They're both packing scatterguns."

"So what? As soon as they move over this way where I can get a clear shot at 'em, I'll knock 'em both off."

When Coy heard Hubbard's warning cry, he hurried eastward along Broadway. As he passed the cut-offs, the officers, who had entered the east gallery, saw him. Officer Virgil Cochenour, nosed his Winchester Riot Gun, loaded with double-O buckshot, through the bars and blasted lead pellets down Broadway.

Only 100 feet from the blast, Coy didn't wait to aim and fire. He turned and raced toward the west end shelter of C-block as the pellets banged and bounced around him.

"Damn scatterguns," he panted. "A guy can't buck them close up. I'll have to pick them screws off from behind the block where they can't see me."

The thunderous roar of the shotgun unnerved Cretzer and Hubbard. Unable to get a clear shot at the gun cage officers because of the bars and the unfavorable firing angle, Cretzer said, "Marv, let's get the hell outta here. Those mother fuckers can murder us with those shotguns. They probably got Bernie, if that's who they was shootin' at."

"Who else? If they were shooting at anyone, it had to be Bernie."

"I didn't hear his rifle, did you?"

"No, he must be done for."

"If he is, we got to get his rifle 'n all that ammunition. I wonder where they dropped him."

"They were blasting down Broadway. Bernie's probably there, close to the Square."

The two men, keeping under the overhang and close to the cellfronts, ran down Seedy Street until they reached Times Square. Behind the west end of the block near the utility corridor door, they found Coy.

"Goddam, Bernie. We thought you were dead," gasped Hubbard.

"I almost got it, but I ducked behind the damn block when those finks started to shoot at me. How did you do, Joe?"

"Bernie, we didn't have a chance to fire. I can't reach the finks from here with this Colt. Maybe you can pick 'em off."

"If I can see them, I can hit them, and I'm sure going to try to see them. Let's get ourselves set. The screws own the east end now, and there ain't nothing to stop them from busting in through the main gate. When they do, they'll probably spread out and come down all

147

ALCATRAZ '46

these alleys. They might even come down behind A-block through the old library. Marv, you watch Michigan Boulevard between A and B-blocks. Joe, you cover Seedy Street and the west gun cage entrance. I'll watch Broadway and try to pick off those two finks in the gun cage."

Darting across Broadway, Hubbard stopped behind the corner of B-block. He hunched down on the concrete and nervously caressed the haft of his butcher knife. "I wish I had a gun instead of this pig sticker," he thought.

In the east gun gallery, Cochenour telephoned the armory to report the encounter with Coy, then the two officers stayed out of sight behind the waist high gallery wall and watched for signs of the armed convicts.

Unable to see the officers, Coy held his fire. "Joe, if I could just see a little bit of them finks, I'd blast them to hell right through that tin wall they're hiding behind."

"How come your little rifle bullets go through that steel, and my .45 slugs just bounce off it?" asked Cretzer.

"I don't know, Joe, but they do. I almost got one of them a while back, right through the gun cage door, but the bastard ducked behind the concrete wall, and I missed him. These rifle bullets will go through steel and bulletproof glass, but they just bounce off concrete."

A half hour passed with no opportunity to shoot at the officers in the east gun cage.

"They know we're laying for them, Joe. They ain't going to show themselves so we can shoot them," Coy said. "Let's get back to D-block and see if we can spot any screws through the windows."

Seeing his two partners disappear through the D-block door, Hubbard left his lookout position and followed them. The inmates in D-block were not happy to see the escapees.

"For Cri-sakes, Joe," protested an inmate locked in an open-front cell on the flats, "Every time you guys come in here you get them screws all stirred up. You fire a couple of lousy shots at them, and suddenly there's a hundred guns out there shooting at us. And they throw tear gas, too. Look at all them burned out gas bombs on the flats. If the ventilation system wasn't working, we'd all choke to death."

"Get under your bunk and pull your mattress over you. You'll be safe enough, and you'll get used to the gas. We have," smiled Coy.

The three inmates hurried upstairs to the top tier where they lay flat on the deck to stare through the windows in the south wall. They could see a great number of boats loaded with people, cluttering the surface of the bay just beyond the marker buoys.

"Look at all those rubbernecks," exclaimed Hubbard.

"The bastards came to see us get killed, Marv. We got a real live audience. I bet half the goddam reporters in the country are out there. Now, if we can just knock off a few of them screws hidin' out there in the bushes, they'll have somethin' to write 'bout."

"I can't see no screws to shoot at," said Coy. "Maybe I ought to take a few pot shots at those fat cats on those damn boats. They're no better than the finks that work here."

"They're too far away," said Cretzer. "Dammit, since there ain't no screws to shoot at, there is someone I wanta get in here."

Cretzer got up and ran along the tier to cell 47 near the east end where Henri Young cowered behind his mattress. Cretzer and Young had been feuding for many months, but no inmate knew what had caused the feud.

Cretzer stood in front of Young's cell and stared vindictively at the terrified inmate. Resting his .45 on a crossbar, Cretzer aimed directly at Young's head and snapped off the safety.

"Say a prayer, you rotten little punk."

Then, as abruptly and impulsively as he had come, Cretzer flipped the safety on and spat at the inmate. "You ain't worth wastin' a bullet on, louse," he said, turning away.

When Cretzer returned to the tier where Coy and Hubbard were waiting, Coy said with approval, "Now you're being smart, Joe. Our job is to kill screws, not convicts."

* * *

When he arrived at the armory, Bergen learned that Wright was already armed and posted. Jesse Shannon was helping Fish with the communications because the shortwave radio and telephone trunk lines were demanding constant attention. As Bergen received his favorite Colt .45, Cochrane arrived.

"I'll take one of those pistols and plenty of extra clips," said Cochrane. "Give me a box of tracers, too."

Fish handed the pistol and ammunition to him. Cochrane asked, "What's happened since we talked to you, Cliff?"

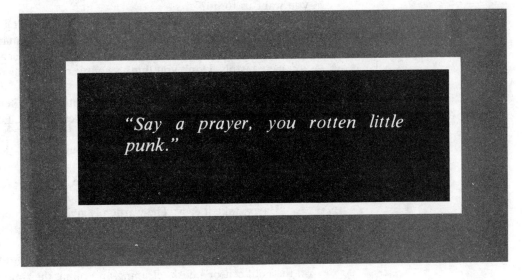

"Say a prayer, you rotten little punk."

"We put Cochenour and Zubke into the east gallery, and we've got men covering the cellhouse from the main gate and the visiting room. We had a little action in there a few minutes ago, but luck ran against us. Cochenour spotted Coy coming toward him with the rifle, so he opened up with a riot gun. Double-O buckshot fell all over Broadway, but Coy managed to escape. Not long before that, Coy fired a shot at Faulk through the gun gallery entrance door. The shot just barely missed him."

"It seems as though Coy is the only con that has been seen in the cellhouse with a gun in his hand," Bergen said thoughtfully. "Miller saw him. Faulk saw him. Now Cochenour and Zubke saw him. Didn't anybody see any other con carrying a gun in there?"

"Not that we know of, but there's bound to be more than Coy in on this. Thirty or forty of the worst cons in the prison are in that cellhouse with him. It figures that some of them, maybe all, are in on the escape."

"Now that the east gallery is manned, the cons have probably run down to the west end," said Cochrane. "I'll bet that's where they are now."

"They could be anywhere in there," said Bergen. "But I think you're right, Harry. They're probably holed up around the west end where they can watch that entrance to the gun gallery and all the aisles leading from the east end."

Associate Warden Miller entered from the warden's office and beckoned to them.

"For Cri-sakes, Ed, what happened to your face," exclaimed Bergen.

"I ran into my own gas billy. It looks worse than it is."

"Fish has been filling us in on what's been happening. What do you want us to do?"

"The warden said for you two to wait here. Don't go wandering off looking for trouble. As soon as Faulk gets the inmates from the work area into the yard, we'll be going into the cellhouse. I see both of you have pistols. Don't you think a couple of riot guns or a Thompson would be better?"

Bergen and Cochrane looked at each other, then Bergen replied, "Let the other guys carry the choppers and scatterguns, Ed. We prefer the pistols, if you don't mind."

"What do you think happened to our men in there?" asked Cochrane.

"We won't know until we get in there."

"Well, why don't we go in there right now?"

"Harry, take it easy. The warden is giving the orders. When he says go, we go, but not before. You'll get all the action you want before long."

Miller returned to the warden's office. Cochrane and Bergen sat on the mail censor's desk, cleaning and oiling their pistols.

"Let's reload these clips with fresh ammunition, and put a couple of tracers in each clip," said Cochrane.

Bergen agreed with the suggestion because the visibility in the cellhouse would be poor with all the lights switched off.

In the armory, Shannon and Fish struggled to answer the flood of calls which jammed the small switchboard. When they received a call from one of the officers on the mainland, the caller was advised to rendezvous at Dock 4 and wait for transportation to the island. The shortwave radio buzzed, crackled, and delivered staccato messages from military and police agencies.

From time to time, an officer from the security perimeter hurried into the building seeking a cold drink of water, additional ammunition, or a trip to the officer's rest room. The supply of tear gas dwindled to a few cannisters.

* * *

For a period of time, there was no gunfire. An uneasy silence engulfed the prison.

Miller emerged from a long conference with the warden and beckoned to Bergen and Cochrane. They holstered their weapons and followed him into his office.

"The warden feels that we don't have enough officers available to risk an assault on the cellhouse just yet. We have a detachment of Marines on the way from Treasure Island. When they get here, we will put them on the yard wall to relieve our officers. Then we should have enough men to go for an assault party."

"How many men does the warden think it'll take, for Cri-sakes?" sputtered Cochrane. "How many guns do those cons have? Two? Well, here's two guns and two men who know how to use them. You already have this end of the cellhouse covered by armed officers in the east gallery. Why in hell don't we just go in and take the guns away from those bastards? They've been shooting at everybody they could lay their sight on and missed them all. All, except Besk, and I hear he got hit by a ricochette."

"The warden gives the orders, Harry. I just pass them on. He thinks it's best to wait. So we wait."

Bergen, taking Miller's arm, said quietly, "Other people are waiting, too, Ed. All those officers in there. If any are alive, they're waiting for us to do something. I agree with Harry. We're stalling around too damn long."

"I feel the same way, but like I told you, I'm not running the show. The warden says wait."

A disgusted look appeared on both Bergen's and Cochrane's faces. Miller continued, "The boys in the east gallery can see everything at that end and in all of the aisles. There hasn't been anything moving in there since Cochenour fired at Coy and missed. Those damned old World War I brass shotgun shells we're using must be defective."

"If Cochenour missed Coy at that range, defective ammunition must be the reason. Better dump those brass shells, Ed, and replace them with loads that go where you point them."

"We will. A gun that don't hit what you aim at is worse than useless. Now if you guys are ready, the warden wants you to do a little spying. He wants information on what is going on in the west end of the cellhouse. You can look through the windows that open on the west end."

"Anything is better than sitting here doing nothing," said Cochrane.

Bergen agreed although he wasn't enthusiastic about an assignment that offered a maximum of risk and a minimum of strategic value. To get to the windows which were 24 feet above the level of the roadway alongside the building, the two officers would have to locate a ladder and place it against the side of the building in an area that was an open line of fire from the cellhouse.

After checking their pistols once more, the two men snapped the safeties on, jammed the weapons firmly into the holsters belted around their waists, and closed the button-down safety flaps.

Officer Joe Pascal cautioned them as they passed his post in a sheltered corner guarding one of the basement sallyports, "Careful, Lieutenant. They've been firing through those windows up there. We've been keeping out of sight waiting for a chance to hit one of them, but they stay back away from the windows when they shoot. But we haven't been shot at lately."

"Joe," said Bergen jokingly, "the warden thinks maybe you sharpshooters killed them all, and he wants us to take a body count. Keep us covered while we count them."

Pascal laughed, then watched in disbelief as Bergen looked for the fire ladder he knew was located with a number of red-painted fire buckets and a reel of firehose in the area. When the ladder was found, Cochrane and Bergen dashed across the roadway and lifted it into position below a carefully selected window.

"Those guys are nuts," said Pascal to a nearby officer. "They'll probably get shot off that ladder before they get half way up to the window."

"No they won't," said the other officer. "You and me'd get shot, but not those two. Lady Luck rides on their shoulders."

"Yeah, Cochrane would go out of his way to get into a scrap. He sure is hard nose, alright. He's a natural born fighter."

"But that Bergen's different. He's a glory hunter. Look at him go up that damned ladder. He knows that'll impress the warden."

"I don't see the warden out here being impressed."

"Oh, he'll hear about it."

With Cochrane steadying the long ladder, Bergen climbed to the top rung and squinted into the cellhouse. In marked contrast to the bright daylight which bathed the exterior of the building, the interior was dim and hazy. An unpleasant, eye-irritating cloud of tear gas hung in the aisles and mingled with the sharp odor of burned cordite. Bergen drew his pistol and snapped off the safety. As his eyes slowly adjusted to the interior light, he saw that the entire area was empty.

"See anything, Phil?" asked Cochrane.

"Not a damned thing. No people. No bodies. Nothing."

"Well, then, come on down. Let's get out of here. We're a couple of clay pigeons."

Bergen didn't hesitate. Holstering his pistol, he slid down the ladder. "Harry," he said. "That sure was a waste of time. I hope the old man doesn't get any more bright ideas like that one. Now what'll we do with the ladder?"

"Leave it where it is. The warden will probably send us back to take another look before long."

"Hey, you guys," shouted Pascal. "Was it worth looking at?"

The two officers dashed back across the roadway and Bergen laughed, "Nobody moving around in there, Joe. Either you guys finished them off, or they've crawled back into their holes."

As they made their way back to the office, Cochrane asked, "Do you think they'll give us the go ahead now?"

"No, we're going to have to wait for the Marines."

"What the hell can those sea-going soldiers do here that we can't do better?"

"Harry, we don't call the shots. We only get to deliver them."

By the time they arrived at Miller's office, several officers had assembled in the waiting room. Bergen and Cochrane exchanged pleased glances. It looked like the action might start.

Miller asked, "See anything in there?"

"Not a thing, Ed," Bergen replied. "It's dark in there and full of tear gas, but there wasn't anybody in that end of the cellhouse. The D-block door and the dining room gate were open, but the gate to the basement was closed. Oh, yes. The C-block utility corridor door was wide open."

Cochrane pleaded with Miller, "Ed, go ask the warden if we can go in now. We're just wasting time out here."

While Miller went to talk with the warden, Cochrane, Fish, and Bergen discussed a tentative plan of action.

"Phil, when we go through the gate, should we split or stay together?"

"I'd say stay together, Harry, unless the boss has other ideas. The other guys can have Broadway and the A-B aisle. We can go down the C-D aisle, stay under the overhang, and cover each other as we check each cell. If we find them in the library, we can end this thing in a hurry. If they aren't there, we'll just keep looking until we find them, or they find us."

Turning to Fish, Bergen asked, "What are they doing about picking up the evening shift officers? Have they sent the Johnston over?"

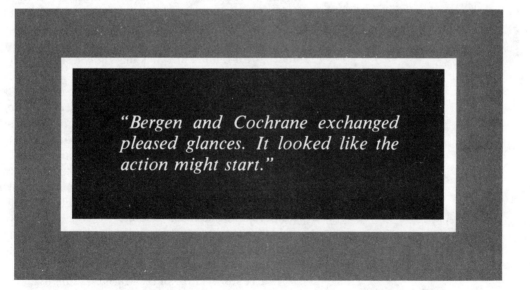

"Bergen and Cochrane exchanged pleased glances. It looked like the action might start."

ALCATRAZ '46

"No. The Johnston is still circling the island. Have you seen the fleet out there? Some of the boys have been checking it with field glasses. Just about all the water taxies and rubberneck cruisers on the waterfront are there. Reporters, cameramen, radio commentators. They all want to come ashore. The Johnston is keeping them herded away outside the 200-yard buoys."

"Those characters better stay out further than that. If Coy turns his rifle on them, they'll wish they were a mile away."

"That's what the men on the Johnston are telling them, but they don't seem to believe that a rifle can reach them. Some have even come up to the dock. Rychner is having a hell of a time keeping them off. If it weren't for Comerford in the tower with his machine gun, they'd be swarming all over the place."

Bergen sat down at the captain's desk. "Harry, I'm going to phone my apartment. I promised the women I'd call them."

After placing the call, Bergen sat down next to Cochrane. With a surprised look on his face, Cochrane nudged Bergen in the ribs and pointed toward the armory. "Look, Phil, that damned Anthony is here in uniform. Looks like he is trying to get a gun. That's all we need to even the odds, a drunk running around here with a gun."

Bergen jumped to his feet and strode to the armory issue window where Fish was trying to persuade Anthony to leave without the firearm he was demanding. Fish saw Bergen and awaited the inevitable explosion, because the lieutenant was notably intolerant of drunks. Drinking or drunkenness on duty was an unpardonable offense in any prison.

"Norman, you're drunker now than when we left you on the dock. By God, you'd better not have any booze on you," said Bergen, searching the protesting officer. No bottle was found.

"I don't know how the hell you got away from the dock lieutenant, but now that you're here, haul your drunken ass into the waiting room and stay there." Turning to the armory officer, Bergen ordered, "Cliff, don't arm this man under any circumstances."

"He won't get any weapons from me, lieutenant."

Bergen returned to the captain's desk where he could observe Anthony through the glass wall in the officer's waiting room.

* * *

For the waiting officers, time seemed to move slowly. The Johnston continued to move in and out among the increasing number of bobbing vessels on the windward side of the island. A light, westerly breeze had sprung up, and many of the people on the vessels were developing stomach trouble.

"Look at that time," grumbled Cochrane glancing angrily at the office clock. "It's nearly 5:00 p.m., and we're still sitting here. How much longer is this going to drag on?"

"We're still waiting for the Marines, I suppose. Look. That idiot, Anthony, is on the loose again. This time he's got a rifle."

Cochrane jumped up and stared out the window. On the tiny lawn Anthony slowly paced back and forth with a .30-06 on his shoulder. Racing out of the office, Cochrane and Bergen disarmed the man and marched him to the armory. Fish stared in open-mouth amazement as the lieutenant thrust the rifle, butt first, through the issue window and growled, "Dammit, Cliff. Didn't I tell you not to arm this drunk?"

"He didn't get that rifle from me," said Fish, turning to the communications officer. "Did you arm this clown?"

"No."

"Well, somebody did and . . ."

An officer rushed in from the waiting room. He was excited and angry. "That's my rifle, lieutenant," he boomed. "This drunk sneaked off with it when I wasn't looking."

Disgusted, Bergen recovered the weapon from Fish and handed it to the angry officer. "Here, hang on to it," said Bergen, his eyes narrowing upon the officer. "I know this drunk is stupid, but what's your excuse for losing your rifle?"

The communications officer interrupted, "Lieutenant, the Marines are here. They'll be on the yard wall in a few minutes."

"It's about time. Harry, lock this bum in the clerk's office so he'll be out of our hair for a while."

"There's no locks on those doors, Phil. Let's have one of the clerks watch him."

Bergen detailed one of the unarmed clerks to guard Anthony.

"Lieutenant," called Fish. "The associate warden wants you and Harry in his office, right away."

Miller greeted the two men with a grin and said, "As soon as the Marines are on the wall, we're going in, but there's been a change in plans. The warden wants the west gallery secured before he sends men into the cellhouse. We've made up two teams. The three of us are going as a team into the west gun gallery. Lieutenant Johnson and some other officers will cover us. As soon as we occupy the gallery and have the west end under control, Faulk will take the other team through the main gate. The warden figures it'll be safer to hunt for the captives if we first control both ends of the cellhouse."

"You want me to say something or just agree with you?" asked Bergen.

"If you have something to say, spit it out." retorted Miller.

"I know the warden is the boss, and I'm ready to do it his way, but I think we're just wasting more time. We should take the cellhouse now. Hell, if he wanted the west galley manned, we could have done that over an hour ago. It should have been done right after you manned the east gallery."

Cochrane nodded in agreement.

"Another thing, Ed," continued Bergen. "If you go into the gun gallery with us, who will be left out here to run things? You belong out here to select the men, the right men, for the jobs and to see that the jobs get done."

"It's a cinch we're going to draw fire when we open that gun gallery door," said Cochrane. "If you are hit or get pinned down in there, we'll be in real trouble."

"Let's make a deal," suggested Bergen. "Harry and I will take the gallery while you stay outside and cover us. If we get knocked off, send in the reserves. But stay the hell out of there yourself . . . unless you don't have confidence in us."

"Of course I have confidence in you. The warden selected you guys himself," said Miller. He thought about the proposal, then said, "O.K., I'll detail a few more guns to support you. How about Harold Stites, Herschel Oldham, and Fred Mahan. What do you think of them?"

"They're the best, Ed, but they've got families."

155

ALCATRAZ '46

"They would never let us bypass them for that reason. It's the safety and welfare of their families they're fighting for," said Miller. "Let's round them up and add a few other officers. Your team will go in the minute the Marines are properly posted on the yard wall."

Fish opened the armory issue window and handed the gun gallery entrance keys to the associate warden. Looking at Cochrane and Bergen, he said, "Jesse and I would like to go in with you, but the boss says no. Good luck, you guys. Be careful, and remember that the gallery walls are not bulletproof. Those .30-06 bullets can bore right through the steel without slowing down very much."

The eight-man assault team, led by Associate Warden Miller, gathered its weapons and hurried across the plaza to the south side of the building. As the men passed the waiting room, several officers, who had been told to stand by for an imminent assault on the cellhouse, crowded into the doorway to watch. Very little was said. Each man was preoccupied with thoughts of the potential gun battle. As they watched, no one noticed that Anthony had quietly vanished, but one officer, pallid and worried, frantically searched for the rifle he had left in a corner of the waiting room.

* * *

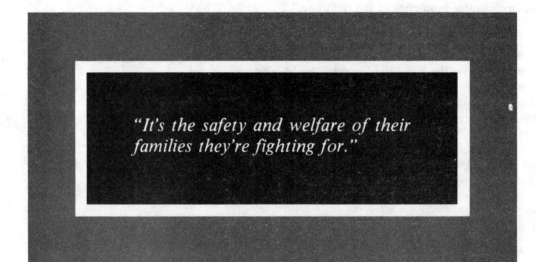

"It's the safety and welfare of their families they're fighting for."

Soon after the first assault team departed, Fish telephoned the tower and yard wall officers. "The associate warden and several armed officers are on their way to the west gun gallery along the south wall. Hold your fire. I repeat. Hold your fire," he warned. "Pass the word to all officers below you on the hillside. All firing must stop. Officers are moving along the wall to the west gallery entrance."

The word was quickly passed from one man to another. The officers who had been firing into the cellhouse through the windows, rested on their weapons to watch the assault team work its way along the catwalk and around the corner of the building. Norman Anthony, armed with a rifle, crawled slowly through the shrubbery, 50 yards east of the Road Tower. Intent on keeping away from the other officers, he found a suitable firing position on the hillside, but he did not hear the cease fire order.

Staying close to the wall of the building, the heavily armed men of the assault team moved quietly along the catwalk. To their left in the small boats on the bay, spectators and reporters aimed telescopes and cameras at them. To the reporters, it seemed the warden had finally deployed his officers for the long-awaited assault on the fortress prison.

Inside the prison, Coy moved swiftly from cell to cell along the top tier of D-block. He was unable to detect the hidden officers on the hillside below, but as he neared the west end where Cretzer and Hubbard were waiting, he could hear the clamor from the penned up inmates in the recreation yard.

"Sounds like the screws are herding all the cons from the work area into the yard, doesn't it?" observed Hubbard.

"Yeah, it figures they'd do that," said Coy rubbing his chin. "They'll have to have a bunch of screws in the yard with them."

"Won't be no place for those screws to hide," said Cretzer. "Maybe we can plug 'em from the dinin' room windows. My .45 would be all right there."

"Hey, listen," interrupted Hubbard. "Sounds like a bunch of screws out there on the catwalk. I bet they're going to bust in through the west gun cage."

"You're right," said Coy, smiling. "I can hear them sneaking along out there. We'll kill every screw that tries to come through that door."

"I'm with you," said Cretzer. "Let's get down on the flats and ambush 'em. We could clobber 'em easy from the alley behind this block or maybe from the end of C-block."

Coy said, "I think we better get into the main cellhouse. Too much chance of getting trapped in here. Out there, we got a hundred ways to go."

* * *

The entrance to the west gun gallery was located in the west wall of the cellhouse, approximately 30 feet north of the southwest corner. Grouped round the double-door entrance, the members of the assault team were exposed to possible gunfire from the nearby dining room windows. Although they could not see into the dimly lit room behind the windows, the men knew they were clearly visible in the evening sunlight. Aware of the hazard, Associate Warden Miller ordered two officers to cover the window area with their machine guns and to open fire on any inmate who approached a window with a firearm.

157

ALCATRAZ '46

Exterior entrance to the west gun gallery. Through this doorway Lieutenant Bergen and five-man assault team entered at about 5 p.m. on May 2nd.

Forty yards to the west, and forty feet below, nearly 200 excited inmates moved restlessly and noisily about the crowded recreation yard. On the yard wall, the small Marine contingent and several prison officers maintained a grim semi-circle of armament around them. In the yard with the excited inmates were Officers Amende, Henry, Manry, and Orr under the supervision of Senior Officer Walter Hansen.

Most of the inmates in the yard were men who were earnestly trying to work their way back to a less restrictive institution. But intermingled with them were the much less tractable men who were released to the yard for their daily recreation period at 1:15 p.m. These men were considered to be possible escape risks. Many were trouble makers who were always ready for open rebellion. If Coy, Cretzer, Hubbard, and the others had reached the yard with a ladder and guns, many of these men would have joined the bid for freedom.

Scattered throughout the crowd and becoming relatively face-less among the more tractable inmates, the trouble makers stimulated a continuous jeering, cursing clamor directed at the grim-faced Marines and prison officers. Only the machine guns on the wall and in the surrounding gun towers kept the crowd under control as they watched the armed assault team prepare to storm into the west gun gallery.

Bergen, Cochrane, and Stites were poised and ready when Miller unlocked the outer door. Lieutenant Frank Johnson, Fred Mahan, Herschel Oldham, Alvin Bloomquist, Joe Maxwell, and Fred Richberger lined up behind them as reserves. Miller, who had reluctantly agreed to remain outside, posted them so they could support the three-man team and stop any would-be escapees who might try to blast out when the doors were opened.

Unlocking the outer grille gate enabled Miller and the team to reach the solid steel inner door. Although there was a small vision panel in the inner door, it was not safe to utilize. The team would have to go in blind and expose themselves to gunfire from the inmates who could be anywhere inside.

"Before you enter," advised Miller, "one thing you guys better remember. Coy was wearing an officer's uniform when he shot at me. The other cons are probably in officer's clothing, too. They might even put convict clothes on our men. Don't make any mistakes and shoot our own officers."

When the large steel door swung open, the three men plunged into the rectangular section of concrete, steel, and tool-resistant bars which formed the ground level of the west gallery. Stites moved to the left and Bergen and Cochrane moved to the right to avoid being silhouetted in the doorway. The men listened, motionless. The interior was silent.

As their eyes adjusted to the darkness, the officers scanned the D-block area from the wide open, main cellhouse entrance door to the wide aisle between the block and the south wall. To their left, the D-block door was open enough to allow a tightly restricted view of the southwest corner of C-block. Directly ahead, mounted on the endwall of D-block, was the wide open control box. To the left of the box, under the middle tier walkway, was the partially open door to the D-block utility corridor. To the right, near the corner where the barred gallery front angled along the south wall of the cellhouse, the officer's desk was a disorderly mess. Drawers and their contents, record books, papers, pens, pencils, and paperclips were scattered about. The polished concrete floor was littered with shattered window glass, empty cartridge brass, and more than a dozen burned-out tear gas cannisters. A thin, unpleasant haze of eye-watering gas lingered in the air.

Cochrane and Bergen headed toward the south wall where the flight of narrow steel stairs led to the middle level of the gallery. From the base of the stairs, they could see most of the long, triple-tiered face of D-block. Many of the cell doors on the two upper tiers were open, but no inmate or captive officer could be seen. The openfront cells on the flats were closed and presumably locked. The outer doors of the six solitary confinement cells were open.

Bergen whispered, "The guns are in here somewhere. Coy and the other bastards could be holed up in any of those cells."

"Then why aren't they shooting at us?" asked Cochrane. "I'll bet the tear gas ran them out of here. They're probably in the big cell-house."

"Stites is covering that area through the doorway with his Thompson. Wonder if he can see anything?"

"I can't see anyone," whispered Stites. "I don't like this. It's too damn quiet."

* * *

"*The guns are in here somewhere. Coy and the other bastards could be holed up in any one of those cells.*"

ALCATRAZ '46

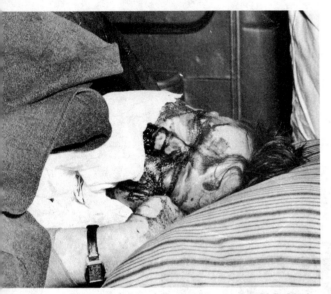

Dramatic photo of Corwin en-route to U.S. Marine Hospital in the Presidio. Notice his wrist watch, indicating 12:10 a.m.

Beyond the D-block entrance door, Coy and Cretzer hid in the shadows near the west end of C-block. As the two inmates readied their weapons, Coy smiled, "They'll have the daylight at their backs, and it's so dark in here they won't even see us."

Through the partly opened D-block door, the convicts saw the grey-uniformed officers moving quickly across the beam of sunlight coming through the gun cage entrance. Waiting until the officers were clearly in their gun sights, each inmate fired one carefully-aimed shot. Simultaneously, the guns of the assault team roared, and a barrage of bullets swept across the west end of D-block. The immediate area filled with gunsmoke and the acrid fumes of burned cordite. Sub-machine guns, shotguns, rifles, and pistols thundered incessantly. Tracers illuminated the darkness with streaks of light. A seemingly endless cacophony of explosions echoed and reechoed from the walls and ceiling as bullets whined, smashed, and ricochetted off unyielding steel and concrete. The intolerable din and smoke made it impossible to tell the directions from which shots were coming.

Bergen gasped, "Harry, I can't see a damned thing to shoot at, can you?"

"No. And I can't see who's shooting at us. Nobody showed at any of those cellfronts. Maybe we'd better get upstairs. We're sitting ducks down here, and the air is getting too foul to breathe."

"Hey, Stites," Bergen shouted. "Let's move upstairs. We're doing no good here."

The three officers moved toward the stairs as the thunder of gunfire continued to envelope them. Glancing back, Bergen saw several officers crowded in the gun cage doorway firing aimlessly into D-block.

"For Cri-sakes, don't shoot wild like that," yelled Bergen, but no one heard him over the deafening sounds.

The barrage surprised and frightened the ambushers. Coy hadn't expected to face so many guns at once. Before they fled, they fired two more hastily aimed shots at the officers in the gun cage.

Cochrane suddenly veered away from the stairs. Bergen reached out to guide him, and his hand came away from the officer's shoulder, wet with blood. Cochrane's bullet-shattered arm hung uselessly at his side.

"Harry, you're hit."

"Caught one in my arm. It ain't bad. Let's get upstairs."

"Upstairs, hell. You're getting out of there before you bleed to death."

* * *

In the darkness of the main cellhouse, Coy shouted to Cretzer, "Goddammit, Joe. We can't stop them. I think we hit some of them, but the dumb finks just keep coming. Some ran to the stairway. They got out of sight before I could lay my sights on them. These damned old bolt-action army rifles ain't no good for fast shooting."

"We need a spot where we can see them before they see us, Bernie. How about the hospital or maybe the kitchen?"

Hubbard, who had been standing near the utility corridor door, said, "Duck in here, you guys. We can hide behind this thick steel door and knock them off when they come through the door in the gun cage wall."

"Good idea," said Cretzer. "We got all our stuff from the gun cage stashed in there — flashlights, clubs, gas-bombs, gasmasks, everythin'."

The three inmates entered the C-block utility corridor and pulled the entrance door almost closed. It was dark in the long, narrow alleyway except for the thin line of light through the slightly open door. Coy and Cretzer, with guns ready, pressed against the opening to watch the padded door in the middle level of the gun gallery.

* * *

Police vehicles rushed heavily armed, San Francisco policemen to vantage points on docks and boat landings. Fisherman's Wharf, the Marina Yacht Harbor, and the ferry slips north of Telegraph Hill were strategically staked out against an invasion of Alcatraz inmates.

At first, only a handful of fishermen and picnickers showed interest in the unfolding drama, but as radio broadcasters filled the airwaves with exaggerated accounts of the event, a sizeable number of people gathered at various viewpoints. The island's women, children, and evening shift officers assembled at the dock to await the 3:35 p.m. launch. Informed of the battle and concerned for the safety of friends and loved ones on the island, they crowded against the creosote-soaked pilings and strained to see and hear the action across the water.

Sightseers watching Alcatraz from a good vantage point.

ALCATRAZ '46

When 3:35 p.m. passed, it became obvious to the waiting officers that the prison launch would not abandon its island circling assignment to pick them up. Using the dock telephone, one of the men contacted the prison armory, then reported to the others at the launch gangway.

"I talked to Fish," he said. "We are to wait here until they can send for us. The women and children will have to stay in town. Fish says it's getting rougher all the time. They're afraid the prisoners might try to blastout of the cellhouse at any minute. They're going to keep the launch on patrol to stop them if they get as far as the water and try to swim for it."

"Did Mr. Fish say anything about anybody being hurt?" asked Mrs. Cochrane.

"Nothing was said about casualties, but he did say that bullets were flying all over the place."

* * *

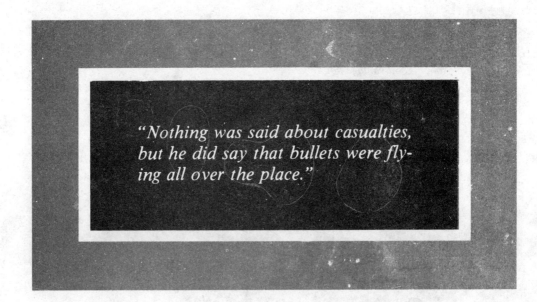

"Nothing was said about casualties, but he did say that bullets were flying all over the place."

The Third Day of Riot

'THE BLASTED ROCK'

Behind these battered walls of Alcatraz, its barred windows shattered by two days of pounding by rifle grenades, one of which is shown exploding in the large circle on the right, rioting convicts were still holding out against combat Marines and prison guards this morning. In the circle at the left is a Marine firing squad, one of the many which has been pumping hot lead into the citadel since Thursday afternoon. —Associated Press Photo.

TO 'ROCK'

Four doctors from the Marine Hospital in San Francisco are shown near government dock at the foot of Van Ness avenue before they went aboard boat for Alcatraz Island. Left to right: Doctors John S. Haines, Albert Myatt, Romaine Trainor and Kemp Dowdy. —Call-Bulletin Photograph.

BATTERED WALL

This close-up shot shows the shell-pocked wall of Alcatraz in the immediate area of Cell Block C, where the convicts are making their last stand today. —Call-Bulletin Photograph.

REINFORCEMENTS ARRIVE

Flown here from government prisons at Leavenworth and McNeil's Island, these men are prison guards arriving at the government dock at the foot of Van Ness avenue to reinforce Alcatraz guards and Marines who have been battling the besieged prisoners on "The Rock" since late Thursday afternoon. —Call-Bulletin Photograph.

FEDERAL PRISONS CHIEF

James V. Bennett, director of federal prisons, checks his tickets before taking off by plane from Washington last night for San Francisco to aid in quelling and later investigate revolt at Alcatraz federal prison. He was to arrive at airport here this morning. —Associated Press Wirephoto.

MARINE MAJOR TELLS STORY

Marine Major Albert Arsenault uses Call-Bulletin to illustrate his description of battle of Alcatraz when he returned from the Island.

THE PRESS GOT THIS CLOSE TO THE 'BIG STORY'

Newspapermen and photographers are shown on landing boat that brought them to dock at northeast end of Alcatraz yesterday. Part of prison wall can be seen at top of hill on left. This is as close as the men were allowed to approach the island "to cover" the story of one of the worst convict uprisings in United States penal history. —Call-Bulletin Photograph.

The May 4th Issue of the San Francisco Call Bulletin describes the action at Alcatraz.

ALCATRAZ '46

Bergen shoved Cochrane toward the entrance doorway and again shouted for the officers to stop firing. When the shooting stopped, several officers helped lead Cochrane into the sunlight. The seriousness of the wound was obvious, so he was immediately escorted to the administrative office where a first aid station had been hastily established. Fred Richberger, hit in the leg at almost the same time, hobbled along the catwalk with him.

Inside, the west end of D-block was laced with choking smoke. Officers and escapees were holding their fire. Mahan and Oldham cautiously followed Bergen and Stites up the narrow stairs to the middle level of the gallery. At this level, the air was breathable, and the waist high steel of the gallery front offered some protection.

The window sills in the south and west walls of D-block were approximately 10 feet above the cellhouse floor. Along the west wall and for 20 feet along the south wall where the west gun gallery clung to the cellhouse walls, the window sills touched the metal deck of the gallery's middle level. This construction was one reason for the semi-darkness in the entrance area. The upper decks, however, were almost as brilliantly sunlighted as the catwalks on the other side of the walls. Anyone in the gallery who came close to the windows was easily visible to the officers outside the building.

* * *

Armed with a rifle and stubbornly determined to aid in the defense of the island, Anthony found a comfortable firing position on the rocky slope below and to the south of the prison building. He had listened to the gunfire inside D-block and had watched intently as the assault team and its support group hurried along the catwalk to the gun gallery entrance. When he saw Cochrane and Richberger led away, he became more resolved to join the battle. He was sure he had seen Coy and the others behind the cellhouse windows. Staring intently at the windows, he rested his rifle on a convenient rock and waited.

In the gun gallery, where the head of the stairs reached the middle level deck, was an L-shaped junction. Stites and Oldham rushed along the leg of the L that extended across the south wall windows. Bergen and Mahan hurried around the corner of the stairwell and moved toward the padded door between D-block and the main cellhouse. All four officers crouched against the steel wall and squinted over its top edge. From here they had an unobstructed view of the cells on the middle and top tiers of the block. Nothing moved in the vicinity of the cellfronts or on the tiers.

On signal, the men of the support group again provided a covering fire into D-block from the gallery entrance. Assuming that the assault team would move into the main cellhouse section of the gallery during the covering fire, Stites, in a half crouching stance, inched around the corner of the L-shaped junction toward Mahan and Bergen. As he squeezed through the narrow space between the stairs and the gallery face, he was silhouetted for a moment in the sunlit window. A single shot, indistinguishable in the thunderous roar of cover fire, hit Stites. The officer suddenly straightened up, dropped his Thompson, and made a futile gesture to his companions. He slumped to the floor upon his unfired weapon.

Bergen and Mahan crawled to where he had fallen in the constricted passageway. Stites was unconscious and bleeding profusely.

Mahan leaned into the stairwell and called for help.

The two officers freed Stites from the tight passageway and started him, feet first, down the narrow steel stairs. Realizing how difficult it was for them to handle Stites, Oldham left his position near the control box and crawled forward to assist. When he stood up to move past the window, a bullet smashed into his arm, spinning him around against the face of the gallery.

"My arm!" he cried.

"Stay low, Herschel," yelled Bergen. "Stay down and crawl over here if you can. That gun must be high up on the top tier of the block. I didn't hear the shot, did you Fred?"

"No. Too damn much noise below."

"Maybe Coy rigged up some sort of silencer. We can't see or hear him, but he's still knocking us off, right and left."

Officers Maxwell and Bloomquist, who had been sent to replace Cochrane and Richberger, climbed the stairs and carried the unconscious Stites from the area. Gritting his teeth to conceal the pain in his shattered arm, Oldham refused assistance and walked to the exterior catwalk on his own. He and Stites were rushed to the improvised medical unit in the administration office. Oldham's wound received prompt attention. With a rifle bullet in his kidney, Stites was dead on arrival.

* * *

Officer Harold B. Stites was liked by fellow officers, and he was judged to be more courageous than most. His courage had served him well during an attempted escape by three inmates in 1938.

Stites was on duty in the Model Tower when James 'Toughy' Lucas, Rufus 'Whitey' Franklin, and Tom Limerick battered their work detail officer to death with a hammer. The three men, armed with hammers and heavy iron bolts, then approached the Model Tower. As Limerick lead the attack, Stites calmly drew his pistol and fired through the shatterproof glass of the tower wall. The bullet crashed into Limerick's forehead, slamming him back into the maze of barbed wire surrounding the tower. Franklin raced toward the tower with a heavy sledge hammer, presumably the one with which he had beaten the shop officer to death a few minutes earlier, and reached the shatterproof glass wall before Stites saw him. Again the .45 roared. Its heavy, copper-jacketed bullet caught Franklin in the left shoulder, knocking him off the tower catwalk. Almost instantly, the berserk killer recovered and scrambled back to smash at the tower with his hammer. Stites fired again, hitting Franklin in the right shoulder. This time, the inmate cowered helplessly in the wire.

Meanwhile, Lucas had circled to attack from the south side. He reached the tower door undetected and tried to wrench it open. Stites whirled and fired a hastily aimed shot. He missed, but Lucas saw the muzzle of the .45 and the blood-spattered bodies of his pals sprawled out in the wire and decided to give up. He dropped to the roof below the tower and rolled under a wooden ramp. He was cowering there when a shotgun carrying patrolman raced across the roof to cover him. Harold Stites had stopped one of the most desperate escape attempts in Alcatraz history.

Following the event, Stites testified, "Limerick? Well, I took my .45, and I took aim, and I fired a shot at him. I got him over the right eye. He dropped and never moved again. I had to use two shots to

Officer Harold P. Stites was apparently accidentally shot through the kidneys by one of his fellow officers during the first assault on the west gun gallery.

165

ALCATRAZ '46

stop Franklin. He really wanted to bust into my tower with that hammer. Lucas? I fired a warning shot through the tower door, and he quit cold."

The event left a lingering mark on Stites. Fellow officers noted that he began to travel different routes to and from his apartment, day or night. He took care to never leave his back unprotected. He confided to friends that he thought all Alcatrz convicts were continually scheming to get him.

In an interview, his brother-in-law, D. O. Epue of Vallejo, recalled, "Harold was always waiting for the possibility of an ambush, a withering burst of deadly fire from a convict who might slip from regular duties and wait to kill. The inmates have nothing to think about except revenge. Harold never talked much, but he did say that he would never take a man's life when it wasn't necessary. He could have killed both Franklin and Lucas that time in 1938, but he didn't."

One of the most difficult tasks Warden Johnston ever had to do, was inform Stites' wife and children of his death.

* * *

U.S. Attorney General Tom Clark presents Mrs. Harold Stites with a plaque commemorating her husband's performance.

On the slopes below the prison building, Norman Anthony stared into the empty receiver of his weapon. He had fired five rounds. Rising to his feet, he shouldered the empty rifle and stumbled uphill along the narrow single lane road to the administration building.

"Gotta get more bullets," he mumbled. "Damn gun's no good without bullets."

When he reached the officer's waiting room, he looked for unguarded bandoliers of ammunition, but there were none. While he quietly wandered around the office area, Lieutenant Martin Klein emerged from the warden's office and beckoned to several officers who were awaiting instructions.

"We're going on the roof," said Klein. "The warden thinks we can keep an eye on the cons in the yard from up there, just in case they get any wild ideas about tackling those Marines on the wall."

Unobtrusively, Anthony joined the group. The men passed through the main gate and up several flights of stairs to the roof where Harry Manderville was stationed in the Main Tower. Klein posted the officers at vantage points behind the parapet overlooking the recreation yard and returned to the warden's office. Within a few minutes, Anthony had borrowed several five-round clips of .30-06 ammunition and reposted himself in a sheltered spot on the hospital portion of the roof. From here he could not only watch the inmates milling about the yard but could see the activities at the entrance to the west gun gallery within the building.

* * *

All guns were silent. Bergen and Mahan were alone in the gallery.

From the catwalk at the entrance gate, Miller shouted to them, "We'll have more men up there in a few minutes. Can you guys hang on for a while?"

"Don't worry about us, Ed," Bergen replied.

"Maybe we can stir the bastards up a little with a few bursts from Stites' Thompson," suggested Mahan grinning at Bergen.

"Not yet. We don't want to let them know we've got a machine gun up here. If you crawl over to the corner and cover me with the Thompson, I'll fire a few tracers along the tiers. Watch the cell fronts for Coy. If you see him, then use the Thompson."

Mahan holstered his .45 and armed himself with Stites' machine gun. He slung the canvas sack with its 20-round clips of ammunition over his shoulder.

Bergen eased his .45 through the bars and sent seven quick shots down the tier walkway. There was no reaction along the cell fronts.

"Cover me, Fred," said the lieutenant. "I'm going to use that telephone on the wall."

The gun gallery telephone was mounted shoulder-high on the west wall. Bergen reached it in one swift move and dropped the receiver from its cradle. It dangled a few inches above the floor. Because the dialing mechanism was still in the open, Bergen picked up the handset close to the floor and listened.

"If there's no answer, they're probably taking a coffee break," quipped Mahan.

"They'll answer as soon as someone notices the gallery number

ALCATRAZ '46

"We're going to leave this telephone off the hook. It's too risky to stand up and talk, so keep your line open and just whistle if you want us."

light up on the board. When they answer, I'll order mine hot and black. How about you?"

"Tell them I prefer to take mine in the officer's waiting room. It has a more congenial atmosphere."

"There sure ain't anything congenial in this rat trap."

The telephone receiver suddenly buzzed. A voice asked, "Burch, is that you?"

"No. It's Lieutenant Bergen. Is that you, Washington?"

"Yes, sir."

"Fred Mahan and I are in the west gallery on the D-block side. No one has fired at us for nearly five minutes. Tell the warden I'm going to find out what happened to Burch. Mahan will stay here near the phone."

"Hold on, I'll tell the warden."

In a few minutes, Washington returned and said, "O.K., lieutenant. The warden says to go look for Burch. Be careful, but try to locate the captive officers if you can."

"I'll try. Now listen. We're going to leave this telephone off the hook. It's too risky to stand up to talk, so keep your line open and just whistle if you want us. We'll do the same when we have something to report."

Leaving the phone, Bergen loaded a fresh clip into his pistol and headed toward the sound-resistant door which opened into the main cellhouse.

* * *

International News Photo depicting a dramatic sequence during the action.

In the C-block utility corridor, the three escapees watched and waited. Using a cigarette lighter for illumination, Hubbard took stock of the materials on hand.

"Bernie, we got everything here but the keys. We left them on the floor near the yard gate."

"I still got the D-block keys," smiled Cretzer.

Coy felt in the pockets of the uniform jacket he was wearing. "Hell, I got all the keys we'll need right here."

Cretzer wondered, "What's the matter with those fucking screws? It's been quiet for quite a while. What do you suppose they're up to?"

"Take it easy, Joe. They're just playing it smart, not showing themselves," said Coy.

As they watched the door to the gallery, it quickly opened and closed, but they saw no one to shoot at and no one shot at them.

"They're trying to sucker us into shooting so's they can find out where we are," said Hubbard.

"You're probably right," said Coy. "I could shoot right through that tin wall up there, but then they'd know where we are. Well, we'll outsmart them. No more shooting for a spell."

* * *

Inside the main cellhouse section of the gallery, Bergen was enveloped in darkness.

"Wish I had a flashlight," he thought, then told himself, "No, if I had one, I wouldn't dare use it. Coy would zero-in on the light."

Even though his eyes adjusted to the darkness, he could barely make out the general configurations of the long, narrow walkway. Pistol in hand, he inched forward, moving slowly on his elbows and thighs. His eyes strained to see what, if anything, lay in his path. About 10 feet into the gallery's darkness, his elbow contacted an obstacle. Holding the pistol in his right hand, he felt the obstacle with his left and realized a cold body was stretched out before him on the steel deck.

"Who . . . who is it?" asked a faint but familiar voice.

"It's me, Phil Bergen, Bert. What the hell happened to you?"

Bergen pointed the muzzle of his pistol away from his friend, but kept it ready. Burch's rigid limbs relaxed slightly.

"I don't really know what happened, Phil. I came in here from D. Something hit me and knocked me down. I was fighting with someone. I guess I got knocked out. When I came to, I was here on the deck, like this."

"Was it Coy?"

"Yes. I think it was. I remember seeing his face after he jumped me. He was naked. Covered with grease. He was here in the gallery, but I don't know how he could get in here."

"We don't know either, Bert, but we'll find out. You don't suppose he's still in here, do you? Some son-of-a-bitch has been shooting at us, but we can't figure out where the shots come from."

"I'm not sure about anything, Phil. He might still be here. Maybe on the top deck. He must have come in that way."

"Do you have any idea where Bill Miller is? He's missing. A lot of other guys are missing, too — Weinhold, Simpson, Baker, Sundstrom, several others."

"Phil, I must have been out cold for a long time. I haven't seen anybody except Joe Cretzer and some other inmates down there at the end of C-block. I didn't get a good look at any of them except Joe. He shot at me, and I've been laying here, playing dead ever since."

"Pretty cold on that steel deck, isn't it?"

"Yeah, but not as cold as being on a slab in the morgue."

"Coy must have wanted your uniform."

"Yeah. He took almost everything, even my cigarettes. Give me a cigarette, will you Phil?"

"Sorry, Bert. You know I don't smoke."

"Dammit, I forgot. Here I've been waiting for hours for someone to come in and rescue me, and when he gets here, it has to be the one man in the joint who doesn't smoke."

"Cheer up. Mahan is in D. He'll fix you up with a smoke. Do you think you can make it over there all right?"

"I think so. I got a lot of bumps and bruises, but no broken bones that I know of."

"O.K. Be as quiet as possible, and don't stand up. We'll crawl back into D."

When they reached the D-block side of the gallery, the two officers sagged against the wall and waited for their eyes to adjust to the sunlit area.

"Who the hell is that beatup bathing beauty you got with you, lieutenant?" asked Mahan in mock seriousness. "Is it alive, or do I see a ghost?"

"He's alive, but just barely," replied Bergen as he unbuttoned his uniform jacket. "Put this on, Bert. It's too big, but it'll keep you warm. With all the broken windows in here, it's pretty breezy."

"And here's a .45 to help warm you up," added Mahan as Burch slipped into the jacket. "You shouldn't be going around naked and empty handed like that. You'll catch something."

"It's Coy that I want to catch."

"Well, stick around," Bergen said. "We'll flush him out sooner or later."

"Maybe you shouldn't stay up here, Bert," said Mahan. "You've been beatup, and you're probably cold and hungry."

"I want to stay. I'll never get a better chance to fix that damn Coy. Just tell somebody to send me some clothes. All I need is a pair of pants and my shoes."

"Fred," said Bergen, "I know just how he feels. Let's let him stay. Contact the front office. Tell them Burch is alive and full of fight. Ask them to send some clothes for him. Also let them know that Bert saw Cretzer running around with a .45 in his hand."

Mahan unbuckled his belt with its holster and clip pouch and tossed it to Burch. Mahan then crawled to the telephone and whistled. A listener in the front office answered and took the report.

* * *

At 4:30 p.m., the army steamer, Coxe, arrived at Dock 4. The anxious and frustrated evening watch officers hoped that the promised transportation had finally arrived.

A few military passengers disembarked, bursting with eye-witness accounts about the Alcatraz escape attempt. The steamer embarked passengers for Fort McDowel, but the captain refused to allow any Alcatraz personnel to come aboard. Disgruntled, the officers milled about as the steamer quietly drew in its mooring lines and eased away from the dock.

As more time passed, the number of spectators on the dock and on the nearby Municipal Pier increased steadily. Most of the island's school children had arrived by 5:00 p.m. Several island women, who were employed in San Francisco, had joined Mrs. Bergen and Mrs. Cochrane. Some found their frightened and bewildered youngsters waiting for them, while others with pre-school children in the care of baby sitters on the island were frantically concerned.

* * *

Satisfied that D-block was under control, Bergen again entered the main cellhouse section of the gallery. He paused just inside the padded door and listened while his eyes adjusted to the darkness. He wanted to call out to let any captive officer within earshot, know that help was coming, but he knew that his voice might draw gun fire from the escapees.

Keeping as quiet as possible, he crawled along the cold, steel deck until he reached the north end where the flight of stairs led up to the top tier. Cautiously, he studied the stairs leading upward. Light from adjacent windows in the north wall illuminated the area, and he realized that climbing the stairs to make certain no armed convicts were above, would be hazardous. Taking a deep breath and holding the pistol pointed ahead of him, he bounded up the stairs and threw himself flat on the deck of the top level with his head and pistol arm pointed toward the south end of the tier. The long walkway was empty.

Bergen raised to a kneeling position to study the barred face of the gallery. Almost directly overhead was the small opening in the bars through which Coy had squeezed. The lieutenant peered over the top of the steel wall and scanned the cellblock tiers on both sides of Michigan Boulevard, the A-B aisle, and what little he could see of the tops of B and C blocks. Then, in a half crouch, he ran across the long, dimly lit gallery. At mid-point, he paused for a quick scrutiny of the cellblock tiers on both sides of Broadway. Hurrying toward the padded door which opened into the D-block section of the gallery's top level, he anticipated an encounter at any moment. At the door he again dropped to one knee and took a long, searching look down Seedy Street toward the east end.

From his position, the tops of A and B cellblocks stretched out in front of him. Each was fenced with tool-resistant bars from the block top to the ceiling. Bisecting the two blocks were the topless utility corridors. Although the cellhouse lights were turned off, the barred and screened skylights in the cellhouse roof above the aisles admitted some natural light, thus Bergen could see the cellhouse interior reasonably well. There was no one on top of the blocks, in the aisles, or on the tier walkways. All six of the west end utility corridor doors were closed.

Bergen turned and gave the padded door a tentative push. As he expected, it was latched from the D-block side. Moving back a few paces, he hit the door with his shoulder and crashed through. The D-block area was well lighted by the windows in the south wall. A quick glance around the corner at the head of the stairs satisfied him that there were no inmates lurking in the gallery. He leaned into the stair-

Officer Fred Mahan

well and called to Mahan and Burch before he slid down the steep steel stairs to join them.

Mahan asked, "Nothing doing in there, Phil?"

"No. I didn't see or hear anything. There's no sign of life in the big cellhouse. I didn't even see anyone in the east gun gallery, although I know Cochenour and Zubke are there."

"How about Bill Miller and all those other guys?" asked Burch. "Do you have any idea where they are?"

"No. At least they aren't lying around the aisles shot to death as I was afraid they might be. They've been hidden away somewhere. I'll report that we've accomplished our mission. We could use a few more men in here to cover the aisles better from both levels of the gallery, but I'd say we're in control at last. The second team shouldn't have too much trouble checking the cellhouse with all these guns covering them."

A whistle brought a voice to the other end of the telephone line. The lieutenant said, "Bergen, again. We're still in the west gallery. The shooting has stopped. None of us has been hit. Let me talk to the associate warden."

"He's in a conference in the warden's office."

"O.K., tell him we have D-block and the west end secured. We're waiting for orders. And don't forget about getting Burch some clothes. It isn't exactly warm back here."

After a few minutes of silence, the voice returned to the telephone. "The warden says to stand by. Hold your fire, and try to learn where the hostages are being held. He's ordered Lieutenant Faulk and his team to wait. He's afraid they'll get ambushed."

"We'll stand by, but please ask Ed Miller to contact us as soon as the warden turns him loose."

"O.K. And tell Burch that Ray Gaynor went to get some clothes for him."

With a frown on his face, Bergen left the telephone. He was not pleased with the warden's decision to wait.

* * *

"There's no sign of life in the big cellhouse."

Federal Prisons Director J. V. Bennett (right) and Warden Johnston examine bar-spreader and pliers used in break.

ALCATRAZ '46

As the sun set below the Pacific horizon, a cool, moist breeze rippled the glassy surface of the bay and pushed gentle wavelets against the pilings of Dock 4.

The crowd on the dock watched the launch depart from its patrol duty and sail behind the easternmost point of the island, apparently headed for the Alcatraz dock. Twenty minutes later, the high, broad bow of the launch appeared off the point of the island and headed for the mainland. As the waiting officers hastened toward the ramp leading to the landing float, they heard the wail of sirens speeding through the city streets behind them.

Ambulances and other emergency vehicles rounded the curve past the city pumping station and sped onto the dock. The lone military policeman on duty quickly herded the women and children out of the way so the ambulances and a vehicle from the city morgue could maneuver into position near the launch ramp. With sirens off, their flashing red lights cast an eerie intermittent glow across bewildered faces.

A group of people, who had followed the ambulances, was courteously escorted from the government dock by the military policeman. Reluctant to leave the scene of so much excitement, the growing number of spectators clustered around the city pumping station near the dock entrance to observe developments. Some of them were thoroughly disgruntled.

"This is public property," complained one irate woman. "You got no right to push us taxpayers around."

"Yes, Ma'am," replied the military policeman politely. "But it's crowded and dangerous on that dock. Much too risky for public use."

"Then what are all those other people doing out there?"

"Lady, they're Alcatraz people. They're accustomed to danger."

The military policeman returned to the dock landing ramp to meet the prison launch. Suddenly, Betty Cochrane cried, "I knew it! There's Harry. He's wounded, just like I knew he'd be!"

Mrs. Bergen said, "Thank God, he's not dead. Look, they're carrying somebody off in a stretcher. Who is it? I can't see Phil anywhere. Isn't that Mrs. Stites coming out of the cabin?"

Mrs. Stites accompanied the body of her husband to the mainland. Her children were waiting at the top of the landing ramp, unaware that the blanket-wrapped body in the wire basket was their father.

* * *

Once the four casualties were sent to San Francisco, the warden's main concern turned to finding and rescuing whoever might be alive among the captive officers. He called a staff conference to explore how this might be done.

"What's the best way to find the men?" he asked.

"We have armed officers in both gun galleries and in the visiting room," said Miller. "We control all the aisles and all the cellblock tier walkways in the main cellhouse and D-block. I think we can go right in under cover of those guns and find the captives wherever they are."

"I'm not so sure that we have all the escapees pinned down. We don't really know where they are, and they may be waiting in ambush. They have keys which will open all the gates except the sallyport gates and those that must be unlocked from the outside. They could be anywhere in the prison."

174

Wounded Alcatraz guard is placed in ambulance after being rescued.

ALCATRAZ '46

"Well, warden, at least we know they aren't in the hospital," said Miller.

"Perhaps we can find a way to communicate with them and persuade them to surrender," reasoned Johnston. "Surely they must realize that they can't escape now."

"Warden, we've tried in every way to get those cons to talk to us. We've shouted at them through the windows. We've talked to them from the galleries. We've tried repeatedly to make contact by ringing the telephones everywhere inside the prison. Obviously, they don't want to talk."

Johnston turned to his lieutenants and asked, "What do you think we should do?"

Faulk replied, "We should go in there and rescue our officers as soon as possible." Several other lieutenants expressed similar opinions.

"Don't you think we should first try to learn where the escapees are hiding? There is only one way to get into the cellhouse — that's through the main gate. I am certain the inmates are well aware of this fact. It is probable that they are lying in wait to ambush anyone who enters through the gate. One man died and three were wounded in the ambush at the west gun gallery. I can't let that happen again."

Miller said, "I don't see how we're going to locate those killers without going in after them. If they're waiting near the gate, we'll draw fire. That'll tell us where the guns are, and then we can deal effectively with them."

There was a long silence. Johnston mentally reviewed the situation as he quietly studied the determined faces of his aides. Finally he announced, "We will wait. Pass the word to all officers to hold their fire unless fired upon and to make a renewed effort to communicate with the escapees."

When Johnston's decision reached the officers encircling the prison, the reaction was a mixture of relief and dismay.

* * *

Wounded officers Cochrane, Oldham, and Richberger were rushed to the Marine Hospital in an ambulance. Stites was transported to the city morgue in the coroner's van.

As the vehicles departed, the waiting officers boarded the prison launch. Neither the launch operator nor the armed officer who served as deck-hand could provide any information about the conditions on the island.

"Take care," they said to the women on the dock. "Look after the youngsters. It seems like the battle is far from over. You may be stuck in the city for several days."

The bow line was cast off, and the launch swung away and headed toward the island.

* * *

Coy and Cretzer explored the top of the western half of C-block, then returned through the maze of pipes, electrical conduits, and plank walkways to where Hubbard was watching the west gun gallery.

"Not much advantage from up there, Marv," Coy complained. "All you can see is the top of B-block, the wall of D-block, and the west gun cage."

"Ain't there a tunnel under the cut-off that'll take us to the other end of this alley, Bernie?" asked Cretzer. "Maybe that's where we oughtta be. We can see 'em 'n shoot 'em when they come through the main gate. They won't have no place to hide."

Cretzer's idea sounded good to Coy and Hubbard. Carefully drawing the corridor door shut, Coy picked up one of the two gun cage flashlights and played its light over the pile of defensive equipment collected from the west gun gallery.

"We better grab some of these gas masks. If I know them finks, they'll be gassing us again. Let's take them gas bombs, too. Maybe we can toss them into the gun cages from on top of the cellblock."

"Damn," said Cretzer. "There ain't one bit of ammunition here for this .45. I'm almost outta bullets, Bernie."

"How many you got left, for Cri-sakes?"

"Four, I think."

"Well, Joe, it's your own fault. You wasted more than half your bullets on those finks we captured and on that old man in the gun cage."

Although it was dark in the utility corridor, the three men found it even darker in the shallow crawl-space under the cut-off. Guided by Coy's flashlight, they dragged their weapons and gas masks behind them as they made their way to the east half of C-block's utility corridor. Coy and Cretzer each brought several tear gas grenades stuffed into the pockets of their stolen uniform jackets, but Hubbard, who was in his shirt sleeves, brought only the second flashlight and a gas mask.

At the east end, they tried the door and found it locked.

"Will your keys open this door, Bernie?" asked Cretzer.

"I think so. Marv, shine your light over here so's I can check the key numbers. This takes a 109."

"When you open it, we should be able to shoot those finks in the gun cage," said Cretzer drawing his pistol.

"Forget it, Joe," said Coy dejectedly. "I don't have the goddam 109 key." Hubbard clicked off the flashlight to save its power. Coy rubbed his chin thoughtfully then said, "Marv, there's a lot of guys locked in their cells along here. We're going to need stuff like cigarettes and matches. Get some of the guys to shove the things in to us through the ventilators."

"Buddy is in a cell on the middle tier near this end," said Hubbard rubbing his bare arms for warmth. "Even though the punk ran out on us, he ought to be good for something." After a pause, he added, "It's cold and damp in here. Too bad I threw Miller's coat away. Damn thing didn't fit good, but I sure wish I had it on now."

Cretzer smiled, "It fits me O.K. You shouldda got one offa those guys in the cells before I filled 'em fulla holes."

"I got an old blue wool coat hanging down at the other end with the brooms and mops," said Coy. "Next time we go down that way, you can pick it up. Until then, check Buddy's cell while Joe and I crawl up on top of the block to see if there's anything to shoot at."

* * *

The prison's defensive equipment did not include intercoms, bullhorns, or walkie-talkies although the advantages of such equipment had been discussed with the warden on many fruitless occasions. Telephones had been Warden Johnston's notion of sufficient

At Fort Mason's Dock 4 near foot of Van Ness Ave., wives, relatives, and friends await news of the fate of the hostages.

ALCATRAZ '46

communication facilities on the island, however, he did permit the two-way shortwave radios for contacting the prison launch and for emergency uses.

Since the inmates did not respond to the almost continuous ringing of the cellhouse telephones, the warden finally said, "We'll forget the telephones as a means of communication with the inmates, but we'll increase other efforts to talk with them. All officers who are close enough to be heard by the escapees will offer them an opportunity to surrender. We will make no deals, but we will guarantee the safety of any man who chooses to surrender."

Following the orders, Associate Warden Miller and several lieutenants went to the catwalks below the cellhouse windows. Keeping close to the building, they made an effort to establish voice contact with the escapees.

Atop the easternmost half of C-block, Coy and Cretzer listened skeptically to the pleading officers. From both gun galleries and from the catwalks beyond the cellhouse wall, the discordant voices invited the inmates to surrender and assured them safe custody if they did so.

Coy sneered, "How do you like that crap, Joe."

"I ain't ready to die yet, but I also don't trust them finks. They're gonna finish us off one way or 'nother. Here or in the gas-box at Quentin."

"You're right, Joe. I ain't surrendering to nobody, and I ain't going to let nobody put me in no gas-box."

Associate Warden Miller's voice called from outside, "Coy, Cretzer, the rest of you guys. Throw out your guns and give up."

Cretzer screamed, "Give up, hell. Why you stupid old jughead, we've got bullets and food 'nough to last 40 days. You want us, you'll have to come 'n get us."

"I ain't surrendering to nobody, and I ain't going to let nobody put me in no gas-box."

WARNING
KEEP OFF

While the enraged Cretzer screamed at Miller, Coy crept close to the south side of the block. Out of sight of the officers in the east gun gallery, he pointed his rifle through the bars at the cellhouse window and fired two quick shots into the darkness outside.

Almost immediately, the top of the block was blasted with leaden hail. Coy and Cretzer slithered across the concrete slab and dropped into the cavernous depths of the utility corridor. Above their heads, the storm of bullets and shotgun pellets continued to smash and tear into the metal ventilators and the huge motors which served them. Dropping swiftly through the three-tier maze and guided by the dimming beam of Hubbard's flashlight, they rendezvoused at the east end of the cut-off tunnel.

"Did you get any of them, Bernie?" asked Hubbard.

"No, but we sure stirred up a hornet's nest. We let them finks know what we think of their lousy deals."

The officers in the west gun gallery had heard Coy's two shots but were unable to locate his position. From the east gun gallery and the visiting room, it seemed the shots had come from the top of C-block. This information was quickly relayed to the warden's office. Receiving the information, Johnston smiled with satisfaction. He had been right to wait and avoid the ambush. Now his officers knew the location of at least one of the convict gunmen. Coy was undoubtedly holed up in C-block.

"Now if we could only locate Cretzer," thought the warden.

* * *

The Warden's house, looking up from Building 64.

ALCATRAZ '46

Mrs. Philip Bergen

The Alcatraz women on Dock 4 gathered 46 restless, hungry children and crowded them into the dock waiting room. The long, narrow room was not heated, but it did provide some protection from the chilly dampness of the evening air. Several hard wooden benches were lined in rows beneath one unshaded electric light bulb hanging from the ceiling. Inadequate restrooms were located at the back of the room.

"We can't keep these children cooped up in here without anything to eat or drink," said Mrs. Cochrane. "There must be some way to get food for them. I could do with a hot cup of coffee, myself."

The military policeman assigned to the dock emerged from his tiny office with one loaf of bread, all the food that was available. While the loaf was being broken into small portions and shared among the children, the women pooled their financial resources. The total came to $14.97.

A few women contacted friends or relatives in the area and made arrangements for some of the children to be fed and housed, but eight other women and 30 children still needed assistance.

"Why not try the Red Cross?" suggested Mrs. Bergen.

"They'll probably turn you down because this isn't a disaster like a flood or war," said one of the women.

"Call them, Evelyn," urged Mrs. Cochrane. "We never say 'no' when they ask us for a contribution."

When the call was made, the young secretary who answered the telephone was amazed to learn that the disturbance on Alcatraz was causing serious repercussions in San Francisco.

"I know we'll want to do something to help," she said. "If you let me have your telephone number, I'll call our district manager, and he will contact you."

"We're calling from a public telephone on the army dock," explained Mrs. Bergen. She read the number on the dial plate, then hung up the receiver and said, "I think we called the right people. The girl who answered said she would relay our request to the district manager and that he would call us."

"Sounds like one of those 'don't call me, I'll call you' routines," said one of the women. "Why can't they just say 'yes' or 'no'?"

Another woman added pessimistically, "They stall, then call and say, 'Sorry, your disaster just ain't disastrous enough!'"

"What do you think, Evelyn?" asked Mrs. Cochrane.

"I don't know. I've never been on this end of a Red Cross solicitation before. We'll just have to wait and see. A little praying might help."

Several newspapermen and their attendant photographers arrived on the dock. They descended upon the Alcatraz refugees with countless questions and a barrage of popping flashbulbs. The women and children deftly parried the inquiries while the newsmen scribbled impressions of the event as seen through the eyes of the 'callously abandoned refugees'.

During the interrogations, one reporter slipped into the telephone booth and remained there, apparently talking with someone in his newspaper's city room. The monopolizing of the only telephone on the dock seemed designed to prevent other newsmen from contacting their newsrooms.

Worriedly awaiting the call from the Red Cross, the women finally demanded that the reporter leave the booth. He ignored the demand. Mrs. Cochrane appealed to the military policeman for assistance.

"That call from the Red Cross means everything to us," she said. "They might call us any minute now, and that fellow won't give up the telephone."

The military policeman pulled open the door to the booth and explained the situation to the reporter. The newsman turned his back on the soldier and continued to talk into the receiver. The policeman quickly reached into the booth, grasped the reporter by his coat collar, and jerked him onto the dock. To another reporter who moved toward the booth, he declared, "No you don't. That telephone is off limits as of right now. If there's any argument about it, this dock will also be off limits." Most of the other reporters approved of the policeman's action.

A few minutes later, the Red Cross call came through. The district manager assured the women that his organization would be of service.

"We know of the trouble on Alcatraz," he said. "We are making plans to send food and medical supplies to your people on the island and will be happy to help you with your problems here."

Questions and answers were exchanged over the line. Gradually, the picture of the women's problem was clearly defined. When he had jotted down all the information, the manager advised, "Tell the other ladies to keep the party together on the dock where you have light, shelter, and some conveniences. We will send a motor bus to pick you up and take you to a hotel for the night. I don't know which hotel it will be because the city is crowded with servicemen passing through. But rest assured, we will find hotel rooms for everyone, and we will make arrangements to feed your party as soon as we can get you to a good restaurant."

Mrs. Bergen thanked him and turned to the military policeman. "Just one more call. I must let our people on the island know that the Red Cross is taking care of us."

The Alcatraz number was dialed repeatedly, but a busy signal was received each time. Before word could be sent to the island, the Red Cross bus arrived at the dock. The women and children hurried aboard under the watchful eyes and popping flashbulbs of the newsmen and photographers.

* * *

On the catwalk outside the locked west gun gallery entrance door, three heavily armed officers stood watch. In the gallery, Bergen, Mahan, and Burch waited impatiently for reinforcements. D-block was quiet. The inmates, huddled behind blankets and mattresses at the rear of their cells, expected another barrage of gunfire at any moment.

Bergen said, "Bert, you know this gun gallery like the back of your hand. Ease into the main cellhouse section. Let us know if there's anything moving around over there. We'll cover you from here."

Burch entered the other section of the gallery, hunched over, running swiftly on bare feet. When he reached the vicinity of Broadway, he stopped to peer cautiously through the vision panel in the west wall. No one was in sight on the other side. A quick look over the rim of the gallery wall assured him that there was no one on the cell-

ALCATRAZ '46

"We have men on the roof watching the cons in the yard, but they won't be doing any shooting."

house flats or on either of the tier walkways. He moved to where the A-B aisle and the west gallery met at the north wall and took another quick look. Again, the flats and the tier walkways were empty. He caught a fleeting glimpse of a uniformed officer in the east gun gallery, then moved back to the Broadway area where he could look and listen without exposing himself.

Mahan and Bergen posted themselves about 20 feet apart. The telephone, dangling from the west wall, was about half way between them. For a long time it had remained silent, but now it began to whistle. To answer the call, Bergen had to crawl past one of the floor-to-ceiling windows in the west wall.

In the next quarter hour, Bergen made several short round trips to the telephone. He grew irritated because most of the calls were from unassigned reserves in the front office who wanted to know what was going on in the cellhouse. On this third trip, he noticed three pencil-size bullet holes in the steel wall opposite the window. On his fourth trip, he was alarmed to find that the number of holes had increased to four. After another response to the telephone's call, there were five closely spaced holes.

"Fred, I think Coy is zeroing-in on us again," Bergen exclaimed. "Did you see any muzzle flashes up there on the tiers?"

"No. I've been watching. I haven't seen or heard anything."

"Well, someone's shooting at us. Look at these bullet holes."

Mahan crawled over to inspect the punctured wall, then backed away from the window area.

"They're bullet holes, all right. But they aren't coming from up in the block. Just feel those holes, Phil. They're smooth on our side. You know what that means. Some fool is shooting through the window at us."

Touching the bullet holes appraisingly, Bergen said, "You're right, Fred. Let's find out where he is. Hang your cap on the muzzle of your Thompson and wave it around in front of the window."

Keeping out of the line of fire, Mahan waved his uniform cap across the window. A muffled report was heard from outside, above and to the west of the gun gallery window, and another round hole appeared in the steel wall.

"That settles it, Fred. Those shots must be coming from the roof of the hospital. We'll have to get that shooting stopped, or they'll be carrying you and me out here in a basket. Who the hell is out there on the catwalk now?"

"I think Mr. Miller is back, Phil. He had been trying to talk Coy and Cretzer into giving up, but they fired some shots at him. He didn't sound too happy when I heard his voice a while ago."

The lieutenant crept to the edge of the window and shouted to the men on the catwalk below, "Hey, Ed. Are you there?"

"Yeah. I'm here. What's bothering you? Don't you like your ringside seat?"

"You won't believe this, Ed, but some damn fool has been shooting at us from the hospital roof. We don't dare go near the phone. He blasts at us every time we move across the window."

"Come on, Phil. There ain't nobody that stupid. We have men on the roof watching the cons in the yard, but they wouldn't be doing any shooting."

"Well then, tell them to stop what they aren't doing before you have two more basket cases on your hands."

Unable to believe what Bergen had told him, Miller stepped away from the wall to look at the edge of the hospital roof. As he did, Mahan again waved his cap-covered Thompson in front of the window. Miller cupped his hands and bellowed, "You, up there on the roof. No shooting. We have officers in the gun gallery."

As he spoke, a roof-top rifle roared, and another hole appeared in the gallery wall. Miller grabbed Joe Maxwell's machine gun, pointed it to the sky, and fired a short burst to attract the rifleman's attention.

"You crazy son-of-a-bitch," he shouted. "You fire one more shot, and I'm going to blast you off that roof with this Tommy gun!"

Norman Anthony withdrew from the edge of the roof to a sheltered corner behind the water tank.

"Thanks, Ed," Bergen said. "Who do you suppose it was?"

"I don't know, but I'm going to find out. Keep away from that window for a while, will you?"

"Hell, yes. I don't like to answer telephones anyhow."

Miller returned to the administration building. Lieutenant Klein and two officers accompanied him through the maze of gates and stairways to the main roof. Anthony was located, jerked to his feet, and escorted to the captain's office, protesting weakly. In a few minutes, his rifle and ammunition were returned to the armory, and he was marched downhill to the island dock to await the next launch trip to San Francisco.

V.I.P.'s touring prison during more peaceful times.

Another view of the island in 1946.

Associate Warden Miller returned to the gun gallery entrance and called, "Hey, Phil. You can answer your phone now. We found that sniper and ran him off the island. It was Norman Anthony, one of those goddam war service appointees."

"Thanks, Ed. Now, where's our reinforcements?"

"Clark and Bloomquist are at the armory now. When they get their shotguns and portable searchlights, they'll come up to join you."

"Will Faulk and his men be going into the cellhouse then?"

"Not right away. We're still shorthanded. Warden Duffy is sending a squad from San Quentin. We have help coming in from all over the map — McNeil, Englewood, Atlanta, Leavenworth, Lewisburg — they're all flying their best officers out here to help us."

"You mean we're just going to sit on our hands until they arrive? That's crazy, Ed. We've got to get into that cellhouse and rescue those officers before it's too late to help them."

"I know that, Phil. You guys ain't the only ones who are bugging me to let you go charging in there."

"Ed, we're no good at just waiting around. Put someone else in our place who doesn't mind waiting. Maybe we can persuade the old man to let us go in."

"The warden told me to keep you guys right where you are. He thinks you've risked your lives enough already. It really shook him when they carried Stites out of here. It was bad enough seeing the wounded men, but Stite's death really got to him. He just don't want any more dead officers on his conscience."

"Well, we could get killed up here as easy as down there."

"The warden doesn't want any more dead heroes. He may decide to starve those thugs into surrendering."

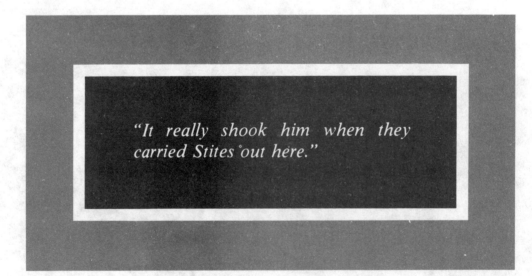

"It really shook him when they carried Stites out here."

"That might be a good idea. I'm all for it, but not until we have found our officers and brought them out. When you put us in here, our understanding was that the second team would get into the cellhouse and rescue them. What's gone sour? Why the change in plans?"

"It was seeing Stites and the wounded men. Like I told you, the old man is sick about it. I don't like what I have to do either, but I take orders, same as you. Now keep your eyes open. Here comes Clark and Bloomquist to help you guys. Post them where you think they'll do the most good, Phil, and keep trying to make contact with Coy and those other thugs. The warden still hopes we can persuade them to surrender."

* * *

ALCATRAZ '46

Rifle grenade striking the cellhouse wall.

Warden Johnston

185

ALCATRAZ '46

In the evening commuter traffic on the bridges, car radios blared, "Hundreds of desperate Alcatraz inmates, with the familiar feel of steel guns in their hands, are fighting their way out . . ."

By 6:00 p.m., newspaper and radio reports had become sensational and exaggerated. Rumors spread quickly. One report stated that Warden Johnston was held hostage by 100 convicts; another told that inmates had stormed the armory and secured all the machine guns and ammunition they wanted; still another reported that inmates were shooting at everybody in sight, a mass escape was in progress, and the entire city was in jeopardy.

Because of the stories, thousands of residents gathered at Fisherman's Wharf, Coit Tower, Aquatic Park, the Yacht Harbor, and other viewpoints. Hundreds more planned to leave the area. Store-owners near the Marina boarded their windows, and hospitals, anticipating the worst, called for increased ambulance service and emergency supplies of food, drugs, and cots. A battalion of National Guardsmen had its May maneuvers cancelled so it could remain on standby. Warden Clinton P. Duffy of San Quentin, sent 12 of his most expert marksmen to Alcatraz.

The dusk of evening changed quickly into the darkness of night. All lights were out in the Alcatraz residential areas. From atop prison buildings and throughout the security area, floodlights cast the cream-colored cellhouse into sharp relief. Along the walkways at the foot of cliffs, patrolling officers with flashlights in hand, seemed to flit like tiny fireflies. Above this scene, the great beacon in the lighthouse swung around interminably.

Even in the chilly darkness, people stayed at vantage points hoping to glimpse anything they could of the siege. On the Bay Bridge, hundreds of sightseers parked their cars and leaned over railings with binoculars to watch the flicker of flashlights and tracer bullets. Those without binoculars could easily see the flares that occasionally drifted slowly in the night. Because traffic piled up beyond the toll plazas, the Highway Patrol's Bay Bridge radio alerted its traffic force to "crack down on the sightseers and keep the bridge traffic moving."

* * *

In the dark interior of the cellhouse, the gallery guns were silent. Only officers' voices, urging the escapees to surrender, could be heard. Then abruptly, the firing began again.

"Sounds like D-block is catching hell. The stupid finks must think we're holed up over there," said Hubbard.

"Let's get outta this goddam alley while it's quiet over here," urged Cretzer. "This ain't no good place to hole up. They got the damn lights shut off, and I'll betcha the drinkin' water ain't runnin'. We'll have a better chance in the hospital or kitchen. We can get somethin' to eat there."

"Marv, you know that kitchen real good. Can we hole up in there and stand them off?" asked Coy.

"It's better than here, Bernie. Plenty of food and hot coffee. Lots of good hideouts. There's some cons still back there, too. I think I saw Harris, Weidmer, Ritter, Hunter, Pugowski, and Audett. That Blackie Audett might throw in with us. He's always bragging about busting out."

"He's long on brag and short on action, but I hear he's real good at cookin'. We'll let him fry us some steaks outta that ice box in the screw's dinin' room," suggested Cretzer.

"Sounds good to me. Let's go," said Coy.

The trio crept through the cut-off tunnel and gathered at the west end of the utility corridor. Hubbard found Coy's wool coat and put it on.

"It fits O.K., Bernie," he said.

"Be careful," whispered Coy. "That gun cage may be full of guns, but we can slip past them in the dark."

"To hell with 'em," snarled Cretzer. "If we wanna go, we go! No lousy screw is gonna stop me."

Coy cautiously opened the door a few inches and whispered, "We'll duck across the Square and get under the gun cage where the screws can't see us. We'll grab all them keys and bust into the kitchen before they know what's happening."

The officers in the west gun gallery heard the inmates when the utility corridor door was opened. They directed their portable searchlight beam at the door and opened fire simultaneously. Shotgun pellets and .45 calibre bullets slammed into the steel door, pounding it shut.

"Christamighty," muttered Coy. "They're just setting there waiting for us to stick our necks out. Them bastards don't want us to surrender. They want us dead."

"We can wait them out, Bernie," said Hubbard. "They'll be doping off after a while. It's only 10 or 12 feet across Times Square. Once we're under the gun cage, they can't get at us."

In the next few hours, the trio attempted to sneak out of the utility corridor several times, but each time, the powerful searchlight and the gallery guns drove them back into their dark sanctuary.

"We've got to get the hell out of here, but we can't do it with that fuckin' light and them guns blasting at us," said Coy. "I'm going up on top of the cellblock. When I get up there, you guys stir them finks up a little so they'll turn on that light. I'll smash it with one of these rifle slugs, and maybe I'll nail a few screws, too. When I start shooting, they'll be so damn busy ducking my bullets, they'll forget all about you guys down here. That's when you bust out of this alley and hightail it to the kitchen. I'll follow, first chance I get. Just leave this door open when you go."

* * *

It was almost 10:00 p.m. when Warden Johnston decided to assemble a second assault team. Calling the associate warden to his office, he asked, "Does Lieutenant Faulk have his men armed and ready?"

"Yes, sir. Some of our best officers, Lieutenants Faulk and Roberts and officers Jones, King, McKean, Mowery, Pollock, Runnels, Sievertson, Wright, and Zubke. They are equipped with guns, flashlights, cellhouse keys, and a well thought out plan."

"Do you think they can effect the rescue without further casualties?"

"Yes, sir. I'm going with them. That'll make 12 of us, and we have good coverage from the gun galleries."

Led by the associate warden, the assault team slipped quietly through the main gate into the dark cellhouse. The officers ran across the east end to the C-D aisle and proceeded cautiously toward the west end, checking each cell visually with their flashlights as they went.

Officer Mowery found the two library clerks, Cooke and Peabody, cowering behind a pile of books in a far corner of the room. After being searched thoroughly, they were locked in their cells.

Moving along the C-D aisle, the officers continued to check each cell systematically in a determined effort to locate the captive officers.

When Coy reached the top of C-block, he heard the muffled footsteps of the officers below him on Seedy Street.

"It's a goddam goon squad," he thought, scurrying across the top of the cellblock to the northeast corner where his line of fire would be least impeded by the concrete and steel cells. Thrusting the barrel of his rifle through the bars, he sought a position from which he could see the officers three tiers below him, but they were somewhat protected by the overhang of the middle tier walkway, and, except for the flickering of flashlights, they were invisible in the darkness.

"Even if I can't see them under the damn overhang," thought Coy as he hurriedly moved to the bars at the south side of the block, "I can ricochet bullets off the D-block wall and hit some of those screws on the rebound."

From somewhere in the darkness ahead of them, the leaders of the assault team heard Carl Sundstrom's voice calling that he and the other captives were locked in cells 402 and 403. At the same moment, Coy began firing. He sent a dozen rifle bullets slamming into the D-block wall, filling the C-D aisle with ricochetting slugs.

At Miller's order, the assault team retreated to the east end of the cellhouse and ran across Pekin Place to the aisle between A and B blocks.

Responding to Coy's rifle barrage, the officers in both gun galleries opened fire on the top of C-block. Covered by this gunfire, the assault team proceeded cautiously along the A-B aisle toward the west end of the cellhouse, again checking each cell to minimize the possibility of an ambush. By the time the team came out from under the protective overhang of the B-block middle tier walkway to cross Broadway, the shooting from the gun galleries had stopped.

Coy crawled to the bars which rose to the ceiling above Broadway. He could hear the officers below as they scurried across the aisle between B and C cellblocks. Thrusting his rifle through the bars, he sent several bullets into the shadowy line. Lieutenant Roberts, hit in the back and shoulder, slumped to the floor. Several officers quickly dragged him to the relative safety of the cellblock overhang.

As the guns in the west gallery opened fire, Coy snake-crawled to the shelter of the utility corridor, calling to Cretzer and Hubbard as he threaded his way downward through the pipes and planks, "Into the tunnel, quick. Them finks know we're in here, now. They'll open that goddam door and blast hell out of this alley. We might have to shoot it out right here."

Cretzer and Hubbard reached the entrance to the crawlspace under the cutoff at about the same time Coy lowered himself to the floor of the alleyway. After hastily improvising a barricade of broken planks, half in and half out of the tunnel, the trio stretched out flat on the cold concrete behind it. They could barely hear the footsteps of officers on Times Square and Seedy Street through the partly open corridor door.

Coy pressed his ear against the grille of a cell ventilator and listened for a clue to the whereabouts of the officers, hoping to get a shot at them through the grille.

When the assault team reached the imprisoned officers, they quickly unlocked the cells. Burdette, Bristow, Sundstrom, and Lageson helped place the seriously wounded men on canvas stretchers.

Through the grille, Coy heard the sound of voices and the moans of injured officers. "Goddam, Joe," he said, disgustedly. "Some of them finks you shot are still alive. That dumb Injun didn't finish them off like we told him to."

"The Kid double crossed us," said Hubbard. "Sounds like some of the screws weren't even hit."

"The hell they weren't," snapped Cretzer. "I killed all of 'em. The Kid said they was dead. Why should he lie? He's the one that hasta worry 'bout witnesses, not us."

"Just use your ears, Joe. Some of them screws ain't dead. We're dead, though, if we don't get the hell out of this trap soon."

After the men of the second assault team carried the wounded officers to the main gate, they returned to methodically check the main cellhouse and to lock every cell door and every control box. Lieutenant Faulk closed and locked the D-block entrance door and the C-block utility corridor door.

*   *   *

"The Kid said they was dead. Why should he lie?"

ALCATRAZ '46

Picture (see roof) shows heavily armed officers trying to re-enter cellhouse.

Officers hug wall and watch apprehensively as one man climbs ladder in order to hurl tear gas grenades through a bullet-shattered window opening in D-block.

The rescue permitted some rest for the tired officers and non-participating convicts. In the recreation yard, approximately 200 inmates huddled around bonfires fed by tables, gameboards, baseball bats, and other recreation equipment from the storage shed under the cellhouse stairs. On the yard wall, U.S. Marines and prison officers shivered in the cool breeze that swept through the Golden Gate. Appetites were appeased by the distribution of sandwiches and coffee furnished by the Red Cross.

Outside the warden's office, Drs. Roucek, Bowden, and Jones of the United States Public Health Service, examined the wounded and worked hurriedly to stop the flow of blood that soaked their clothing and the canvas stretchers. The wounded had been bleeding for many hours. Morphine injections were administered to ease their pain. Weinhold and Simpson were in critical condition. Baker, Corwin, and Lageson were wounded less severely. Bill Miller's bleeding arm seemed to be the least serious of all.

In normal circumstances, the prison hospital facilities would have been available, but because of the blastout, it was impractical to utilize them. With no provision for blood transfusions, the wounded were given emergency treatment in the hastily improvised First Aid Station near the warden's office. They were then rushed to the Marine Hospital in San Francisco.

* * *

Lieutenant Bergen posted several officers on the top level of the west gun gallery to be ready to fire if the escapees got within sight and range. Officers Mowery, Runnels, and Jones climbed to the top of B-block to flood the top of C-block with beams from their portable searchlights. Two other officers, stationed in the visitor's room near the main gate, knocked out the bulletproof glass in the visitor's viewing panels so they could fire into the cellhouse.

Warden Johnston congratulated the officers of the second assault team after they rescued the captive officers. When the wounded men had been sent to the mainland hospital, the warden felt a tremendous sense of relief; however, this feeling was quickly replaced by a sense of anger. His men had been brutally and callously shot at point blank range. Bristow had told him, "When the siren went off and the bullets started whizzing through the cellhouse, most of the inmates scurried back to their cells, that is, except Coy, Cretzer, Hubbard, Thompson, Carnes, and Shockley. Shockley went wild. You know how much he hated us. He screamed for our blood. He finally goaded Cretzer to kill us so that no one would be alive to testify as witnesses."

Information gathered from the officers convinced the warden that he had to subdue Coy, Cretzer, and perhaps several other convicts before he could regain control of the prison. Before deciding on a plan, he pieced together as much information as was available. Officers patrolling the catwalks on the south side of the prison had reported to him that shots were fired from D-block windows. Since the report came after Lieutenant Faulk had locked the door between D-block and the main cellhouse, the information implied that at least one escapee, probably Cretzer with the pistol, was trapped in the segregation cellblock. Johnston also surmised that the other escapees must be in or near the C-block utility corridor.

Based on statements from the rescued captives, Johnston concluded that no more than six inmates were actively involved in the attempted blastout. Officers on the second assault team had found Thompson and Carnes locked in their cells, and Shockley was known to be back in D-block. This information was relayed to the officers in the gun galleries and at other posts surrounding the prison. It was also transmitted to the Office of the Federal Bureau of Prisons in Washington, D.C.

* * *

It was almost 11:00 p.m. when several tear gas grenades were dropped through the roof ventilators into the C-block utility corridor. The trio strapped on their gas masks and crawled deeper into the tunnel as choking, eye-irritating fumes slowly filled both sections of the corridor. From time to time they heard far off voices calling, "Surrender. Surrender."

Coy sneered, "Yeah, surrender and sniff cyanide at Quentin."

"And they don't supply gas masks there," quipped Hubbard.

* * *

At 11:35 p.m., the second airborne contingent of prison officers from Leavenworth arrived at Hamilton Field. Sped to the Sausalito docks by military vehicles, they boarded army crash-boats for the trip to the island. Another 15 officers were due to arrive from McNeil Island, and an additional 25 hand-picked men were standing by at Englewood, Colorado.

In the cutoff tunnel, Coy rummaged through Weinhold's uniform coat pockets. "I got five full clips, 25 shots, and two or three more in the rifle," he said. "How many you got, Joe?"

"I still got four."

"It ain't much, so we sure don't want to waste any. Let's just lay back and make them come to us."

Suddenly, a fragmentation grenade burst in the west section of the C-block utility corridor.

"What the hell was that?" asked Cretzer.

"Sounds like dynamite," replied Coy. "Them fuckers is using dynamite."

"That ain't dynamite," said Hubbard. "They're using hand grenades on us. I never thought they'd do that."

"These finks are worse'n the fucking Japs 'n Germans in the war. They'll use anythin'. They want us dead, 'n they don't have the guts to come in here after us."

"They have to come in sooner or later," said Coy. "They can't reach us in this tunnel with those lousy bombs."

"Sounds like they're droppin' 'em through the ventilators like they did the tear gas."

"I think we'll be O.K. in this tunnel," said Hubbard. "There's no ventilator over the cutoff. There's no way they can drop anything on us unless they chop a hole in the roof."

"I wouldn't put it past 'em to tear off the whole prison roof just to get at us."

"Those bombs will just bounce off this concrete slab. It's a couple of feet thick. We're in the best damn bomb-shelter on the Rock," smiled Coy.

* * *

ALCATRAZ '46

U.S. Marines stand on yard wall guarding non-participating inmates. During entire 36-hour siege, inmates huddled in a corner of recreation yard watching events unfold step-by-step.

Armed with bazookas, flame-throwers, and light machine guns, a second detachment of 30 Marines landed on the island at 12:30 a.m. They relieved the tired, hungry men on the recreation yard wall. Arriving with them on the Navy LCM, were 24 cases of newly developed explosives. Specifically requested by Warden Johnston, the small, deadly, cone-shaped bombs were designed to blow holes in concrete.

While the shadowy forms of 20 men unloaded the explosives on the dock, antipersonnel grenades continued to drop into the cellhouse through the ventilators.

* * *

At the U.S. Marine Hospital in the Presidio, Captain Weinhold was placed in an oxygen tent following an operation that removed two .45 caliber bullets from his body. Simpson was in fair condition after removal of several .45 caliber bullets from his chest and stomach. Hospital personnel said that Corwin would have to undergo extensive plastic surgery for his shattered jaw.

Because of the apparent seriousness of their wounds, Weinhold and Simpson had been given preference on the operating table. Miller, younger and seemingly wounded less seriously, went into shock from a loss of blood. He died while waiting his turn on the table.

* * *

Marine Lieutenant A. L. Smith pencils in assault directions to Privates George Myers and Vernon Weber.

Detachment of U.S. Marines land on Alcatraz.

ALCATRAZ '46

As daylight gradually crept through the bullet-shattered windows and skylights, the inky darkness of the cellhouse changed to a murky grey. In the bomb-blasted utility corridor on both sides of the cutoff, there was nothing but devastation. The catwalks were twisted and torn from their supports. The shattered planks from the walkways above, littered the alley floor. Electrical conduits hung loosely from the walls. The exploding grenades had wrecked the water and sewer lines. Foul-smelling salt water from the sanitary system gurgled into the corridor, and sewer gas fouled the air.

Following a 5:30 a.m. breakfast of coffee and rolls, Associate Warden Miller, seven prison officers, and 15 Marines climbed to the main cellhouse roof to drop more antipersonnel grenades through the ventilators. Other officers worked on the roof with a jackhammer. They were cutting a jagged opening directly above the C-block cutoff.

* * *

Bergen was tired and somewhat irritable after a sleepless night of frustrating inactivity. When he heard a whistle over the telephone, he checked his watch. It was 7:00 a.m. He crawled to the dangling instrument. Bertrand whispered, "Hold on a second, lieutenant. The warden wants to talk to you."

After several minutes of listening to disconnected background conversations, Bergen finally heard Johnston's voice ask, "Are you and your men all right, lieutenant?"

"We're tired, hungry, and dirty, but otherwise O.K."

"Has there been anything happening back there? Have you seen Coy or Cretzer or whoever it is with the gun up there in D-block?"

"No, sir. None of my men has seen any of them except Shockley. He and the other D-block regulars have been out of their cells moving around on the tier walkway."

"Do you have any idea at all as to where the gunman might be hiding?"

"No one up here has seen him. When the shooting was going on, it was impossible to tell where the bullets were coming from because of the ricochets."

"What do the inmates do when they come out of their cells?"

"Some just come out, look around, and go back in. Several, I noticed, seem to be getting together in a cell near the east end of the middle tier of D-block. They've been carrying things in there."

"What things?"

"Mattresses and blankets and pillows. That sort of thing."

"But you haven't seen any of the gang except Shockley?"

"Shockley is the only one, and he's been up on the top tier."

"Did you recognize any of the inmates who were congregating around that cell on the middle tier?"

"Yes, sir. They are all regular D-block inmates including old Stroud. He's been in and out of that active cell several times."

"Which cell is it?"

"About the fourth from the east end on the second gallery. That'd be cell 24 or 25."

"Well, tell your men to keep a sharp lookout. Don't take any unnecessary chances. We're going to flush that gunman out of his hiding place."

* * *

Warden Johnston authorized Marine Warrant Officer Charles L. Buckner to deploy a rifle squad equipped with grenade launchers to the grassy slopes below the south wall of D-block.

The first grenade hit the detention sash of a window and exploded above the catwalk. A second bored through the sash and its protective steel grille and exploded inside the building, showering the cellhouse with fragments of steel.

Less than 100 feet away, Bergen and his men, unwarned of the incoming grenades, were caught by surprise. They flattened themselves on the steel deck and hoped the metallic shrapnel would not penetrate the thin protective wall of the gallery.

Several volleys of grenades, aimed toward cell 25, followed in quick succession. Some exploded harmlessly against the outer wall. A few destroyed the detention sash and its glass panes but did not seriously damage the tool-resistant bars. Many exploded inside the cellhouse. Some, failing to explode, began to litter the D-block flats.

When there was a momentary lull in the bombardment, Bergen peered through one of the bullet holes in the gallery wall. He expected to see much of D-block in twisted, sagging ruin, but was surprised to find little visible damage. The floors of the cellhouse and the cellblock tier walkways were strewn with burned-out tear gas cannisters, fragments, and unexploded grenades. There were blackened areas around a few of the cell fronts on the middle tier. Another barrage began before the damage could be fully assessed.

"What the hell did we do to deserve this?" asked Mahan.

"I wish I hadn't let you guys talk me into staying up here," said Burch. "This is one hell of a breakfast they're serving."

As the morning hours passed, the officers grew accustomed to the continual explosions and choking smoke. Surprisingly, the thin steel wall of the gallery was effective against the flying shrapnel. During lulls in the bombardment, the officers breakfasted on Thursday night's leftover sandwiches and cold coffee.

* * *

The inmates in the 14 cells on the D-block flats were unable to flee the fury of the bombardment. They crouched in cell corners behind doubled-over mattresses and buried their heads in blankets and pillows to muffle the ear-shattering thunder of exploding grenades.

In their abortive attempt to release Franklin and others, the escapees had opened the solid steel outer doors of the solitary confinement cells. Now as bullets and grenades hit in the area of cells 24 and 25, the men in the six confinement cells screamed frantically for someone to close the outer doors so that the shrapnel would not reach them.

The cells on the two upper tiers had been unlocked and left open, but only 12 of the 28 had been occupied. Many of the inmates had wandered around the block, but as soon as the shooting began, they stopped roaming. Two carried pillows and blankets into the D-block utility corridor. Finding the corridor unsatisfactory, they climbed to the top of the block and found sanctuary in a crawl-space beneath the reinforced concrete roof. Other inmates divided into small groups and scattered throughout the two upper tiers. They gathered mattresses and blankets from the unoccupied cells and built barriers against the incoming grenades and bullets. Stroud calmly dropped to the D-block flats to close the protective outer doors of the solitary confinement cells then, just as calmly, returned to his top tier cell and the protection of his doubled-over mattress.

* * *

Generals Joseph Stillwell and Frank Merrill, leader of the famous Merrill's Marauders, arrived at Warden Johnston's office and asked if they could be of service.

The warden thanked them for the men and munitions already provided and told of the arrival of reinforcements from other federal prisons.

"I feel certain my officers can handle things now," said Johnston.

"You're much like a general in the field," said Stillwell. "A siege must be well executed if it is to succeed. You seem to have the situation under control. I just want you to know that we are ready to furnish assistance if it is needed."

* * *

By 8:00 a.m., the officers on the roof had cut a hole directly above the cutoff. Loosened chunks of concrete thudded upon the roof of the tunnel below. Dozens of demolition bombs were dropped through the hole to burst on the concrete floor of the cutoff, directly above the heads of the escapees. The powerful explosives failed to blast an opening through the thick concrete, but the concussions drove the three half-dazed escapees from their sanctuary. Because fallen chunks of concrete from the tunnel roof blocked the west exit, the trio scrambled to the east opening and hurriedly improvised a barricade of broken planks.

In a tight formation, half in and half out of the crawl-space with their guns defiantly pointed toward the far-off east end entrance to the alleyway, they covered their heads protectively with their hands and waited.

Now the antipersonnel grenades which had proved ineffective on the concrete roof of the tunnel, were diverted to the utility corridor. Marine Officer Buckner tied precisely measured lengths of string to the grenades and lowered them through the ventilators. When the suspended grenades reached a predetermined depth, the pins were pulled by other strings. The resulting explosions blasted the utility corridor at carefully calculated levels.

Metal fragments tore into the protective planks of the barricade until, battered and bleeding, the trio was forced back into the tunnel where they were pounded by almost unbearable concussions.

* * *

At 8:30 a.m., the warden called Bergen for a report on the activities in D-block.

"We are still suspicious of inmate activities around cell 25," Bergen said. "But we haven't seen any inmate named by the captive officers except Shockley, and he has not been near the cell. There are 12 inmates loose in here. We've seen and recognized all of them. None had a gun, and we haven't been shot at for several hours. When the shooting was going on earlier, we thought firing came from somewhere close to the east end, but there was so much shooting, so many ricochets, and so much smoke that no one here really knows where the shots came from."

"But you think they may have come from cell 25?"

"Probably from somewhere in that area. We are watching that cell very carefully."

"Good. We will try again to persuade them to surrender."

Johnston dispatched several lieutenants to various points around the prison to reason with the escapees. When there was no reply, the officers returned to the warden's office and the grenading resumed.

* * *

Newsmen interviewed some of the rescued officers at the Marine Hospital in the Presidio.

Lageson related the earlier events, "Coy was the leader. But Cretzer seemed to get the most pleasure out of shooting people down. I played dead for nearly ten hours. With Burch's keys, those rats unlocked all the cells and invited all the other convicts to join them. There must have been fifty or more men in B and C blocks, and about thirty in D, but only twelve joined them. The rest stayed in their cells. Later, I saw Coy pick off three guards with as many shots. All the time those cons kept coming back and looking into the cell where we were laying. I thought sure Cretzer would come back and finish us off."

Baker added more details to the reporters' notes. "I was at my desk in the front office when we got word of the riot in the cellhouse. I ran into the cellhouse, and they jumped me. I was caught off guard. I saw Thompson running around the cellhouse with a rifle. He threatened me, but I didn't see him shoot anybody. He was always threatening someone. I heard Coy yell, 'I got that son-of-a-bitch in the tower,' but I couldn't tell which officer he was talking about."

Cochrane continued, "After reaching the island in a coast guard cutter, I drew a pistol from the armory and was detailed to assault the west gun gallery. I rushed toward D with my .45 pistol in my hand. Stites was covering me as I ducked and ran toward the penned up cons. Then I got hit. Stites went on after them and got killed. No, the cons didn't get to the prison arsenal. They couldn't reach it. It was protected by three steel doors. But they must have gotten at least one rifle from the gun gallery. A lot of shooting was done with that damn rifle. This must have convinced somebody that Coy had a machine gun."

* * *

"*Coy was the leader. But Cretzer seemed to get the most pleasure out of shooting people down.*"

ALCATRAZ '46

Stories of the blastout attempt appeared on the front pages of more than 600 morning newspapers in the United States and on thousands of others throughout the world.

Edward V. McQuade, crime and prison reporter for the San Francisco Chronicle, wrote a dramatic, but somewhat inaccurate, account of the event.

News of the blastout made sensational front page headlines.

ONE GUARD KILLED, NINE INJURED
AS PRISONERS CAPTURE ARSENAL

Rioting desperadoes on Alcatraz island yesterday turned the federal penitentiary there into an inferno of gunfire in one of the bloodiest prison uprisings in California history.

The barricaded prisoners were holding approximately 20, or more than half the normal complement of the island's guards as hostages.

The dead guard was Harold P. Stites. He had been machine gunned in the back at close range, according to the Coroner's office here.

A 'tough guy' convict, Bernard Paul Coy, Kentucky bank robber, precipitated the riot. Convict Coy's job was to clean up gun galleries. It was reported he overpowered a guard there, helped himself to weapons and made his way to the guards' dressing room, forced them at gunpoint into the cell block and threw a master switch opening all cells in the block. He asked the inmates to join him. Sixteen did.

The island was a ring of fire in the night, outlined harshly by search-lights and the blinking beacons of ceaselessly patrolling gunboats.

A cordon of heavily armed Navy and Coast Guard planes and boats encircled the island. Picked San Francisco police marksmen also patrolled the area in the police boat.

An unknown number of women, the wives of guards, nurses and clerical workers, took refuge in the island's air raid shelter — a relic of wartime preparedness.

One of the first wounded guards brought ashore last night, Fred Richberger, said he believed there were many wounded on the island, "but none we can get at." He indicated some were injured in blocked-off, besieged areas under the range of convict fire. "I had three years in Europe without getting shot and then this had to happen," he added.

Late last night Coast Guardsmen shuttling back and forth from the island with casualties reported the situation was 'still out of control.'

'All the cons in that cell block are armed,' a crew member of the prison launch reported.

As the fight progressed, the guards hunched down, ran along a ramp outside the tier windows, stood on tiptoes and fired rifles and tear gas bombs directly through the windows.

With tactics reminiscent of Indian warfare, the guards often would put their caps on the ends of extended rifle barrels, draw the convicts' fire and thus spot their position.

Warden Johnston revealed that a convict somehow had obtained a machine gun and had imprisoned 'most' of the island's officers in the cell house.

It was definitely reported that no prisoner had as yet escaped to the mainland, but police were stationed every block along the waterfront and all police and city emergency hospitals were alerted.

Nine San Francisco police cars, carrying about 20 especially armed officers, patrolled the waterfront to intercept any convict who might reach shore and to be on the alert should Johnston require additional help.

Alcatraz authorities were in radio communication with the police, Navy and Coast Guard boats.

Warden Johnston was believed reluctant to ask for military aid because the convicts were holding most of the prison officers as hostages and a full-scale offensive might incite them to murder the officers.

From the sound of the convicts' gunfire, experts estimated that in addition to the machine gun they had plenty of 45-calibre ammunition. A prison official said he knew definitely that one of the convicts had at least 30 rounds of rifle ammunition.

In San Francisco, anxious wives of Alcatraz officers and employees lined the Aquatic Park pier. Their children, for the most part oblivious of the day's tragic import, romped about.

As the battle still raged last night, Dr. J. C. Geiger, City Health Officer, ordered all emergency hospitals alerted. Harbor and emergency hospitals were expected to bear the brunt of treating the wounded and injured.

* * *

ALCATRAZ '46

An Oakland theater owner advertised in the morning newspapers that he was rerunning *King of Alcatraz,* the "sensational, punch-packed, thrill-crammed story of the man who blasted his way out of the impregnable rock." Made in 1938 by Paramount Pictures, the film starred Gail Patrick, Lloyd Nolan, J. Caroll Naish, Harry Carey, Robert Preston, Anthony Quinn, and Porter Hall. The owner expected large crowds for the performances.

* * *

Movie advertisement for "King of Alcatraz," the C-rated 1942 film starring J. Caroll Naish. Capitalizing on blastout publicity, film was quickly flown up from Hollywood to play in Bay Area theatres.

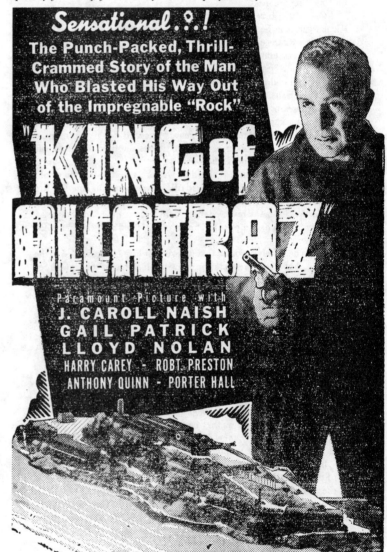

Warden Johnston placed a call to the army authorities. He requested that a Civilian Air Patrol airplane be assigned for duty over Alcatraz. He said he wanted to keep unauthorized civilian aircraft from flying over the island, but the real purpose was psychological.

"Maybe we can unnerve the escapees," said the associate warden. "From inside, they can see the Coast Guard ships. Now they will hear the army plane."

Major Tom Neblett, Wing Liason Officer, and Major Victor Rubon of the Army Air Force, were assigned by Hamilton Field officials to a fast, single-engined AT-6 trainer.

* * *

By 9:00 a.m., an enterprising citizen erected a huge poster on a 25-foot stretch of Aquatic Park waterfront. On the poster was printed the advertisement:

> See this spectacular riot!
> Mothers! See who might have been your son!
> Watch them try to escape and get killed in action!
> It will leave you breathless!
> One hour for one dollar.

* * *

Thousands of spectators crowded at various vantage points for a view of Alcatraz. Many brought lunches and prepared to spend the day. Absenteeism in San Francisco's public schools was high, but the stranded Alcatraz youngsters were present at classes because of the transportation provided by Red Cross busses. Motorists commuting to work, struggled in one of the largest traffic jams in Bay Area history. Cars were stopped bumper to bumper along the Embarcadero. Traffic was tied up on the bridges as hundreds of people hung over the railings to gaze at the island. Endless lines formed on Fisherman's Wharf behind the 10¢-a-look telescopes. Nearly the entire Bay Area population was gripped in attentive fascination.

Observers heard exploding grenades and small arms fire. They saw flashes, flames, and smoke. One woman spectator commented, "If you'd see a movie like this, you'd never believe it was real."

Ten miles away, San Quentin's 3800 inmates followed the events. Having access to daily newspapers from which nothing was censored and being able to listen to radio broadcasts with cell earphone equipment, many of them remained in their cells during the morning to follow the unfolding story. Warden Duffy permitted prison wide dissemination of news about the escape. He said, "Of course the inmates are intensely interested in the situation. I feel it is preferable to let them hear the truth. Otherwise, rumors of the wildest kind would circulate. There is, because of this, no tension in the prison. Everything is quiet and serene. It might serve as a good lesson for others."

At Folsom State Prison near Sacramento, Warden Robert A. Heinze expressed concern. He told reporters, "You never know about these kinds of insurrections. I have to keep in close touch with our own convict activities. This sort of thing sometimes becomes a disease. We had that little disturbance at the Preston School of Industry in Ione over the weekend, then this one at Alcatraz. While everything is quiet and serene at the moment, it takes only a couple of minutes for things to blow up."

ALCATRAZ '46

Headlines from the San Francisco News.

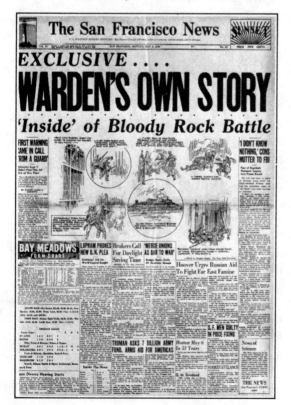

With more than 2200 inmates in his maximum security prison, Heinze revealed that he was short of men on the guard line. He asked the press to announce that there were 14 jobs available for qualified applicants.

* * *

The siege continued throughout the morning. Sharpshooters fired round after round in an attempt to flush out the armed inmates believed to be in D-block.

Observing from a chartered launch, reporter Jack Foisie wrote the following eyewitness account for the San Francisco Call Bulletin.

> The battle of Alcatraz, as it appears from the outside, has settled down to a grim effort to keep rebellious convicts pinned down in the one cell block they hold.
>
> Five stout men, protected by a ledge about 100 yards directly beneath and out from the "hot" cellblock window, are doing the job of keeping the convicts from reaching the window ledge — and a possible dash for freedom through the open shattered bars.
>
> They are doing the job by firing about every five minutes four rifle grenades through the cellhouse windows into D block.
>
> During the hours I watched, other weapons were used — bazookas and mortars. Earlier in the day, a few smoke bombs churned up outside the beleaguered cellhouse.
>
> It is understood that the five men who can be seen operating the grenade and mortar launcher devices with methodical precision, at least one is a Marine. They are preparing to fire, now. The grenades and mortars are attached carefully to the launching devices in the barrels of army weapons.
>
> There are slight reports as they leave the guns but drowned out by the sharp concussions as the projectiles strike the wall. Flashes of yellow flame light up — then curling black smoke.
>
> Each grenade sprays the cell area with jagged metal scraps for a radius of 60 feet, forcing the convicts inside to keep down on the floor, in corners, behind sheltering mattresses and blankets.
>
> Two more mortars are fired, and then the firing party relaxes. The men can be seen lighting cigarettes and stretching out on the beds of bright purple flowers.
>
> Major H. W. Thompson, who commanded a heavy weapons company in the 97th Division, is on the boat. It is his opinion that Warden Johnston has decided using more weapons heavier than grenades, bazooka shells, and mortars even though they can knock in the walls and give the convicts access to freedom during the night.

* * *

During second day of siege, tear gas grenades and smokebombs cast a shroud over main cellhouse.

ALCATRAZ '46

Despite the fact that no return shots had been fired for some time, the grenadiers on the south slope continued to send a seldom interrupted stream of fire into D-block. When the munitions supply diminished, an additional supply was sent from the Benecia Arsenal.

Before the fresh supply of munitions arrived, the associate warden suggested that the Marines use their flamethrowers to flush out the escapees, but the warden adamantly refused to approve the use of the weapons.

Bergen and his men continued to crouch behind the protective wall of the west gun gallery. "I'm about fed up with this mess," he said. "I've got a headache that won't stop. We've been up here for about 20 hours. Burch has been here even longer. It's about time we got relieved."

"Forget it, Phil," said Mahan. "They'll get around to relieving us when they get damn good and ready. Besides, who the hell wants to climb up or down those stairs with all that firing going on. I don't think anybody is anxious to come here and take our place. They aren't forgetting Stites got killed up here."

"We might have been killed too, if you guys hadn't wised up to that fool Anthony shooting at us from the hospital roof," said Burch.

"I've been thinking about that since Fred reminded me that Anthony's bullets were traveling east instead of west. There are other holes in this gallery wall, smooth on our side just like Anthony's bullet holes were. Look at these holes in the corner near where Stites was hit," indicated Bergen. "Three of them. All nice and smooth on our side. They had to come in from outside — from a gun tower or the hillside below the building."

"We might have been killed too, if you guys hadn't wised up to that fool Anthony shooting at us from the hospital roof."

Mahan said, "You're right, Phil. They are smooth on our side, just like the other ones."

"We'd better avoid the windows from now on," suggested Burch.

"Pass the word to Clark and Bloomquist to stay away from the windows," ordered Bergen. "And everybody keep low. We don't know when more grenades will be fired through those windows."

"Who do you suppose gave them the authority to do all that bombing?" asked Burch. "In all my years in the prison service, I never heard of anything like this."

"Well, the Marines brought all that hardware over here with them, and the warden probably thought it should be used. When he decides to do something, he does it. I'll bet he didn't bother to ask the Director of Prisons for permission. Jim Bennett is going to get a hell of a surprise when he arrives."

"Do you think he'll come from Washington for this?" asked Mahan.

"You can count on it. He'll be here asking plenty of embarrassing questions, especially if a lot of innocent inmates got hurt in this goddam senseless bombing."

"How soon do you think we'll find out if anyone got hurt in there, Phil?"

"Who knows? They should be sending in a lock up team soon. I don't like all those duds laying around on the floor. They sometimes explode if they're touched. I better warn them up front about those things."

* * *

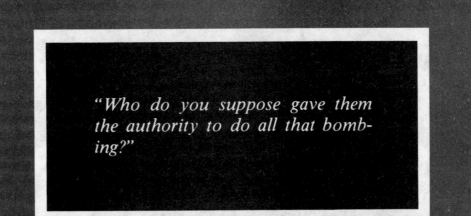

"*Who do you suppose gave them the authority to do all that bombing?*"

ALCATRAZ '46

Late Friday morning, two airplanes landed at San Francisco's International Airport. James V. Bennett, director of the nation's federal prisons, arrived from Washington D.C. Warden C. J. Shuttleworth, of the Federal Correctional Institution at Milan, arrived from Michigan. Shuttleworth was assigned to assist Bennett in an investigation of the blastout. Shuttleworth knew Alcatraz well, because he had been the first associate warden when it was activated in 1934 as a federal civil prison.

In a short interview on the way to a waiting car, the soft-spoken Bennett said to a reporter, "I'm here to look the situation over and find all the facts in the case. I can say this much: the situation is in hand. All the prisoners involved have surrendered with the exception of three. Two of those I presume are Coy and Cretzer. They have three weapons. What food they have, I don't know. We will try to get them out without killing or wounding them . . . if that is possible. Meanwhile, we are considering a starvation siege as one possibility."

* * *

James Bennett, Director of Federal Prisons, arrives at Alcatraz on May 4th.

From his cell on the top tier, Robert Stroud had a ringside seat. Crouched with him behind upturned mattresses was inmate Ed Sharp. They listened to the muffled thunder of exploding grenades in the C-block utility corridor and the clatter of men and machinery drilling through the roof. Rifle bullets and grenades whizzed through shattered windows in the south wall. Nearly all the window panes had been shot out and the waxed floor was littered with broken glass and other debris.

At 58, Stroud was one of the oldest inmates on the island, and he had the unenviable reputation of having been in isolation longer than any prisoner in U.S. history because officials considered him to be a psychopath with homicidal-suicidal tendencies.

While at Leavenworth, he had been allowed to have birds, cages, and laboratory equipment for study. After he was sent to Alcatraz in 1942, requests for such items were continually denied. In 1943 he published a 500-page book, *Digest of Bird Diseases,* and became known as "Bird Seed" Stroud. Without the items he requested for study, his attention turned to the study of law. The Alcatraz library housed the best collection of law books in the U.S. prison system, and Stroud's cell was well supplied with legal books and reference volumes. Finding that 12 inmates had been released from the island prison through writs of habeas corpus, Stroud became determined to be the thirteenth.

While in the Alcatraz segregation section, he received many privileges, including four hours yard exercise per week. He was allowed to subscribe to bird journals and was occasionally permitted to answer queries from teachers, zookeepers, and bird lovers throughout the world.

On this morning of siege, he wondered how much longer he and the 25 other inmates in D-block had to live. In one 10 minute interval, he counted 400 bullets and grenades slamming into the cellhouse.

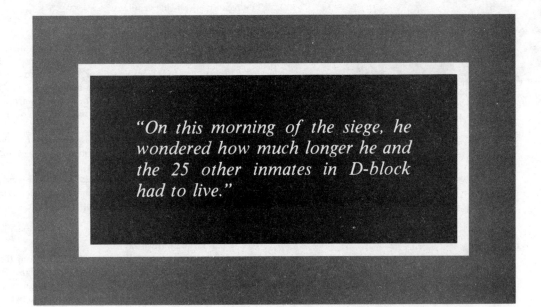

"On this morning of the siege, he wondered how much longer he and the 25 other inmates in D-block had to live."

ALCATRAZ '46

During a lull in the bombardment, Stroud put a box of hand-rolled cigarettes under his arm, stuffed matches into his pocket, and stepped from his cell. In a book* written some years later, he recalled:

The cold water on the flooded catwalk wet his stockinged feet. Ducking from cell to cell, he reached the dangerous stairs between tiers. He waited until a bomb exploded and then quickly ducked into Cell 15, near the gallery.

'This is Stroud speaking,' he yelled. 'What I say is the truth and I will back every word with my life. There is no gun in D block. What you are trying to do is pure murder.'

'I know it's you, Stroud,' said Lieutenant Bergen, holed up in the gun gallery. 'I wish I could believe you, but the evidence is against you.'

'Shut up, you lying old ———,' another guard yelled. 'You cons had your fun and now you can't take it. We're going to blow the block down and I hope you go with it.'

'What do I care,' yelled back Stroud. 'I'm an old man, spent my whole life in these outhouses. You're not beating me out of anything. If you have to kill somebody, I'll step out of here and give you the chance.'

'Take it easy, Stroud,' cautioned the Lieutenant. 'You'll live to write some more books.'

'There are twenty-five men in here innocent of any part in this nightmare.'

'Take it easy,' the guard answered. 'Keep your heads down,' he warned as more bombs hurtled in.

Suddenly the guard who had cursed him shouted: 'If you're so damned brave, why don't you get up there and make Coy throw that rifle down? You know he's up in 25.'

'He's not here and you know it. There is no gun in D block.'

'You're just covering up for him.'

'I just came from 25,' yelled Stroud, still louder. 'I was there all night. There are no guns in D block.'

Stroud waited, coolly thinking it over. Then he called out again. 'Mr. Bergen!'

'Yes.'

'You know the building better than I do. You say shots came from D block last night. I say none were fired inside D block. Now where could they have been fired to appear to come from D block, yet sound to me as if they were out in the cellhouse?"

'You mean the west-side ventilator?'

'Maybe that is your answer.'

The Guard Lieutenant hurried away.

The shooting and bombardment continued. It concentrated on the four end cells of the second and third tiers. The youngest and best educated of the prisoners in D block was 'Crow' Phillips. Stroud shouted for him to leave his cell, before it was blown apart.

'And get shot?' called back Phillips. 'I'm nice and warm in two inches of ice water, under a mattress with two solid feet of books in front of me. I'm O.K.'

Later one of the prisoners cried, 'Crow is hurt. He's bleeding.'

'Bergen,' Stroud called. 'Will you take a message to the warden?'

'Yes, I will. I can phone him. What is it?'

'Tell the warden there is no gun in D block. I back those words with my life. I will step out in front of any man he sends in here. He can use me for a shield. That's offering my life. I can't offer any more.'

Later Bergen returned.

'Stroud!'

'Here. What did the warden say?'

'The warden says tell the boys there will be no more firing through the windows and no more shells without warning. Tell them they can get up and walk around in their cells to keep warm. But no moving out of cell. If anything starts, duck for cover. And if you want to live . . . no wisecracks. We're going to try to take you out.'

Robert Stroud, the "Birdman of Alcatraz."

---

* Gaddis, Thomas E. *Birdman of Alcatraz, The Story of Robert Stroud.* New York: Random House, 1955, pp. 295-301.

Eighteen rifle grenades slammed into D-block in the 15 minutes before 1:00 p.m. Then the bombardment stopped.

* * *

The prison flag was adjusted to half mast. Fresh sandwiches and coffee were distributed to the officers. In small bags, soda crackers, apples, and Hershey bars were lowered from the roof to the men in the prison hospital. The inmates in the recreation yard were fed, and the officers who had remained in the yard overnight were relieved.

In the warden's office, Johnston explained to his staff, "I now believe that all the inmates still actively engaged in this mutiny are in the tunnel under the C-block cutoff. After we remove the other inmates from C-block, we shall continue to try to drive the mutineers out by dropping explosives on the C-block cutoff floor which forms the roof of the tunnel. Although the army sent us bombs that are heavier and more destructive than those we have been using, we are not going to use them. The use of flamethrowers to drive the men out of the tunnel has also been suggested, but I have decided against using such weapons."

After Bergen talked with the warden on the west gallery telephone, he said to his men, "You can relax. It's been decided that the gun we're looking for isn't in D after all. They think all the escapees are in the tunnel beneath the C-block cutoff."

"Too bad they didn't think that one up sooner," said Mahan.

* * *

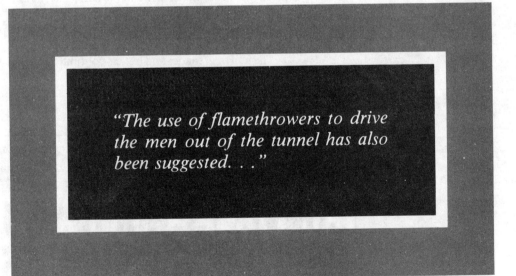

"The use of flamethrowers to drive the men out of the tunnel has also been suggested. . ."

Before the inmates in the recreation yard could be brought into the main cellhouse, some precautionary steps had to be taken. During the next hour, the three escapees were kept pinned down in the cutoff by showers of grenades at both ends of the utility corridor while officers moved the non-participating inmates from C-block and from the Broadway side of B-block into A-block. To accommodate all the men, more than half had to double-up in the one man cells. Because there was only one cot in each cell, extra mattresses were supplied for those who had to sleep on the floor.

While Earl Waller, the prison locksmith, removed the jammed lock the recreation yard gate, the six inmates in the kitchen area were rounded up and locked in cells. Officer Stucker was found unharmed in the basement. The 18 inmates with him were put into cells. Finally, the convicts in the recreation yard were brought in and placed in A and B blocks.

After locksmith Waller removed and replaced the plastered lock on the hospital gate, the civilian stewards, assisted by several officers, prepared sandwiches and coffee for the hungry inmates and officers in the hospital section.

When all the inmates were secured, the bombardment of the C-block utility corridor increased.

* * *

Crouched behind twisted debris in the cutoff tunnel, Coy pointed his rifle at the ventilators above him and fired several shots. Cretzer fired once and staggered in the muck on the floor. Hubbard's butcher knife had fallen into the ankle-deep filth. Each man had been hit several times by grenade fragments.

Slowly, painfully, Coy ejected a spent cartridge and loaded a live round into the firing chamber of his rifle. Resting the weapon carefully on the topmost plank of the barricade, he aimed through the haze at the distant door and curled his finger around the trigger.

"Now let them come," he said hoarsely. "I want just one more before I die."

The hail of grenades and bullets continued, but the corridor door did not open.

* * *

Headlines from the San Francisco Chronicle.

A special edition of the San Francisco Chronicle reached the streets in the early afternoon. The edition contained eyewitness accounts describing what had taken place during the previous 24 hours.

Roy Christiansen, International News Service Special Correspondent, wrote:

Sitting here on top of the cabin of this police launch, I am watching the battle of Alcatraz.

Across there to the west, maybe 200 yards from us, I see six guards creeping along a catwalk, alternately hugging the building to load and then leaning over the far edge of the catwalk to fire into windows a few feet above their heads.

They fire and jump back, fire and jump back.

The shots come to us as a steady, slow fire. We hear the boom of a shotgun, the crack of a rifle, the rat-tat-tat of a machine gun.

That may be the machine gun the convicts have, but at our distance we cannot tell who is doing the shooting and we can see no one at the windows into which the guards are firing.

The fighting is confined to a 50-foot section in the northwest corner of the west wing of the main cellblock.

The crouching guards are directly below the convicts. They fire up at a very sharp angle into the row of windows, apparently hoping their bullets will ricochet down and score a hit.

They go from window to window with their bullets, keeping up a steady drum fire that keeps the convicts back out of sight.

A few minutes ago I saw one of the guards stick his hat on the end of his rifle and lean it out from the catwalk. From this distance I could not tell where he drew fire.

Above and beyond them is another catwalk, and I can see several guards creeping along it on a course that will take them to the center of the fighting.

From here it appears that many of the guard towers no longer are manned because they are exposed to the fire of the felons.

But guards are standing motionless behind buildings, along catwalks out of the convicts' sight, on hidden roof-tops — in fact at every vantage point on the island that Warden James A. Johnston could place them.

From time to time they change station, or two or three of them creep out on the cell house catwalk to take fresh ammunition to the firing guards. When they come to an exposed spot they make a sudden dash.

A dozen of San Francisco's finest policemen, chosen for their marksmanship and courage, are on this launch with me waiting to get into the fight if their help is asked. In charge is Captain of Inspectors Bernard McDonald.

We have aboard tommy guns, tear gas guns, three automatic shotguns, rifles, and pistols.

* * *

After school, the Alcatraz youngsters were bussed by the Red Cross to the Y.M.C.A. and Y.W.C.A. for swimming and organized recreation.

When reporters tried to interview them, the children remained uncommunicative. Mrs. Cochrane provided an explanation of the children's reticence for the reporters, "It's natural for them to refuse to answer a stranger's questions. In addition, people on the island grow up sort of close-mouthed. You don't like to talk about your work guarding men. This may sound silly to you because you do a different kind of work, and you have a lot of strange ideas about Alcatraz, but watching over other men is the occupation of our husbands."

Wives and families of Alcatraz guards keep nervous vigil.

211

ALCATRAZ '46

In the later afternoon, the children spent their free time in the Stewart Hotel lobby, shouting and romping, turning round and round through the revolving door, and traveling up and down the elevators. In the evening, they would attend the 1945 Bob Hope/Bing Crosby movie, *Road To Utopia*, at the Fox Theater.

* * *

Shortly after 5:00 p.m., Joe Steere, the prison electrician, patrolled past the C-block utility corridor door at the east end of the cellhouse. He was startled by a rifle shot, muffled by the steel door and the concrete walls of the corridor. The high velocity .30-06 bullet bored one pencil-size hole in the door and ricochetted off the cellhouse wall in the visiting area, narrowly missing the officer.

When Warden Johnston was informed of this shot, he and his staff immediately assumed that one or more of the escapees had survived the bombardment. He ordered that another attempt be made to reason with them.

"By this time, they surely realize the utter hopelessness of their position and may be ready to surrender," said the warden, hopefully.

Steere unlocked the steel door and carefully opened it a few inches. Three heavily armed officers waited in readiness to prevent any attempt to blast out of the corridor. Standing to one side of the open door, Steere called to the escapees in the dark passageway. For more than five minutes, he pleaded with them to surrender, but there was no response.

The officers at the doorway stepped into the opening and emptied their shotguns into the long corridor. They listened to the gurgle and drip of shattered waterlines in the wrecked passageway, then closed and locked the heavy steel door.

* * *

In recalling the final hours of the siege, Warden Johnston wrote:

We ceased firing, put a watch at both ends of the utility corridor and 'covered' the top of the block so that they could be seen in case they decided to climb back to the spot from which they sniped at our rescue crew Thursday night.

The next thing in order was to relieve the officers who had been on duty continuously through the siege. It was past ten o'clock Friday night, and Mr. Burch had been on duty since eight o'clock Thursday morning, besides suffering from the slugging when his firearms were seized. Lieutenant Bergen and his squad were still in the west gun gallery where they had seen several of their brother officers wounded and one killed. When they were relieved, I asked Mr. Burch and Lieutenant Bergen to sit down and tell me and Associate Warden Miller all that had occurred. Mr. Burch was terribly tired, and his nerves were shattered, but he gave me a detailed account of what had happened to him. Lieutenant Bergen was tired, too, but mentally alert, and he was able to give me a clear picture of the way in which the prisoners were able to pick off the officers as they made their first attempt to regain the gun gallery.

All posts were manned with relief officers and everything was made secure at midnight. I persuaded Ed Miller to go home for a few hours rest. Loring Mills, who with Walter Bertrand, my secretary, had been handling telephones, telegrams, and teletypes, made a bed of blankets on the floor of my office so that he would be available to handle the teletype messages to and from Washington.

I went to my home just a few steps across the road from my office. I told Mrs. Johnston what had happened. She had been alone, locked in her room, since Thursday when the shriek of the siren warned her that

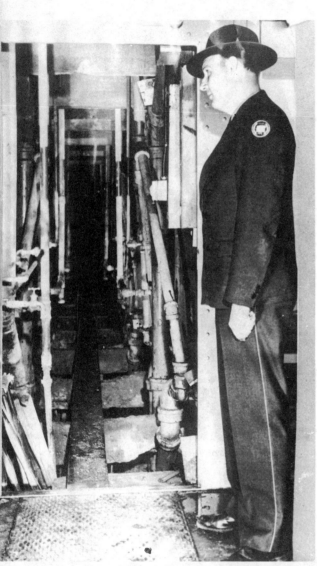

The utility corridor in the east half of C-block, referred to as the "Corridor of Death" by reporters, is where Coy, Cretzer, and Hubbard were slain.

there was trouble. She begged me to rest. I took off my clothes and got into bed, but I didn't seem to be sleepy. I was concerned about our wounded officers. I was wondering about the prisoners who had not participated but may have been endangered by the crossfire of the conflict. I was anxious for daylight. There was important work ahead and I wanted to act. I got up and went back to my office.

When Marine Warrant Officer Buckner was relieved from his duty on the cellhouse roof in the afternoon, he returned to the mainland. During the siege, he had become a tactical advisor to the prison officers.

Arriving at the dock in San Francisco, he was immediately interviewed by reporters. He told them that the siege of the prison was similar to "cleaning out labyrinth pillboxes tenanted by Japs."

"I've been a Marine 12 years," he said. "I fought on Bougainville and Guam, but you can say for me that Alcatraz Island prison is the toughest defensive position I ever saw."

"A group of us Marines went on the Rock Thursday after Warden Johnston called on Treasure Island barracks for help. Some of us dressed in prison uniforms, and we opened up on the cons with anti-tank rifle grenades from the west slope of the island."

"Later we got a hole cut through the top of the cellblock roof and lowered grenades. It was easy lowering grenades down the cell vents on strings. I must have lowered 500. They each would go off at different levels depending on how long the string was. With a second string, I'd pull the pin. Ducksoup. They shattered the vents to pieces. I also fired my anti-tank grenades right down the roof holes. My intent was to riddle a kind of concrete culvert or conduit where the cons were hiding. We'd drop a few grenades at each end of the block and give them a little time to run for this culvert. Then I'd fire the rifle grenades. If there's any cons in C-block, they're sure as hell dead cookies now."

* * *

ALCATRAZ '46

Marine Public Relations Officer points to picture of cellhouse where inmates took refuge.

Unceremoniously, Cretzer's body is carried into a waiting room at Dock 4 in Fort Mason. His crewcut hair is visible under coarse, grey wool blanket.

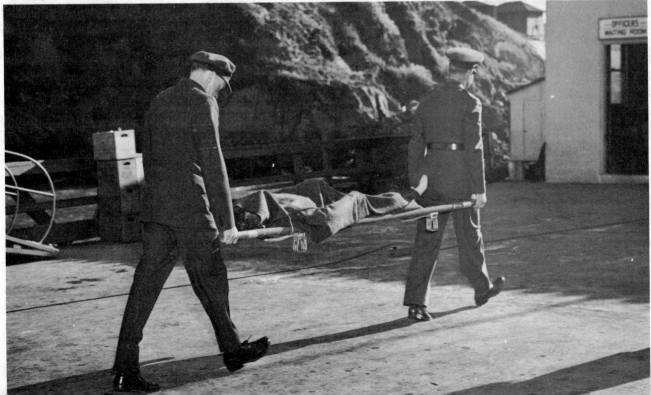

ALCATRAZ '46

Body of Hubbard is moved to a coroner's ambulance. Soldiers, newsmen, and relatives of wounded officers look on.

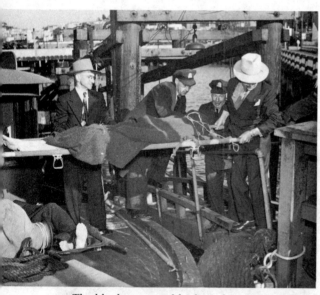

The blanket covered bodies of Coy, Cretzer, and Hubbard are brought to Fort Mason's Dock 4.

At exactly 6:00 a.m. Saturday morning, Associate Warden Miller and several officers converged on the utility corridor. Two officers cautiously opened the steel door. It was dark, damp, and silent inside. The valves which controlled the water lines had been closed during the night, and the sounds of leaking water were no longer heard. The corridor stunk of raw sewage, tear gas, and burned cordite. The floor was covered with liquid filth. Everything had been riddled thoroughly.

Miller shouted into the corridor, "This is your last chance. Get out here, or you're going to spend the rest of your lives dead."

When the ultimatum went unanswered, the officers blasted the corridor with their shotguns. Burst after burst penetrated the darkness until the officers ran out of shells. Again there was no response.

Miller growled, "Looks like we'll have to go in and dig them out."

Officers Steere, Mowery, and Delling volunteered to enter the corridor. Delling carried a portable searchlight; the others were armed with .45 calibre pistols. Cautiously, they waded through the ankle-deep muck, thoroughly soaking their shoes and trousers. When they reached the tangled maze of planks, pipes, and bullet-punctured ventilation ducts, they halted. Even with the searchlight, it was impossible to see what lay ahead in the black recesses of the corridor.

Pushing through the barrier, the officers came upon a grisly sight. The body of Coy, still clothed in Captain Weinhold's uniform jacket, was rigid. His left arm was extended at an angle and his right was flexed at the elbow supporting his weapon in a firing position. Four rifle bullets had torn through his body, ripping through his neck, right shoulder, left cheek, and left ear. There was a fired cartridge in the chamber of the rifle, one live round in the magazine, and 14 more in the pockets of Weinhold's jacket.

Cretzer's cold body was found a few feet behind Coy. He was wearing an officer's coat and belt with holster and ammunition clip-pouch. His pistol had slipped behind some pipes, but his position indicated that he, too, had been in a shooting position when he died. The cocked weapon, with the safety off, contained one live cartridge in the firing chamber and two in the clip. Cretzer had been shot through the left temple above the ear. The bullet had pierced his skull and torn through part of the brain. The path appeared to have been downward.

Behind Coy and Cretzer, lay Hubbard. Dressed in Coy's coat, he was facing the east end of the tunnel. Submerged in the watery filth near him was the butcher knife. He had died from a bullet above the left eye which crashed out through the back of his skull. A second rifle bullet had entered the left side of his head above the ear and emerged through the right ear. Hubbard had not been dead long. His body was warm.

Death had released the men from the prison.

214

EPILOG

"The best way to deflate ego-maniac
individuals is to tell the truth about them.
Had John Dillinger been depicted for the
filthy type of vermin he was, crawling
through holes of our law enforcement,
rather than as one series of articles
portrayed him, a clever and adventurous
individual given a marked degree of chivalry
of Robin Hood proportions, perhaps there
would not be so many stupid boys like
Cretzer laying dead, naked, and unclaimed."

J. Edgar Hoover

"I have no quarrel with society. It ought
not have none with me. I only want what's
coming to me. I've been wrong all my life.
But I ain't bad. Now, in this hole, I fight
the atmosphere, the silence, the bodies.
No one feels the hard misery inside me . . ."

Joseph Cretzer

The Aftermath

Marine Pfc. William L. Pruitt, stationed on Treasure Island, planned to marry Miss Stella Lucille Linscott of Berkeley Saturday afternoon, but he was activated for duty on Alcatraz on Thursday. Miss Linscott was relieved when she learned the siege was over and that Pruitt would be released in time to go through with the ceremony.

* * *

Upon finding Coy, Cretzer, and Hubbard dead, an immediate search was conducted for the remaining participants in the escape attempt. Associate Warden Miller and a team of officers first located Carnes in his B-block cell.

Ordering the cell unlocked, Miller glared at the Indian youth and growled, "Put your hands on top of your head."

Shoving the terrified Carnes onto the tier walkway, Miller forced him to undress.

"Strip down to your redskin ass," he ordered. Turning to the other officers, he said, "Some of you men take him over to A-block and throw him in one of those dark holes. If he makes a false move, blow his rotten head off."

Taking several officers with him, Miller headed for Shockley's cell in D-block. Unlocking the cell door, Miller barked at the three men inside, "All right, Shockley. Get your ass out of there."

"I ain't done nothing. We been in here all the time, ain't we fellows?" The other inmates did not answer.

"Watch him," cautioned Miller. "He may have a knife. Shoot him in the balls if he makes a funny move."

"I been here all the time. I got no knife. Honest, I'm innocent. I never went out of this block."

"Come out of that cell. Pull off your clothes. All of them, and throw them over the rail."

Shockley stumbled onto the tier walkway and stripped. Miller growled, "You rat. We know you were out there helping to kill those officers. Admit it or I'll kick your teeth in."

Shockley moved to escape his captors but was slammed back against the cellfront. Whining and begging, he mumbled, "Honest, I'm innocent. I wasn't no friend of theirs."

One officer asked Miller, "What do we do with this garbage?"

"Take him to A-block and put him in a dark cell. But don't hurt him. Don't put any marks on him. He'll get what he deserves soon enough."

Shockley's bare feet were bleeding as he was roughly led away through the broken glass on the D cellhouse flats.

Opening Thompson's C-block cell next, Miller ordered, "O.K. Get out of there and strip."

"But I ain't done nothing."

"Quit lying, you bastard, or you'll take a dive off this tier. You didn't want any witnesses, did you? Well, we have witnesses, and they're going to send you to the gas chamber."

Handcuffed D-block inmates being transferred to other Federal prisons.

The San Francisco Chronicle carried the following editorial in its morning edition:

PROMETHEUS AT ALCATRAZ

Almost all prison breaks are a matter of desperate chance, but it is probable that in any definitive study of prison breaks the wild thrust at Alcatraz would go down as the most foredoomed of all.

Even had the prisoners managed to shoot or neutralize every official on the island, they would have faced a moat through which perhaps one convict in a hundred would have a chance.

A 'successful' break on Alcatraz, therefore, could lead only to siege, a siege in which convicts might be prepared to be hard to kill but not hard enough to make any conceivable difference to them in the end.

For they were up against the whole weight of their country's society, without even liaison lag between State and Federal authority. Were it necessary, they were up against thousands of men who have spent recent months digging suicidal Japanese out of caves at Saipan and Okinawa. If need be, they were up against flame-throwers, and indeed in ultimate theory against bombing planes and artillery. The adventure of Alcatraz's handful thus moves out of comparison with Canon City and Dannemora and takes on the color of classic drama, when man, dragooned protagonist of death, is driven inexorably toward his goal.

It may be that Bernard Coy and Joseph Cretzer went through the mental motions of weighing their chances. It would have made no difference: they were in Alcatraz because they were men who had failed in judging the odds in the sanguinary adventurer's war against his fellows.

As to why this judgment goes wrong, perhaps William Bolitho was right; that the adventurer is peculiarly drugged by the stuff of adventure and cannot think of failure. It may be, as Sigmund Freud had it, that there are men in subconscious search of death.

And it could be a mixture of all: the caged adventurer "thinking out" his last, lost adventure with a judgment ruined by the corrosion of confinement, extravagantly magnifying his minuscular chances and feeling for death, if not welcome, at least something very different from that felt by those picnicking on the green Marina a few hundred yards away.

In any case, it was an epic drama of man bound upon a rock, and Aeschylus would have lifted it to the plane of universal tragedy and grandeur.

* * *

Thompson removed his clothing and stood naked on the cell-block tier walkway.

"Get on to A-block, pimp," snarled an officer. "I hope you make a false move, just one false move. I'd like to tag you, personally."

When coffee and sandwiches were passed around to the non-participating inmates later that day, Carnes, Shockley, and Thompson each received only a handful of soda crackers and a cup of water.

* * *

Late Saturday morning, Warden Johnston held the first press conference in Alcatraz's history. He escorted a large group of newsmen to his island office where weapons, bandages, and paraphernalia of an improvised First Aid Station lay on his desk. Tired, stubble-bearded officers grinned modestly as Johnston spoke about the courage of his men. He then provided reporters with a list of weapons used during the siege:

1. Shotguns — 12-gauge, Remington automatic. This weapon is deadly with buckshot at 50 yards and might do serious injury at a greater distance. It holds four shells in the magazine and one in the chamber.

2. Tear Gas Launcher — snubnosed barrel 1½ inches in diameter, mounted on a short stock. Operates on principle of Very pistol. Shoots two types of tear gas shells. One is long range (up to 200 yards), which explodes on contact. Other is for close range shooting gas for 50 feet directly out of barrel.

3. Springfield .30-06 Rifle — a very accurate weapon at up to 1000 yards but can kill at greater range. Bolt action, high power, carries five cartridges in magazine and one in chamber.

4. Garand M1 Rifle — Standard .30-06 caliber weapon of Marines and United States Army. Best accuracy at 500 yards. Semi-automatic, clip holds eight shells.

5. Pistol, .45 Cal. — semi-automatic, hard-hitting standard side-arm of U.S. Armed Forces. Fifty yards is a long shot with this one. Cartridge clip holds seven rounds.

6. Thompson Sub-Machine Gun — fires 600 to 800 rounds per minute. Cal., 45. Range best at 75 yards. Clips hold either 20, 50 or 100 rounds.

7. Carbine — light, handy, 15-shot semi-automatic weapon widely employed by armed forces. Best accuracy is had at distances not over 150 yards. Its .30 Cal. cartridges are not high velocity.

8. Fragmentation Grenades — these are the famed "pineapples." Weighing less than two pounds they can be hurled on an average of 35 yards. Their effective radius is about 15 yards but sometimes the fragments kill at much greater distances. These were dropped through holes in the roof into the utility corridor in C Block.

9. White Phosphorous Grenades — spray of burning particles shot forth by these grenades renders particularly demoralizing ef-

fect. In addition they hinder breathing, hurt the eyes and conceal movement.

10. Rifle-Grenades — these are launched from a rifle or carbine equipped with a small "adapter" device. They will penetrate armor or masonry and can be hurled 300 to 400 yards, with remarkable accuracy. These were shot into D via windows and dropped through holes in the roof into the C cut-off area.

For nearly two hours, Johnston described, chronologically, the details of the battle. Occasionally he answered questions from the reporters.

"Yes, Coy had a crude bar-spreader made out of toiletbowl fittings and pipes. Nobody knows how long ago he made it or how he smuggled it into the prison. He might have had it for months. He also had a Stilson wrench from the cellhouse maintenance tool kit. Where he hid those things, we don't know. It's funny, too, because we searched his cell only a few days ago on a routine inspection."

When he finished recounting the story, Johnston rose and led the newsmen and photographers through the main cellhouse. Along Broadway he said, "The first thing an escape-minded prisoner does is 'case the joint.' He watches everything, every officer. He looks and looks for a weak point. Sixty-five of our prisoners were transferred here as too tough to keep in other prisons. They are considered high escape risks and are closely watched so they don't have an opportunity to try anything. Then, just when things look safe, along comes a well-behaved inmate like Coy, whom you try to trust, and he winds up tearing the place apart. But all our officers come into this lion cage knowing that the inmates appraise their moves. Coy must have watched Burch for days to know his exact routine and movements."

Warden Johnston points to the top of the west gun gallery while explaining to reporters how Coy spread bars to enter the gun cage.

Warden Johnston examines cell where officers were held captive.

ALCATRAZ '46

"The maximum security prison still maintained its 12-year escape proof reputation."

Reporters noted that the concrete walls and several of the steel doors were bullet-nicked. Bulletproof glass observation windows were scarred as though frosted. As they walked down the aisle between B and C blocks, the inmates yelled and cursed from their cells. Johnston ignored them. Quietly, the warden led the reporters to the east entrance of the C-block utility corridor. The 30-inch wide passage, dark, narrow, and wet with sewage, still smelled of tear gas and burned cordite. Above the cutoff, in the prison roof, was the jagged hole through which anti-tank grenades and other explosives had been dropped.

"In there," pointed Johnston, "the three mutineers died, barricaded in a tunnel below the cutoff. A pretty good fox hole, but we outfoxed them. Our attack drove them farther and farther back into the bowels of the block. At the end, they were deeper in the rock than any prisoner ever had been before."

Inmates again rose behind their bars and hooted and jeered. Johnston disclosed that a number of them had demanded medical care for a variety of injuries allegedly sustained during the fighting. Only one inmate, James Grove, who complained of a shrapnel wound in his wrist, was sent to the prison hospital. It was later determined that his wound was self-inflicted in the hope of getting transferred to a mainland hospital from which he might escape.

"The situation is almost normal, now," continued the warden. "In fact, as you can see, our regular routine is being restored rapidly. This was a bitter incident, but I'm satisfied there was nothing irregular, nothing we can criticize in the conduct of our personnel."

As the reporters and photographers departed, Johnston gave a final comment. "I hope you remember that this wasn't a riot in the sense your newspapers have headlined. It was simply a plot for a mass escape, a blastout in the old fashioned sense. But this incident in our history has demonstrated that this is a pretty tough place to get out of."

The maximum security prison still maintained its 12-year escape-proof reputation.

* * *

Late Saturday afternoon, Mrs. Cochrane stood on Dock 4 with a group of women and children waiting for the prison launch to take them home. Her two daughters were with her.

The launch was 200 feet off the dock when the women noticed the three blanket-wrapped bundles on its bow. Mrs. Cochrane stared at the bundles and shuddered.

When the boat docked, the women and children boarded the launch, but Mrs. Cochrane stopped at the gangplank and asked the launch operator if there would be another boat at 6:00 p.m. When she was assured there would be another boat, she and her daughters returned to the dock waiting room.

Army enlisted men from Fort Mason carried the three wire baskets to the waiting vehicle that would take the bodies to the San Francisco Morgue.

"Now we can go home and get some sleep," said Officer Marshall Rose stepping back onto the prison launch. He and Officer Marvin Orr had not slept for two days.

* * *

A Marine Corps Public Information Officer in San Francisco disclosed that during the peak of fighting, he received numerous telephone calls from ex-Marines who offered to re-enlist if they could be sent to fight on the island.

* * *

Kay Benedetti, shocked and upset, begged newsmen and photographers to leave her alone. Her husband pushed reporters away from their Hunters Point housing project apartment.

"Stop bothering her," he said. "She was no gun moll. She wants to lead a decent life. She told the coroner she won't go to the morgue to claim or even see Cretzer's body, even though Cretzer named her as the person who should get the body if he died in prison. She doesn't want anything to do with this. It's all over."

* * *

Late Saturday afternoon, the government announced that if the bodies of Coy, Cretzer, and Hubbard remained unclaimed after 30 days, it would contract with a local funeral parlor for inexpensive burials.

* * *

"The launch was 200 feet off the dock when the women noticed the three blanket-wrapped bundles on its bow. Mrs. Cochrane stared at the bundles and shuddered."

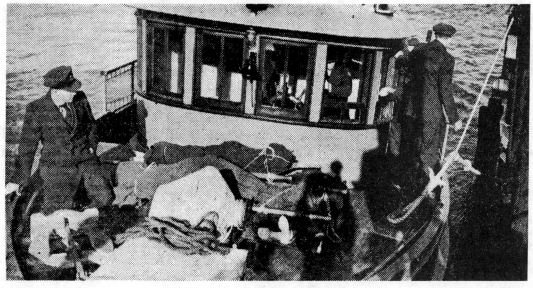

ALCATRAZ '46

On Sunday morning, inmates silently watched while prison officials posed for newspaper and newsreel pictures below the bombed-out windows. Officers reenacted battle-episodes for the cameramen.

Nearby, Army personnel with steel detonation boxes collected unexploded grenades. False rumors spread among the inmates that two-inch shells had been fired into the prison from Navy destroyers and Coast Guard gunboats.

* * *

Dr. G. T. Kerhulas invited newsmen into the shade-drawn Kingston Alley Morgue. Assistant Chester Goodwin wheeled the bodies of Coy, Cretzer, and Hubbard into the room one at a time while Kerhulas, wearing surgical rubber gloves, identified the wounds on each of the convicts.

"I would estimate that all three men died about the same time, late Friday night or early Saturday," Kerhulas said. "Death was instantaneous in all three cases. Goodsized rifle bullet holes. High velocity bullets. Range could have been a hundred yards . . ."

On Monday morning, the San Francisco Examiner carried the headlines:

'BIG SHOTS' OF ALCATRAZ RIOT LIE ALONE, UNMOURNED IN S.F. MORGUE

Autopsy Surgeon Finds Bullets That Wrote Final Chapter in Sordid, Unglamorous Life of Crime

Some reporters, noting that Coy's body was extremely thin, inferred that all Alcatraz inmates were being cruelly starved. One newsman observed, "I saw the concentration camp at Dachau, and these men look as starved. This kind of hunger doesn't just happen during a forty-hour battle. It had to be systematic."

Without checking further, stories were quickly published. These stories, which described imaginary mistreatments of prisoners, contributed to the public's misconception of the Alcatraz prison.

* * *

In the afternoon, U.S. Attorney Frank J. Hennessy announced he would seek to indict the surviving mutineers for the murder of Officer William Miller. Twenty-four inmates, who allegedly participated in the escape, would be included in the conspiracy indictment. Assistant U.S. Attorney Daniel C. Deasy added that Warden Johnston, F.B.I. agents, and Alcatraz officers would be called as witnesses, but no inmates would be asked to testify for the prosecution.

"Where one or more participants in a conspiracy to escape actually killed someone, the others would be part of that conspiracy and could also be charged with murder," explained Deasy. "If the men are convicted and sentenced to the death penalty in a Federal Court trial, they would be executed in California's gas chamber at San Quentin. Since the Federal Government has no facilities for executions, it uses the facilities of the State in which the Federal crime occurred. At this time, the F.B.I. is investigating and taking statements from prisoners as well as guards. When the material is assembled, the matter will be presented. There is a good chance that the evidence will be sufficient to at least indict Carnes, Shockley, and Thompson for murder."

* * *

In the Bay Area's 9 newspapers, only one Letter to the Editor was written concerning the escape attempt. Bill Banning of Oakland wrote:

> Editor: The Alcatraz fight is not finished. It remains for the F.B.I. to browbeat some prisoners into involuntary confessions. Life in prison is difficult enough without being prosecuted for refusal to squeal.

> Very few prisoners voluntarily talk to guards or officials; among those at Alcatraz I'd say there are none. There is one reason why they are at Alcatraz, they won't cooperate with the officials.

> The F.B.I. is not interested in truth and justice, but in prosecution and conviction.

* * *

Special agents for the F.B.I. routinely interviewed the entire prison population. Agents Alan Trichak and Ivan Baier told reporters that little information was obtained because they encountered a "wall of silence as cold and hard as the walls of a cellblock."

* * *

From his *Digest of Bird Diseases* book royalties. Stroud authorized $200 to be forwarded to court appointed defense attorneys for Carnes, Shockley, and Thompson. Other prison inmates turned down prison jobs, transfers, and other advantages in order to be available to testify at the trial.

An angry Stroud claimed that the indiscriminate bombardment of D-block and the 34-hour delay in rescuing non-participating inmates was as scandalous as Teapot Dome. He wanted to inform the courts and press that D-block was a private purgatory where a few carefully chosen victims could slowly be driven mad.

* * *

Robert Stroud (center) contributed $200 to defense of Carnes, Shockley, and Thompson.

ALCATRAZ '46

During the days after the siege, editorials appeared in most local newspapers. The San Francisco Examiner challenged the value of Alcatraz:

WHY ON ALCATRAZ?

The latest — and worst and bloodiest — uprising on Alcatraz underscores an issue of long concern to San Franciscans: What is a maximum security Federal penitentiary, for the Nation's most hardened desperados, doing on San Francisco's doorstep?

WHAT CAN BE MORE CONDUCIVE TO HATCHING AN ESCAPE PLOT IN THE MIND OF AN EMBITTERED FELON, SERVING OUT VIRTUALLY HIS LIFE THAN THE LOCATION OF ALCATRAZ?

He sees the city's skyline before him, continually. It is so near — the FREEDOM, LIFE, and LIGHTS. Days, months, he lives with it. It looms up, a constant mirage before him.

The island, itself, is impractical for a maximum security prison. Its confines are cramped. Men are caged like wild animals, in despair.

A prison's chief purpose is to change criminals into useful men.

BUT ALCATRAZ, WITH ITS HISTORY OF BLOODY REVOLTS, APPEARS ONLY TO AGGRAVATE CRIMINALITY INTO HOPELESS, VENGEFUL SAVAGERY.

San Francisco is not the place for this institution. San Francisco, with its wide area in which an escaping convict could hide out; with its population which could be menaced by a successful mass break.

The Alcatraz penal institution is a blot on the bay. By now, Federal authorities should realize this — and transfer it elsewhere.

* * *

A citizens committee demanded that Alcatraz prison be transferred elsewhere. With the slogan "Banish the Blemish of the Bay", they based pleas to federal officials upon three factors:

1. The location of Alcatraz is such that prisoners are constantly stirred with the idea of escape.

2. The proximity of San Francisco offers an escaped convict every opportunity to be able to hide if he gets off the island and to shore.

3. If such institutions as Alcatraz are desirable, they should be located in an isolated place — far from the center of population.

* * *

Mrs. T. W. Cahill pleaded with the Berkeley City Council to change Alcatraz Avenue to Eisenhower Avenue. She argued, "Because of the publicity and disgrace, no one on the street is proud to live on Alcatraz Avenue. San Francisco has suffered a lot of adverse publicity over the prison revolt — a publicity that we do not deserve. How do you think we like living on this street?"

Mrs. Cahill's request was referred to a sub-committee of the City Council. The name of the avenue was not changed.

* * *

Dr. Henry Grady, former Chamber of Commerce president and Chairman of American President Lines stated, "I think I am speaking for many San Franciscans when I say that I would rather see a plain, natural, and beautiful island out there than a prison surrounded by walls."

* * *

Warden Johnston ordered the interior of the prison to be repaired and repainted as quickly as possible. The landscaping budget was increased to make the exterior of the prison building appear more attractive to residents of the Bay Area.

After surveying the damage, Bureau of Prisons Construction Engineers began repairing and improving the interior of the cellhouse. The jagged hole cut in the ceiling was sealed immediately. Crossbars were installed in the face of the west gun gallery. Cyclone wire fencing was stretched across the bars of both gun galleries to provide additional protection.

The most extensive damage was found in the C-block utility corridor and in the crawl-space under the cutoff. The cellblock's utility lines were almost totally destroyed. Electrical conduits, fresh water lines, salt water lines, sewer lines, and ventilation ducts were completely inoperable. The plank catwalks on the middle and upper levels of the utility corridor, and their steel supports, were grotesquely twisted. Much of the structure had fallen to the floor of the narrow passageway or was precariously suspended in space. Atop the block, the huge D.C. motors, which operated the ventilator fans, had been changed into useless junk by grenades and bullets. The reinforced concrete rear walls of the C-block cells, although scarred and scorched by the exploding grenades, had not been pierced by the hail of shrapnel and bullets.

During the rebuilding, inmates who had been assigned to C-block, were housed temporarily in A-block. After checking the prison behavior records, officers reassigned inmates to the old cellblock. To make this block functional, the long unused sanitary facilities in the 126 cells had to be reactivated. Fortunately, the electrical circuits and the sewer lines were operable, and the water lines were intact, however, the wash basins and the water closets in many of the cells were inoperable. Because of this, it was sometimes necessary to place two men in one cell. To the administration, it was clear that a reduction of the inmate count was imperative.

In the following weeks, approximately 30 of the non-participating inmates, most of whom had previously been recommended for return to other federal penal institutions, were transferred from Alcatraz. This enabled the prison administration to return to its single-occupancy cell system.

* * *

Throughout the week following the battle, reporters haunted Kay Benedetti. She denied having knowledge that Cretzer was going to break out of prison. She said she last saw him during a brief prison visit more than 16 months earlier.

"Even if he made it, I wouldn't have helped him," she declared.

* * *

After an investigation of the escape attempt, James V. Bennett, Director of the Federal Bureau of Prisons, held a press conference. Praising all the Alcatraz personnel for the way in which they handled the emergency, he stated, "There was not the least indication of negligence or carelessness or inefficiency in this affair. The felons found and took advantage of a weakness which not the most experienced and able prison man could anticipate. When the emergency broke, it was handled intelligently, courageously, and with great devotion to duty. Casualties were kept at a minimum. After the first half hour or so, there were no casualties except among the rioters. What was to have been a mass escape, failed utterly. Warden Johnston deserves high commendation."

To the press and all personnel in the Federal Prison System, Bennett distributed copies of a tribute to the officers killed in action.

A Tribute to
William A. Miller and Harold P. Stites

When men of courage and steadfastness lose their lives in the faithful performance of their duty, there is little that need be said by those of us who did not face the danger. Their deeds speak far more eloquently. But I am sure there is no one in the entire Federal Prison System whose heart is not quickened with pride and at the same time saddened with a very real sense of loss when two such heroic men as William A. Miller and Harold P. Stites make the supreme sacrifice. Perhaps the best memorial we can erect to these men is an invisible one: a conscious dedication of our own efforts to bring to reality the principles and objectives for which we have striven so long and which they so well exemplified in their final unselfish devotion to duty. Let us so dedicate ourselves, let us so perfect our procedures and build so well that no such tragedy may ever again come to any of our people. That, I think, is what these men would wish.

After the press conference, Democrat George P. Miller, Representative from the Sixth Congressional District in Alameda and Contra Costa Counties, told newsmen, "I don't believe either Bennett's or Johnston's story of the rioting and its causes. When I return to Washington, I will ask the Department of Justice to undertake a further and fuller inquiry into what the prison is doing to men out there. If I am not satisfied, I'll call upon Congress, by resolution, to dig to the bottom of the whole affair."

* * *

In Washington D.C., Attorney General Tom Clark announced, "I am extremely proud of the officers who advanced into the cell-block under heavy fire and brought out their wounded comrades. These were acts of heroism worthy of the finest traditions of the prison service."

Washington, May 13, 1946

My dear Warden Johnston:

Mr. Bennett has just given me an account of the manner in which the courage, bravery and quick thinking of you and your staff prevented the mutiny at Alcatraz from becoming a truly serious calamity.

I would like you and every member of your staff to know of my appreciation and admiration for the outstandingly courageous and intelligent manner with which you and your officers coped with the revolt. All of you performed a signal service in protecting the public from the desperate criminals with whom you must deal and showed a devotion to duty which I am sure will command the admiration of every good citizen. The fine job you did under extremely difficult and dangerous circumstances will add further to the excellent reputation the Federal Prison Service has earned.

Our sincerest sympathy goes forward to the families of those officers who died shielding the lives of others and our best wishes for a speedy recovery are extended to those who performed their tasks so unselfishly.

Sincerely yours,
TOM CLARK,
Attorney General.

ALCATRAZ '46

Hubbard's body was claimed by his wife and shipped to Alabama for burial.

"If only he had bided his time and hadn't participated in the escape," commented Hubbard's attorney, James E. Burns. "It might have been a different story for him today."

Assistant U.S. Attorney Karesh moved for dismissal of Hubbard's habeas corpus petition. Karesh stated, "In all probability, the petition would have been granted and Hubbard would have been returned to Tennessee for retrial."

* * *

Officer Harold Stites was buried near San Francisco. His wife and children moved to Santa Rosa, California. Mrs. William Miller accompanied the body of her husband to Philadelphia by train. Both women paid for funeral expenses out of family savings because the Federal Bureau of Prisons never paid for the funerals of prison officers, even for those who died in the line of duty.

Prison officers throughout the Federal Prison System took up a collection. $6,900 was divided equally between Mrs. Stites and Mrs. Miller.

* * *

After more than a week's delay, Kay Benedetti claimed the body of Joseph Cretzer.

"I told Joe I was going to marry a good man, and I wouldn't be seeing him anymore," she told reporters. "I really wanted to start a new life. But because he loved me, I'll see to his burial. He was really a good man, once you came to know him. He would have meant no harm if he had gotten a few decent chances in his life."

Kay had the body cremated at the Cypress Lawn Cemetery. She and an unidentified man were the only people present at a brief service.

Following the service, Kay and her friend, Helen Wallace, pleaded not guilty to a shoplifting charge before Municipal Judge Daniel R. Shoemaker. The two women were charged with stealing a $19 hat and a $40 coat from a Market Street department store.

* * *

Bernard Coy was buried in a local cemetery at government expense.

* * *

"He was really a good man, once you came to know him. He would have meant no harm if he had gotten a few decent chances in his life."

Many of the men who had been flown from other federal prisons, remained at Alcatraz for several weeks to help maintain order and to facilitate the much needed repairs.

No immediate changes were made in the routine operation of the prison except for those considered necessary to maintain security — a second officer position was restored to the west gun gallery day watch.

* * *

In the next month, the wounded officers, one after another — Roberts, Besk, Richberger, Lageson, Cochrane, Baker, and Oldham — returned to duty. Captain Weinhold and Lieutenant Simpson remained in critical condition for a long period of time. After a slow recovery, they became eligible for disability retirement.

* * *

Captain Weinhold

Lieutenant Simpson

ALCATRAZ '46

Handcuffed and under heavy armed guard, Carnes, Shockley, and Thompson were arraigned before Federal Judge Michael Roche seven weeks after the escape attempt. Before the three neatly dressed men entered the courtroom, the chains which linked them together were removed.

With 14 deputy marshals posted in and outside the room, the murder indictments were read. No emotion was shown by any of the three inmates.

* * *

When the trial opened on November 20, 1946, the prosecutor built his case around two charges: first degree murder of Officer William Miller; conspiracy to commit murder. The inmates had not been indicted for the death of Officer Harold Stites.

Defense attorneys developed their case around inhuman prison conditions and negligence of officers. Speaking in defense of Thompson, Attorney Vinkler told the jury, "The convicts had been deprived of proper food and had not been given the proper medical treatment. They were deprived of newspapers. Their mail, incoming and outgoing, was censored. The guards, because they are guards on Alcatraz, have an innate sense of hostility to the prisoners. They acquired the prison point of view. Petty peeves that you and I would not pay any attention to were magnified in their minds. Whenever a prisoner said something that might not just set right, the guards, having the position of authority and feeling they were superior, naturally took advantage of these men. I am not telling you that the inmates were angels. The men obviously have been convicted of certain crimes. But what I am trying to tell you is that any break that took place in Alcatraz was the result of the mistreatment and the indignities inflicted upon these men.

The accused — Thompson, Shockley, and Carnes.

"Cretzer who is now dead is far better off. He was going blind. He knew he was going blind. Coy had long planned the so-called break. Coy told one of the prisoners a long time ago that he was going to escape from Alcatraz, and when this prisoner said to him, 'How are you going to do it, Coy?' he said, 'See,' pointing to the west gun gallery where Guard Burch was walking along, 'that is the way I am going to escape.'

"The witnesses who are going to be produced by the defense will be convicts. But the prosecution or the Government's testimony will be supplied, naturally, by guards. The Government has not called one convict as witness. It is practically an issue of convicts against guards. Who is going to tell the truth? These convicts hate those guards just as much as these guards hate the convicts. There is going to be some lying here.

"The Government is going to present its testimony before the defense naturally puts in its testimony. They have the first punch. As a matter of fact, there are a good many prisoners who were in Alcatraz on May 2, 1946, and some officers who are now scattered all over the United States. These men could testify probably to the advantage of the defense, but we do not know where these men are. We cannot subpoena these men until we have spoken to them. The Government knows where all these witnesses are but will only produce witnesses in favor of the prosecution.

"But I am especially concerned that many inmate eye-witnesses are at this moment being dispersed throughout prisons in the U.S. and only prison officials know who is being sent where. I charge that this is a conspiracy to keep us from the truth of who killed Stites and Miller."

* * *

Throughout 10 weeks of testimony, Judge Goodman repeatedly ruled that conditions within the cellhouse and officer attitudes and motivations were irrelevant and immaterial. The prosecution insisted that all three defendants were involved one way or another with the death of Officer Miller, but it did not ask for the death penalty for Carnes.

In summarizing the case for the prosecution, the U.S. Attorney concluded his plea for a death penalty by saying, "They that live by the sword shall perish by the sword."

* * *

After 14 hours of deliberations, a jury of six men and six women returned its verdict at 12:40 p.m. on December 22, 1946.

Brushing aside a number of defense motions, Judge Goodman passed sentences: death in San Quentin's gas chamber for Shockley and Thompson; another life sentence for Carnes. Upon the jury's recommendation, Carnes' life was spared because of the mercy he showed the captive officers before and after they were shot.

* * *

As payment for his defense fees, Thompson gave Attorney Spagnoli a piece of soiled paper upon which was written a "fool proof system" for winning at dice tables. Later, in Reno, Spagnoli won $200 using the system.

* * *

Prison Guard Bert Burch testifying at coroner's inquest in San Francisco on May 10th.

ALCATRAZ '46

On Thursday evening, December 2, 1948, Shockley and Thompson spent their last hours in the two holding cells on Death Row, San Quentin.

Thompson conversed with Mrs. Bessie Clayton, a San Francisco church volunteer, and Rev. Gladsden, the San Quentin chaplain. Thompson's wife and daughter had not visited him for nearly a year. As he waited for death, he fervently embraced religion.

At 10:00 p.m., he nibbled a chicken dinner. Unable to sleep, he requested banana cream pies at 2:00 a.m. and at 5:40 a.m. During the night he scrawled a letter to his wife and wrote a note that willed his library of law books to a social worker who had befriended him. By 7:00 a.m., he trembled visibly and hardly touched the coffee and orange juice served to him.

Shockley refused spiritual aid. He slept a full eight hours and ate a meal of bacon, eggs, toast, coffee, and orange juice.

When Chief Deputy U.S. Marshall John Roseen entered Thompson's cell at 8:15 a.m., Thompson asked, "What happened to my telegram to the Supreme Court?"

"There's been no answer. I'm sorry."

"Can you delay the gassing?"

"No. I'm sorry."

"That's a helluva note. I was in my cell throughout the whole damn thing. Convict alibi witnesses supported me."

"I'm sorry," repeated Roseen.

* * *

The apple-green, octagonal, glass and steel chamber with its two straight-back metal chairs, takes up a third of the room where executions are performed. The steel and glass separates witnesses from the condemned. Venetian blinds on two of its seven windows prevent visual contact between the man who is about to die and the man who must pull the red lever which sends a bag of cyanide pellets into a well of sulphuric acid.

* * *

At 10:00 a.m., Thompson and Shockley were taken from Death Row, accompanied by Associate Warden Harley Teets and two prison officers. It was a six-story ride by elevator to the gas chamber.

Shockley was strapped in the chair at the right of the entrance door. He spat contemptuously at the officer who strapped him in. Thompson, in the other chair, kept his head erect with some effort as the 10 straps were cinched around his body. As required by law, a U.S. Marshall, George Vice, supervised the proceedings.

Just before the cyanide pellets were dropped, Thompson turned to Shockley and said something, but the words were inaudible to the nine official witnesses (three newspapermen, four Alcatraz officers, and two San Quentin officials) who watched through the thick windows.

At 10:12 a.m., Dr. L. I. Stanley, the San Quentin physician who had been listening to their heartbeats through a remote stethoscope, pronounced them dead.

CONCLUSION

"To my mind, a man can have no greater
ambition than the one which forms my sole
desire to give my existence as a member of
an army of decency enrolling itself against
the battalion of darkness. I hope there are
thousands of others within the sound of my
voice who feel likewise.

To combat crime, there must be a constantly
growing band of missionaries who shall go
into the highways and byways carrying with
them the fearlessness and the crusading
spirit so badly needed in a hand-to-hand
combat with a predatory beast. Its name
is CRIME!"

J. Edgar Hoover

"Look, I know I've been involved with crime
all my life. I've hardened to it. Maybe it's
because I ain't had any education, any
chance for a decent way of living. Maybe
if I had been trained to work at something
I wouldn't have been so bad."

Miran "Buddy" Thompson

The Final Years

During the investigation following the escape attempt, Warden Johnston had shown reporters a bar-spreader, contrived from miscellaneous brass toilet fittings, and declared that it was Coy's. To knowledgeable officers, it was obvious that the brass device was not substantial enough to spread the bars, however, the warden's claims were not challenged by newsmen or investigators, and the toilet-fixture bar-spreader became generally accepted as being Coy's.

For many years, officers made attempts to find the actual bar-spreader. In their search, many contraband items such as tools, keys, saws, knives, and money were found. But no bar-spreader.

When it was finally discovered in 1953, it was quietly added to a large collection of contraband. Although it was exhibited, it was not identified as Coy's 'key' to the escape.

* * *

Less than a year after the attempted escape, Associate Warden Edward J. Miller, reknowned throughout the prison service as "a good man with bad men", retired and returned to his home in Leavenworth, Kansas where he had entered the Federal Prison Service many years before. Suffering from a heart condition and diabetes, he died soon after retirement.

* * *

When the trial was over, Carnes was placed on lock-up status for more than six years. During this time, he played chess continually with Robert Stroud. When Carnes was released from lock-up in 1952, he won the institution chess championship and retained the title for the next 10 years.

* * *

Philip Bergen was appointed Captain of the Guards. He served in that capacity for several years and became known as 'counselor' to some inmates because of his efforts to help them solve their difficult adjustment problems. To a few, he became known as 'Ice' Berg-en because of his firm enforcement of prison regulations.

From the time he was volunteered for transfer to the Rock, Bergen heard the rumor that preparations were being made at the Bureau level to close the island prison.

"Don't bother to uncrate your furniture when it arrives from the East," said the prison's business manager when Bergen and his family arrived on the island. "We'll be closing this prison in a month or so."

During his subsequent years on the Rock, Bergen and every officer learned to live with this ever persistent rumor.

* * *

At the age of 72, Warden James A. Johnston retired on April 30, 1948. Upon retirement, he was appointed to the United States Board of Parole. For several years, he served as one of the board's most distinguished and effective parole judges. Warden Johnston died in San Francisco in 1958.

* * *

Edwin B. Swope, a veteran of the Federal Prison Service who had served as warden of several federal and state prisons, was named warden of the Alcatraz Prison on May 2, 1948.

Under Warden Swope's direction, the operation of the prison underwent several notable changes. Inmate privileges were gradually increased until they approximated those enjoyed by inmates at other federal prisons. B and C cellblocks were wired so that radio earphones could be used by each inmate in good behavior status. Tailor-made cigarettes, three packs per week per inmate in good status, were issued in addition to the unrationed supply of cigarette and pipe tobacco. The distinctive Alcatraz inmate uniform of well-tailored coveralls was replaced with standard blue denim trousers and chambray shirts. The entire interior of the prison, which had been painted 'prison grey' with black trim, was repainted 'shocking pink' with bright red trim. Inmates were allowed to repaint their own cells in colors of their own choosing. Black inmates were assigned to the kitchen detail, thus ending the segregation of blacks in the main cellhouse.

* * *

After 26 years of prison service, including 16 years on Alcatraz, Captain Bergen was promoted to Correctional Inspector, Federal Bureau of Prisons, Washington, D.C.

"Although there is no truly escape-proof prison," he commented, "Alcatraz, because of its unique moat of cold, turbulent, shark-infested water, comes as close as any. Of course, the San Francisco Bay sharks are not known to be man-eaters, but the majority of inmates believe that they are. Future close custody prisons — the Alcatrazes of tomorrow — will be only as secure and effective as their carefully selected locations and the competence of the men who staff and administer them."

In 1955, Bergen was promoted to the position of Associate Warden and transferred to the Federal Correctional Institution at La Tuna, Texas.

* * *

Warden Swope retired on January 30, 1955 to accept the wardenship of the state penitentiary at Santa Fe, New Mexico. Paul J. Madigan, who had served as Lieutenant, Captain, and Associate Warden at Alcatraz, succeeded him. Warden Madigan ruled the Rock with a firm, but humane hand until November 26, 1961 when he was transferred to the United States Penitentiary, McNeil Island, Washington. He was replaced by Olin G. Blackwell, the island's fourth and last warden.

* * *

ALCATRAZ '46

In a check of the prison structure during Blackwell's administration, it was discovered that the prolonged bombing during the seige in 1946 had insidiously taken its toll on the reinforced concrete structure of the prison. Unsuspected by the earlier inspectors, the concrete floor of the utility corridors of both B and C blocks, resting on huge steel beams which supported the great weight of the two cell blocks, was fractured in thousands of tiny places by the bombing. Hairline cracks, almost invisible to the naked eye, penetrated the floor concrete and the concrete overlay which masked the supporting beams in the unused basement space below the cellhouse floor. The salt water leakage from the sanitary lines had been seeping imperceptibly through these cracks for more than a decade. Absorbing the leakage like a giant sponge, the thick concrete covering which had been intended to protect and beautify the huge beams during the Army Disciplinary Barracks days when the prison basement was used for offices, storerooms, and a row of solitary confinement cells, enveloped the steel beams like an invisible corrosive blanket and gradually weakened the structures.

According to estimates, it would cost $5,000,000 to replace the rusted-out beams and repair the sagging catwalks, rusting watchtowers, and exterior concrete walls of the prison. When officials admitted that Alcatraz was already costing taxpayers $13,000 a year per prisoner, it was decided that it was not practical to renovate the prison, especially since a newer maximum security prison had been constructed on a 1250 acre reservation at Marion, Illinois.

* * *

Alcatraz Prison was always a difficult penal institution to staff and administer, partly due to the prison's undeserved aura of ill repute and partly due to the ever present danger of possible assault by some vicious, disgruntled inmate who decided he had nothing to lose. The difficulty in recruiting suitable officers and the potential for violence increased during the prison's final years.

Violence and/or the threat of violence hovered over the Rock like the heavy fog from the Golden Gate. Officers were assaulted from time to time, but only three — Cline, Miller, Stites — died in the performance of duty. Once placed in this tense environment, most officers chose not to remain on the island for more than a few years.

Some critics claimed that the assaults, the attempted escapes, the strikes, the homosexual rapes, the incidents of arson and sabotage, and the cold-blooded murders of fellow inmates occurred because of the effect of the isolation imposed upon the prisoners. Officers who had to face the men committing the offenses, contended that most of the offenders were simply following long-established behavior patterns that would have surfaced wherever they were confined.

Because the FBI and other law enforcement agencies had long since captured most of the major bank robbers, train robbers, kidnappers, and other desperadoes whose headlined exploits in the 20's and 30's had helped persuade law enforcement officers to establish Alcatraz Prison, by the mid-50's most of the criminals had been returned to less restrictive federal prisons. Some had even rehabilitated themselves and were living productive lives in society. As they were transferred, the prison gradually received in their place, a collection of overly aggressive sociopaths and emotionally immature individuals who needed psychiatric care as much as they required close confinement and constant supervision. Thus the character of the inmate population slowly changed.

With the change in the nature of the inmate population came disparaging comments by eminent penologists in and out of the Federal Bureau of Prisons. These comments focused upon the negative aspects of Alcatraz within the Federal Prison System. Their widely publicized pronouncements made officer recruitment and the retention of recruits even more difficult than it had been. Finally, it became necessary for the Bureau to establish an in-service training program on the island to select trainees from totally inexperienced applicants.

* * *

Inmates were not slow to take full advantage of the supervisory weaknesses that developed because of the high turnover and inexperience of new officers.

On the night of Monday, June 11, 1962 three prisoners — Clarence and John Anglin and Frank Lee Morris — disappeared from Alcatraz. All were bank robbers serving long terms.

For several months the three men had plotted the escape and carried out the preliminary steps. First, they dug holes through the concrete at the back of their cells. They covered the holes with cardboards artistically painted to resemble the air ducts that they had removed to begin the holes. Next, they fashioned dummies and improvised Mae West jackets from pieces of rubber raincoats. When the holes were completed, they had access to the utility corridor behind the cells. From the utility corridor they climbed to the top of the cellblock where over a period of time, working a few minutes each night, they loosened the bars guarding a vent in the roof.

Sometime after the 9:00 p.m. count, they placed the dummies in their beds, exited from the cells, and escaped from the cellhouse through the roof vent. They let themselves down to the ground, climbed a 15-foot fence, and made their way to the beach. They were never seen or heard of again. Only traces of a few pieces of debris were found at widely scattered points around the bay. The men were presumed to have drowned in the 54° water due to the cold or the currents.

On December 16, 1962 two inmates sought to swim the watery barrier between the island and the mainland. Assigned to the kitchen detail, Paul Scott, serving 30 years for bank robbery, and Darl Parker, serving 50 years for bank robbery and an escape from an Indiana jail, over a period of months surreptitiously weakened the bars on one of the windows in the storage basement under the kitchen. Their tools were a serrated spatula and a butcher's twine soaked in wax and covered with coarse scouring powder to serve as an abrasive.

Late in the afternoon, a few minutes after they had been counted, they wriggled through the window opening. Out of sight of the gun towers, they climbed to the roof on some exposed piping. On the other side of the building they let themselves down to the ground with a length of stolen electric cord. As they reached the island shore, the escape alarm sounded. Hurriedly they inflated some surgeon's rubber gloves, wrapped them in their pants legs, and tied the improvised flotation gear around their waists.

ALCATRAZ '46

Once in the water, Parker found he was unable to breast the swift current. A launch picked him up, thoroughly chilled and clinging to a rock 50 feet from the island shore. Scott managed to float and swim into the outgoing tide which swept him onto some rocks near the Golden Gate Bridge. Officers lassoed and hauled him to the top of the 20 foot sea wall near the bridge. He was rushed to the hospital, nearly dead from exposure.

* * *

After his retirement in 1967, Bergen stated, "I sincerely believe that an Alcatraz, by whatever name, is as necessary today as it was in the 1930's when the Congress established it as an integral part of the newly created Federal Bureau of Prisons and that there is urgent necessity for similar arrangements in the several states.

"No prison system, state or federal, which seriously proposes to rehabilitate any sizeable percentage of its inmates can hope to do so unless it has an Alcatraz — a penal institution of maximum security and minimum privilege dedicated to the effective segregation of convicted criminals who cannot be rehabilitated. Alcatraz Island Prison is gone, but the Alcatraz concept lingers on, and rightly so because it is a valid concept."

Just before the prison closed, Carnes was transferred, on January 16, 1963, to Springfield for a gallbladder operation.

"I could hardly believe they were closing the place," he said when he was transferred. "There had been a lot of skepticism about the closing because it had been a rumor a couple of times a year through all the years it had been a federal prison. The fact is, the night I got to Alcatraz, one fellow said to me, 'I don't know why they sent you out here. This place is closing next month.' Those words made me happy at the time. I didn't know I would hear them again and again, many, many times as the years passed."

Following a successful operation, Carnes was sent to Leavenworth where he worked in the mail room and at other jobs. He enrolled in one of the prison's school programs and took courses which gave him the equivalency of a high school diploma. He then successfully completed a college program arranged through Highland Junior College, Highland, Kansas.

"From the confinement of my cell," he once said, "I have been given a view of life and history such as I would never have known otherwise, and I think I have come to an understanding with myself — a thing that is priceless. If I die before I get out, and at the instant of my death someone asked if I would rather have died with Shockley and Thompson, I would answer, 'No, I am glad that I have lived.'"

* * *

An end to the prison's operation was eventually brought about by the combination of a large number of factors: the increase in assaults and other types of violence; the turnover of officer personnel; the increase in the number of inexperienced officers; the general drop in officer morale; the pressure from a public concerned about the location of the prison; the pressure from critical penologists; and the vast deterioration of the prison's structure and surrounding facilities.

On May 15, 1963, Alcatraz Island Prison was officially closed.

During its 28 years as a Federal Civil Penitentiary, Alcatraz experienced 14 escape attempts involving 39 inmates. Of the 39, 26 was quickly recaptured. Seven were shot to death by prison officers, and six were drowned or lost in the turbulent waters of the bay.

The inmate population turnover was fairly consistent through those years. It never exceeded 300 at any given time, and the daily population average was about 250 men. Less than 1% of the total population of the Federal Prison System ever reached the island prison. At its close, the highest register number was 1041 Az.

ALCATRAZ GLOSSARY IN 1946

APE. Derogatory term for a Black male.

ARCTIC. Isolation, or solitary confinement.

B & W. Bread and water.

BEATING THE GUMS. Talking, screaming, shouting.

BLAST. Shoot with firearm.

BROADWAY. Wide, east-west aisle between B & C cellblocks.

BUM RAP. An excessive sentence.

CELL. An inmate housing unit.

CELLBLOCK. Two or more cells, in one section, or "block".

NOTE: At Alcatraz there were:
124 cells in A-Block
168 cells in B-Block
168 cells in C-Block
42 cells in D-Block

CELLFRONT. Front wall of a cell, usually barred.

CELLHOUSE. A room enclosing one or more cellblocks.

CLEAN. Free from contraband articles.

CON. A convicted criminal.

CROAKER. A physician or prison medical officer.

DECK. Steel floor of Gun Galleries, Towers, etc.

DOG BLOCK. D-Block (segregation and isolation).

DOUBLE TEAM. Two officers guarding an inmate.

EASY-GO. Easy prison job.

FAIRY. A sexual pervert.

FINK. Contemptuous term for law-enforcement officer.

FLATS. The ground floor of the cellhouse.

FOOD-PASS. An oblong 4″ x 12″ opening in a cell front.

FRESH FISH. A newly arrived prisoner.

FRISK. A quick, superficial body search.

GENERAL POPULATION. Majority of inmates not in isolation or segregation.

GRADE. Lesser form of punishment.

GUN CAGE. Term for Gun Gallery.

GUN GALLERY. A secure, elevated, enclosed walkway from which an armed officer supported unarmed officers.

SEGREGATED. Confined apart from others.

SHAKEDOWN. Search.

SHITTER. A water closet. A cell toilet.

SHOOTING GALLERY. Term for Gun Gallery.

SOLITARY CONFINEMENT. Housed apart from others, usually in an unlighted cell.

STOOLIE. Stool Pigeon. An informer.

TICKET. Inmate's record or discipline report.

TIER. A row of cellblock cells, con-

HACK. Officer.

HIT THE BRICKS. Escape to San Francisco.

HOLE. Term for Solitary Confinement cell.

HOLED UP. Hidden in a defensive position.

HOT BOX. Solitary confinement.

ISOLATION. Housed apart from other prisoners. In most instances, a synonym for Segregation.

JIGGERS. Keeping a watch against officers.

JUG HEAD. A derogatory term for a stubborn, unyielding official.

JUNGLE. Recreation yard.

KITE. An illicit communication, usually a letter.

LAG. "Jailbird", of long standing.

MEAT HEAD. Synonym for Jug Head.

MICHIGAN BOULEVARD. Inmate nickname for the A-B aisle in cellhouse.

MONKEY-SUIT. A prison officer's uniform.

ON THE CARPET. Disciplinary action.

PAPER-HANGING. Passing bad checks.

PEKIN PLACE. Inmate nickname for the north-south aisle across the east end of cellhouse. The visiting area.

PIG STICKER. A knife.

PISS & PUNK. Bread & Water diet.

PUNK. An inexperienced criminal and/or a young male playing the female part.

QUARANTINE. Segregation.

QUEER. A sexual pervert.

RACK. Operate a mechanism to open or close a cell door.

RANGE. A row or tier of cells.

RAT. An informer.

RIDGE-RUNNER. A woodsman, or "Hillbilly".

RUMBLE. Rumor.

SALLYPORT. A specially designed and safely controlled entrance-exit.

SCRAPPLE. Prison food.

SCREW. A prison officer.

SCREW-DRIVER. A prison official, usually the captain.

SEEDY STREET. Inmate nickname for C-D aisle in cellhouse.
structed atop another row of cells.

TIMES SQUARE. The north-south aisle, across the west end of the cellhouse, where cellhouse clock was located.

UNDERDOGS. Inmates.

UPPERDOGS. Officers.

WALKWAY. The elevated pathway in front of a tier of cells on the upper tiers of a cellblock.

WOLF. An aggressive homosexual.

YARD BIRD. Cleanup man assigned to prison yard.